THE COMPLETE
Horse &
Rider

THE COMPLETE
Horse &
Rider

A PRACTICAL HANDBOOK OF RIDING AND AN ILLUSTRATED GUIDE TO TACK AND EQUIPMENT

SARAH MUIR & DEBBY SLY
Photography KIT HOUGHTON

HERMES HOUSE

This edition is published by Hermes House
Hermes House is an imprint of Anness Publishing Ltd
Hermes House, 88–89 Blackfriars Road, London SE1 8HA
tel. 020 7401 2077; fax 020 7633 9499

www.hermeshouse.com; www.annesspublishing.com

If you like the images in this book and would like to investigate
using them for publishing, promotions or advertising, please visit
our website www.practicalpictures.com for more information.

Publisher Joanna Lorenz
Managing Editor Judith Simons
Project Editor Charlotte Berman
Indexer Helen Snaith
Designer Michael Morey
Illustrators Diana Breeze and Rodney Paull

Previously published in two separate volumes,
Saddlery & Horse Equipment and *Practical Rider's Handbook*.

7 9 10 8

Contents

Introduction

Horse riding is a demanding yet ultimately fulfilling pastime that has brought a great deal of pleasure and fun to many. It is important to remember that whatever your ambition, whether it be to compete at the highest level or to go on a gentle hack through beautiful countryside, riding should be enjoyable for you and your horse. The relationship between the rider and his or her mount should always be a partnership.

If you have never so much as sat on a horse or pony, there will be a great deal to take in to start with. Riding, like many other activities, requires specialist clothing and equipment. A visit to your local saddlery or tack shop will confirm the bewildering array of tack and equipment on sale – not all of it necessarily essential. With this in mind we have provided a detailed guide to **Saddlery and Equipment**, focusing on the everyday saddle and bridle, as well as explaining how and why many of the more unusual items of equipment are used.

The Saddle is an essential piece of riding equipment and one of the most expensive items the owner has to buy for his or her horse. There are saddles designed to suit every style of riding, so we explain which is the best for you and your chosen type of riding. There is also a section on essential saddle accessories including girths, stirrups, breastplates and saddle cloths, as well as a guide to saddle care.

The bridle is an equally important piece of equipment, and like the saddle should be chosen carefully, with the comfort of the horse and the safety of the rider firmly in mind. The subject of **Bridles and Bits** is a

Horses are very vulnerable to minor injuries when traveling on the roads. This horse is wearing all the necessary equipment; tail bandage and tail guard to keep the tail clean and protect it from damage by rubbing; felt hock boots to protect the hock joint; travel bandages to protect all four legs; cooler rug, to keep the horse warm, fitted beneath a day rug and held in place with a surcingle and breastgirth; lead rope to secure horse in trailer; poll guard to protect the horse's head; and a leather headcollar or halter, which is safer when travelling than a nylon headcollar because it will break more easily in the event of an accident.

complex one and it is important to choose the right combination of tack to suit the horse and the rider – too mild a bit and you could be left with an unstoppable horse, too strong and you could unwittingly inflict pain on the horse. We explain the different types of bridle and noseband, and look in detail at bits and bitting, describing the various bit groups and the different actions they have on the horse.

As we place greater demands on the horse, expecting improvements in athletic performance and transporting horses to and from competitions, the need for special horse clothing and equipment has increased. From boots to protect your horse's legs, to rugs and blankets, the

range of horse clothing is enormous. We guide you through the maze of clothing and equipment available, as well as providing a step-by-step guide to putting on boots, bandages and rugs, so your horse will be protected from head to tail.

Learning the art of horsemanship requires the dedication and patience of the pupil – the rider never stops learning. Horses are individuals, and we can learn as much from them as they can from us.

The **Learning to Ride** section will prove invaluable to anyone with an interest in riding, including first-time riders. We look at where to learn, how to prepare the horse for riding, and how the rider communicates with his or her horse.

Although there is no substitute for actually being on a horse, when you are learning to ride the time spent in the saddle is often relatively little (it may be only an hour a week), so it is useful for the budding equestrian to be able to read and learn more about horsemanship. Such knowledge will hopefully be put into practice the next time you ride.

Firstly we examine the means of communication with the horse, through the use of the legs, seat, hands and voice. The art of riding lies in learning to feel what the horse is doing underneath you, and understanding how to influence what he or she does by mastering this subtle form of communication.

In **Mastering the Paces** we look at how the horse moves, showing the four paces – walk, trot, canter, and gallop – in detail, as well as the transitions between these paces. As the rider gains confidence and balance and learns how to coordinate himself, he can develop his skills and

One of the best ways to encourage an independent seat is to be lunged. To help build up your confidence and balance, practice riding without stirrups. Spread your arms out to either side then twist your body, first to the left then to the right.

learn more about influencing the horse – for example, the half-halt, lateral work, and the counter canter – creating and building upon the all-important rider-horse partnership.

Preparing for Take-off is a useful section on learning how to jump. Starting with simple exercises over trot poles and low fences in the arena, we progress to the exhilaration of riding around a cross-country

course, how to cope with difficult terrain and preparing yourself for the unexpected.

As your riding skills develop further you may want to take part in competitions, so in **The Competition World** we describe the wide variety of equestrian sports that exist, and how to choose one that suits you and your horse's temperament. From the pleasure and excitement of jumping or mounted games, the grace of dressage or the acrobatics of vaulting, to the special demands of endurance riding, or the thrill of taking part in a race, there's something for every rider in this section – along with the idea that the main aim of competing should be fun.

We hope that you enjoy this book and that it will prove to be an invaluable source of information for horse riders and horse lovers alike. Whatever your equestrian ambitions, never forget the pleasure and satisfaction that being involved with horses can give.

In a sitting trot the rider retains the correct classical position, allowing her stomach and lower back to absorb the movement of the horse. Note the straight line through the shoulder, hip and heel as well as from the elbow to the bit.

Horses competing in show jumping competitions have to be taught to jump *over* water in order to jump a clear round, whereas in cross-country riding, as shown here, you are always trying to encourage your horse to jump *into* water.

Saddlery and Equipment

The Saddle

The saddle is one of the most important pieces of equipment for the ridden horse, and, because of the skill and craftsmanship involved in producing a saddle, it is usually the most expensive. The earliest type of saddle, first developed thousands of years ago, was nothing more than a simple blanket kept in place with breastplate and girth. The modern saddle, however, is a sophisticated piece of equipment. It has evolved as a result of the demands of modern equestrianism, whether it be the Western saddle designed to withstand the rigors of cowboy life; the dressage saddle designed to give the rider an elegant yet effective position; or the minuscule racing saddle.

The saddle's design and fit can have a tremendous effect on both the horse's performance and the rider's position. An ill-fitting saddle can cause the horse considerable discomfort and even physical damage. When choosing a new saddle, therefore, it is always advisable to seek professional help – a trained saddler will be able to ensure that the saddle fits the horse correctly.

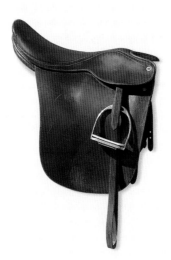

I OPPOSITE
The saddle is an important and costly piece of equipment, and should always be well cared for.

I LEFT
The Saddlebred saddle, specially designed for showing American Saddlebreds and other gaited horses.

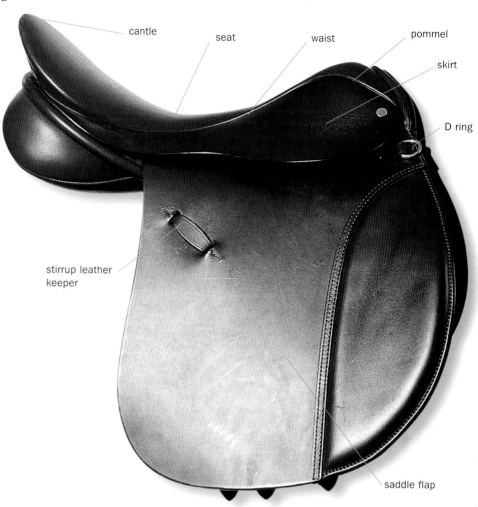

cantle · seat · waist · pommel · skirt · D ring · stirrup leather keeper · saddle flap

Points of the Saddle

Virtually all saddles are built upon a solid framework called a tree. This framework was traditionally made from beech wood but is now available in laminated wood, and even fiberglass and plastic. It is the shape of the tree and the placing of the metal stirrup bars riveted to the tree which determine the size and shape of the saddle. The seat of the saddle is given shape by stretching a webbing and cotton fabric over the tree. Serge or a synthetic fabric is stretched to form the seat shape and a wool or synthetic stuffing provides the padding below.

▌ ABOVE
The general purpose saddle is the standard model for the sport. The moderate features make it suitable for all riding disciplines at a non-professional level. Specialist saddles develop individual characteristics of the general purpose saddle according to the needs of the particular discipline.

▌ BELOW
Under the saddle flap. Most saddles have three girth straps. The first two are fixed to the web strap attached to the tree and the third is fixed independently.

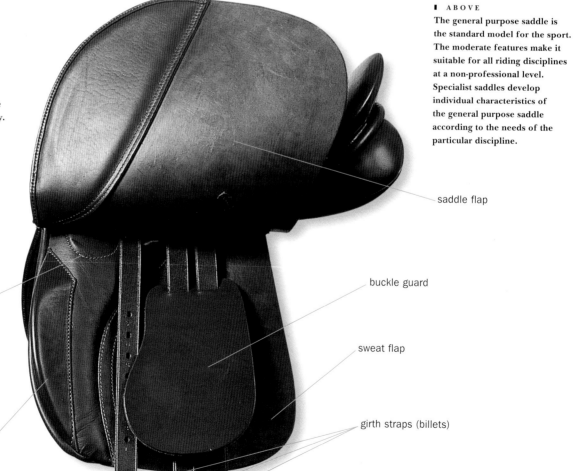

saddle flap · buckle guard · sweat flap · point of tree · knee roll · girth straps (billets)

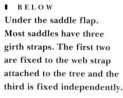

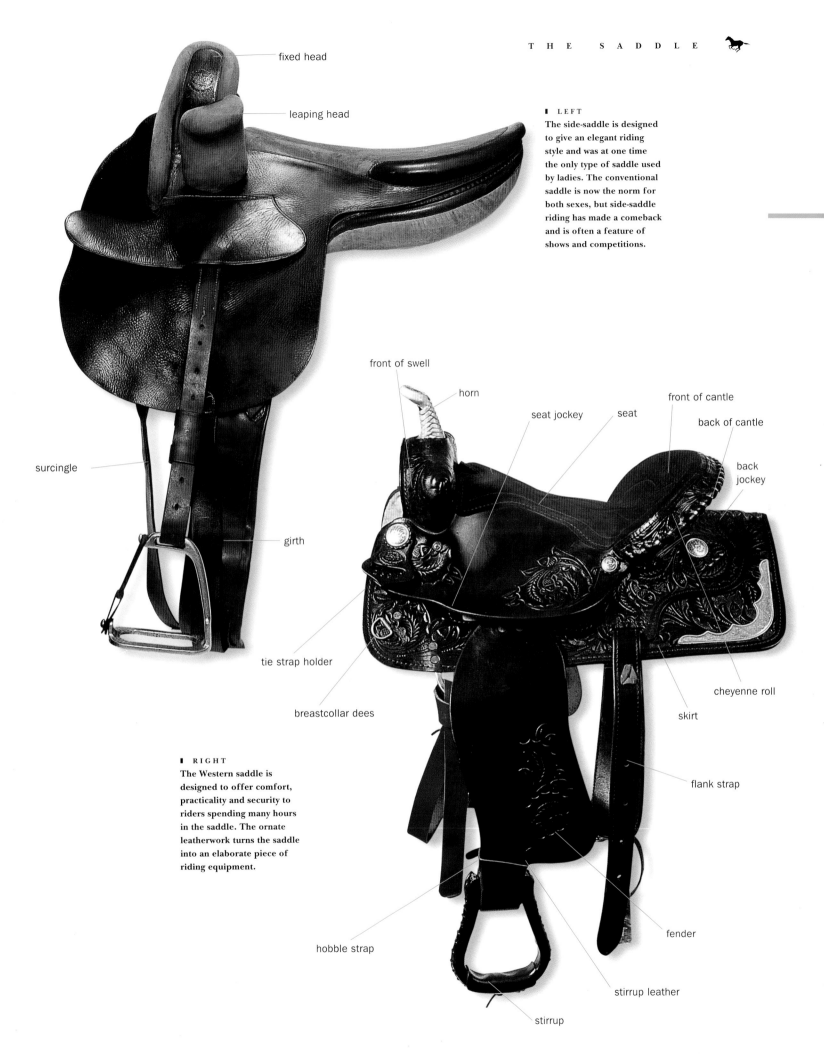

fixed head

leaping head

surcingle

girth

The side-saddle is designed
to give an elegant riding
style and was at one time
the only type of saddle used
by ladies. The conventional
saddle is now the norm for
both sexes, but side-saddle
riding has made a comeback
and is often a feature of
shows and competitions.

front of swell

horn

seat jockey

seat

front of cantle

back of cantle

back
jockey

cheyenne roll

skirt

tie strap holder

breastcollar dees

flank strap

■ RIGHT
The Western saddle is
designed to offer comfort,
practicality and security to
riders spending many hours
in the saddle. The ornate
leatherwork turns the saddle
into an elaborate piece of
riding equipment.

fender

hobble strap

stirrup leather

stirrup

13

Riding and Competing Saddles

Saddles are available in a number of shapes and styles to suit the many equestrian disciplines at every level of competition from novice to professional.

The **leather general purpose (GP) saddle** is designed to be used across the board of riding activities. It is ideal for pleasure riding, hunting, novice cross-country and show jumping and basic dressage. A less expensive alternative to the leather saddle is the **synthetic general purpose saddle**, which is lighter in weight than the leather type, and easier to clean.

For most riders, the general purpose saddle is perfectly adequate for jumping. However, if you are riding at a competitive level and tackling larger fences, you may prefer the specialist design of the jumping saddle. The saddle flaps of the **Crosby close-contact jumping saddle** are more forward cut than those of the general purpose saddle. This enables you to keep your legs close to the saddle even when riding with a short stirrup length.

The **event saddle** is very similar in style to a general purpose saddle and can be used for all phases of horse trials, although some riders prefer to have an additional saddle for the dressage phase. Many famous riders have become involved in the design of saddles and the event saddle illustrated was developed by the international eventer, Mary King.

The **Albion Selecta** is a multi-purpose saddle which aims to combine the general purpose saddle with a dressage and a jumping saddle. It features easily removable knee pads which allow the saddle to be adapted for all riding disciplines from pleasure riding to jumping, dressage, cross-country and working hunter events.

The **polo saddle** has a relatively flat seat, extra-long sweat flaps and no knee and thigh rolls. It is designed specifically for the game of polo, during which the horse travels at speed and the rider needs to be able to move with ease to hit the ball.

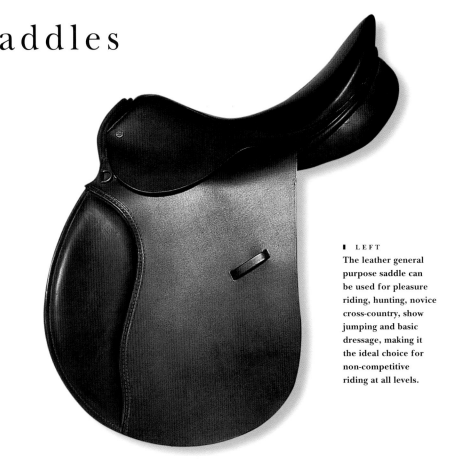

▮ LEFT
The leather general purpose saddle can be used for pleasure riding, hunting, novice cross-country, show jumping and basic dressage, making it the ideal choice for non-competitive riding at all levels.

▮ RIGHT
The synthetic general purpose saddle is a modern alternative to the leather saddle. While it can be put to all the same uses, the synthetic material means it is cheaper, lighter and easier to clean.

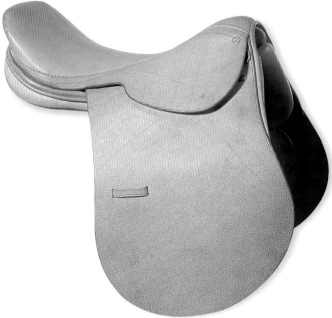

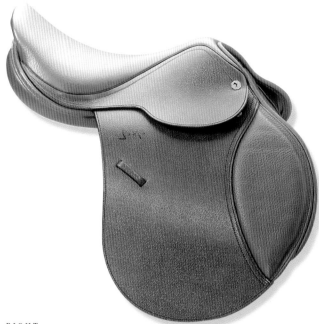

■ ABOVE
The polo saddle has a flat seat, extended sweat flaps and no knee or thigh rolls, all of which allow the rider freedom of movement when striking the ball.

■ BELOW LEFT
Event saddle. This is similar in style to the general purpose saddle and can be used for all phases of horse trials.

■ RIGHT
The Crosby close-contact jumping saddle. The saddle flaps are more forward cut than those of the general purpose saddle. This allows the rider to carry his legs closer to the saddle, and makes his position more secure.

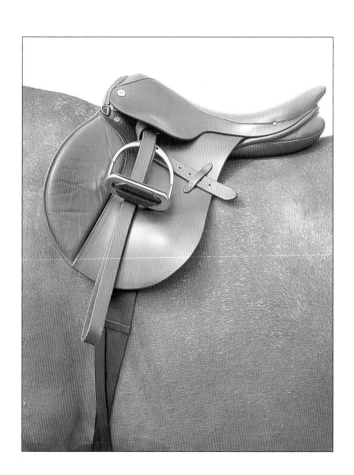

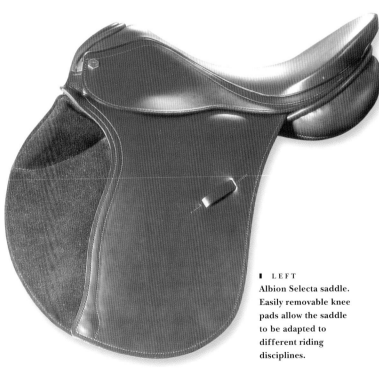

■ LEFT
Albion Selecta saddle. Easily removable knee pads allow the saddle to be adapted to different riding disciplines.

Showing Saddles

There are a number of saddles designed specifically to improve the horse's performance in showing competitions.

The purpose of the **showing saddle** is primarily to enhance the appearance of the show horse rather than to increase the comfort of the rider. The saddle is straight cut to show off the horse's shoulder and is simple in design, since it is the horse rather than the tack that is being judged. The showing saddle is a specialized piece of equipment and not always very comfortable; many riders prefer to use a dressage saddle for showing classes.

The **dressage saddle**, designed for riding and schooling horses on the flat rather than over jumps, has longer and straighter flaps than the general purpose saddle. This allows you to carry your legs in a longer position and closer to the horse's body. To eliminate bulk under your legs, longer girth straps (billets) are fitted and used with a short dressage girth.

The **Saddlebred saddle** is for showing American Saddlebreds and other gaited horses. It features a cut-back pommel (called a "cow-mouth") and very wide saddle flaps, which enable the rider to sit much further back in the saddle than usual.

For showing classes in which the horse is required both to jump and to be ridden on the flat, the **working hunter saddle** is ideal. The seat is deeper than the showing saddle, and padded knee rolls give a more secure seat which is helpful when jumping.

The **side-saddle,** first developed for ladies in the fourteenth century, allows the rider to carry both legs on the near (left) side of the horse, with the left foot in a stirrup and the right leg hooked over the pommel. The flat seat has a suede or doeskin cover for extra grip. Although no longer in general use, shows often feature ladies' hunter classes for side-saddle riders.

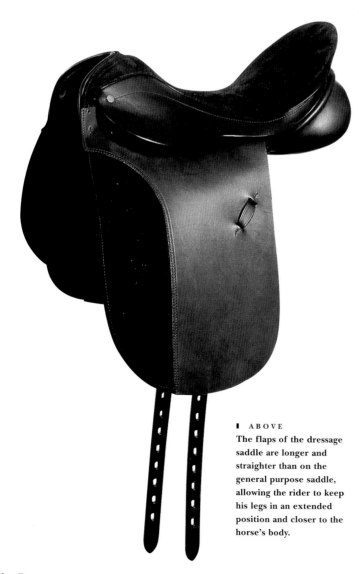

■ ABOVE
The flaps of the dressage saddle are longer and straighter than on the general purpose saddle, allowing the rider to keep his legs in an extended position and closer to the horse's body.

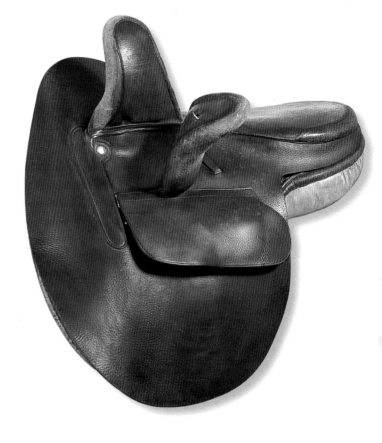

■ ABOVE
The shape of the side-saddle allows the rider to adopt a more elegant position, with both legs on the near (left) side of the horse.

Trail-riding and Working Saddles

addles which are to be ridden over long periods of time need to have an element f comfort incorporated into the design.

The **endurance saddle**, as its name ggests, is designed for long-distance les. The seat has extra padding and the ddle panels have extra width, thereby eading the rider's weight over a greater a and reducing the risk of localized ssure points on the horse's back. ditional D rings are fitted to the saddle hat equipment, such as lead ropes and nges, can easily be accommodated.

The **Australian stock saddle** is a tarian saddle designed for the comfort of both horse and rider during the hours spent driving cattle. The weight distribution properties mean that modified versions of this saddle can also be used for endurance or trail-riding.

The **Western reining saddle** is higher in front than the standard Western saddle, preventing the rider from being thrown forward when the horse performs the characteristic sliding stop. **Western pleasure saddles** are lighter in weight than working saddles and have only one cinch attachment. Comfortable and secure, these saddles are ideal for long-distance or trail-riding.

The **parade saddle** is an ornate working saddle featuring highly intricate metal and leatherwork. These decorative saddles are specially designed for use in carnival or rodeo parades.

The **trooper** or **Cavalry saddle** is built around a steel and wood tree and is the traditional choice of the armed forces because of its strength and durability.

The **military fan saddle** is designed for working horses, such as those used by the mounted police. The saddle tree distributes the rider's weight evenly for comfort during long periods of work, often when the horse is stationary.

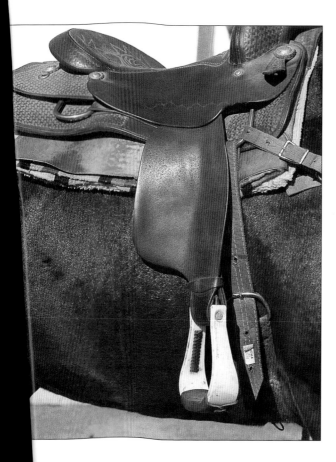

an stock saddle is built for **comfort** and durability. The rider may l hours driving cattle on the **plains**, and the even spread of his saddle will become a **significant** factor for both horse and rider.

❚ ABOVE

The high front of the Western reining saddle prevents the rider being thrown forward and out of the saddle when the horse performs the dramatic reining halt, which is a feature of this riding style.

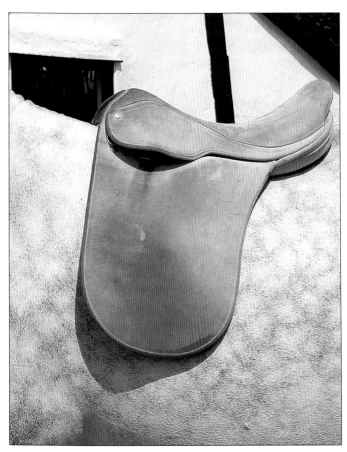

■ ABOVE
This showing saddle in split hide, designed by producer and rider Lynn Rusell, is specially shaped to suit larger show horses such as cobs and hunters.

■ RIGHT
The design of the Saddlebred saddle enables the rider to sit far back in the saddle. In a show this riding style will help to enhance the well-shaped conformation of the Saddlebred horse.

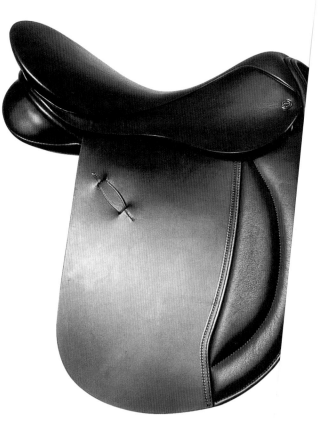

■ RIGHT
The working hunter saddle is a compromise between a showing saddle and a jumping saddle.

■ ABOVE
The Austral
spend seve
weight in th

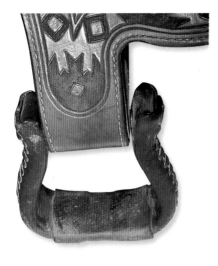

ABOVE
inlaid wood Western stirrups

ABOVE
leather-covered Western stirrup

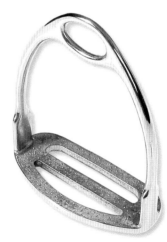

ABOVE
Polymer and Flexi-ride stirrups are designed to increase foot comfort when endurance or trail-riding.

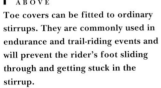

ABOVE
Toe covers can be fitted to ordinary stirrups. They are commonly used in endurance and trail-riding events and will prevent the rider's foot sliding through and getting stuck in the stirrup.

LEFT
Carbon-fiber stirrups are lightweight but extremely strong.

ABOVE
The round eye of the side-saddle stirrup allows the lower leg greater flexibility.

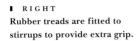

RIGHT
Rubber treads are fitted to stirrups to provide extra grip.

SAFETY STIRRUPS

In the event of a fall, the rider risks serious injury if his foot becomes caught in the stirrup. Safety stirrups are designed to prevent this by allowing the foot to be quickly released from the stirrup.

The **Australian Simplex** or **bent-leg stirrup** has a bent outer leg on the iron, encouraging the early release of the foot. The **Peacock safety stirrup** has a strong band of rubber fitted to the outside of the stirrup, which is pulled off if the foot gets caught. The **precision riding stirrup** is a new design which self-aligns to the position of your foot to increase comfort and security.

STIRRUP LEATHERS

English leathers are traditionally made from top-quality English dressed hides. **Extending leathers** have a small hook attachment which allows the stirrup to be lengthened for mounting. **Racing leathers** are lightweight and made from leather and nylon web. **Jumping** or **double-sided stirrup leathers** are reinforced with nylon to strengthen the leather and prevent it from stretching. The **side-saddle leather** has a hook adjustment to alter the length at the base, near the stirrup. **Dressage leathers** are a smart single thickness of leather with a buckle at the base, allowing the legs to be carried closer to the horse.

■ ABOVE
Australian Simplex safety or bent-leg stirrups. The bent leg of the iron is fitted to the outside.

■ ABOVE
Peacock safety stirrups. In the event of a fall, the rubber is pulled off to release the foot.

■ ABOVE
Precision riding stirrups self-align for safety and comfort.

■ RIGHT
Jumping stirrup leathers, also known as double-sided stirrup leathers, are reinforced with nylon for extra strength under extreme pressure.

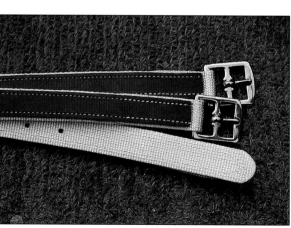

■ LEFT
Top to bottom: synthetic stirrup leathers, racing stirrup leathers, English stirrup leathers

■ RIGHT
Side-saddle stirrup leathers.

Numnahs and Saddle Cloths

Numnahs and saddle cloths are fitted under the saddle to stop the saddle rubbing the horse's back and to absorb the concussion caused by movement. They help to keep the underside of the saddle clean by absorbing sweat and grease from the horse's body. Numnahs are saddle-shaped whereas a saddle pad or cloth is normally square or rectangular. A numnah or saddle cloth should never be used to make an ill-fitting saddle fit, and if not kept scrupulously clean they can rub the horse's back, leading to sores and even skin diseases.

Lightweight **quilted cotton numnahs** are ideal for protecting the saddle from sweat. They are held in place with straps which go round the girth and girth tabs. Available to fit general purpose and dressage saddles, they come in a variety of colors, although white is traditional for competitions.

The materials from which numnahs and saddle pads are made are chosen for their comfort-inducing properties. The **wither pad** is a small, oval pad in fleece or sheepskin which is placed between the wither and the saddle. The **pure new wool numnah**, fully washable with a cotton backing, is designed to relieve and prevent pressure sores. The **sheepskin numnah** absorbs impact and allows heat from the horse's body to pass through it. The **non-slip numnah**, made from neoprene, is designed to absorb concussion and to prevent the saddle from slipping.

Modern choices often include unique features which make them more attractive to the rider. The **Poly pad** is a thick, quilted pad which provides extra protection for the horse's back. Unlike many other numnahs or saddle cloths, it stays in place without the need for straps or loops. The **Coolback numnah** or saddle cloth features a special lining which draws sweat away from the horse's back. The **Proteq saddle pad** is a unique concept,

BELOW
A Poly pad is a thick quilted pad which provides extra protection from the saddle. It is also available as a wither pad.

ABOVE
A quilted cotton saddle cloth and numnah for a dressage saddle.

LEFT
Navajo fleece pad

BELOW
pure wool numnah (*left*) and sheepskin numnah

ABOVE
fleece wither pad

BELOW
The Navajo saddle blanket is often used with Western or polo saddles.

31

incorporating thousands of tiny polystyrene beads. When the saddle is in place the air is pumped out of the pad, so that the beads mould to the configuration between the saddle and the horse's back.

Western and polo saddles are traditionally fitted with the **Navajo saddle blanket**. The **Navajo fleece pad** is a Western blanket pad with a fleece lining.

The **racing weight cloth** is fitted between the numnah and the saddle. It features a series of pockets in which lead weights can be placed to ensure that the rider is carrying the correct weight for the race. Weight cloths are also used in the speed and endurance phases of horse trials.

New products designed to fit between the saddle and the numnah now make use

of highly effective synthetic materials. These include the **Pro-lite relief pad**, which incorporates a visco-elastic gel and latex rubber to absorb impact, and the **gel pad**, which contains thermoplastic elastomer gel for shock absorbency. Flat or molded **shock-absorbing pads** can be placed under the saddle to help distribute the rider's weight more evenly over the horse's back.

▮ ABOVE
Aerborn Coolback numnah. This saddle cloth has a special lining which absorbs sweat from the horse's back.

▮ ABOVE
The gel pad contains a thermoplastic elastomer gel to aid shock absorbency.

▮ ABOVE
Placed under the saddle, the molded shock-absorbing pad helps to distribute the rider's weight evenly.

▮ ABOVE
The flat shock-absorbing pad is used to help distribute the rider's weight along the horse's back.

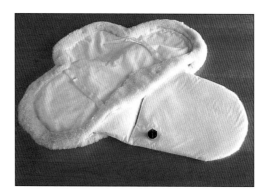

▮ LEFT
The Proteq saddle pad incorporates thousands of tiny polystyrene beads, which help mold the pad to the horse's back.

▮ ABOVE
The Pro-lite relief pad uses visco-elastic gel and latex rubber to absorb impact and concussion.

▮ ABOVE
Lead weights can be added to the pockets of the weight cloth to ensure the jockey carries the correct weight for the race.

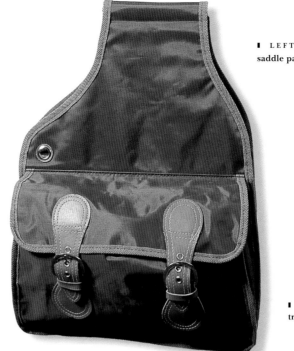

Saddle Bags

Saddle bags, pouches or panniers are lightweight bags which can be fitted to the saddle, positioned behind it and hung over either side of the horse. They are functional accessories used to carry the provisions needed on rides of several hours or more.

The **trail pad**, a fleece pad incorporated into a canvas cloth with pockets, is ideal for endurance and long-distance pleasure rides. The fleece numnah sits comfortably on the horse, while the canvas overlay is suitably sturdy.

As its name suggests, the **hunting canteen** was traditionally used to carry the refreshments necessary for a day's fox hunting. The smart leather pouch is just the right size to hold a flask of warming liquor.

Argentinian saddle bags are handwoven from wool in traditional patterns. They are used by *gauchos* to carry food when riding for days at a time out on the *pampas*.

■ BELOW
trail pad

■ LEFT
hunting canteen

■ ABOVE
Argentinian saddle bag

Saddle Care

A good saddle is a costly piece of equipment and it is important to look after it properly, not only because it is expensive to repair but because a damaged saddle may harm your horse's back.

HOW TO CARRY A SADDLE

▌ LEFT
The saddle should be carried in either of the two ways shown: over the forearm with the back of the saddle nearest the elbow (*far left*), or against the side of the body with the hand holding on to the pommel (*left*).

HOW TO STORE A SADDLE

Once you have removed the saddle from the horse, it can be placed over a fence or saddle rack before being returned to the tack room. (If you leave the saddle over a stable door, the horse will most probably nudge it off.)

You can also put the saddle on the ground, pommel down and with the seat facing the wall. Place the girth between the pommel and the ground to protect the leather.

Saddles are best kept on saddle racks in a clean and dry tack room – damp conditions will damage the leather. Do not leave sweaty numnahs or girths attached to the saddle; remove and clean them before putting them away separately.

HOW TO CLEAN A SADDLE

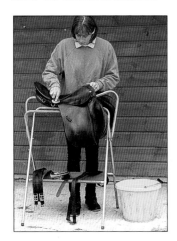   

1 Place the saddle on a stand. Remove the stirrup leathers, girth and numnah. With warm water and a dampened sponge, work all over the saddle removing any mud, sweat and general dirt. Take care not to let the leather get too wet.

2 While cleaning, check the saddle for wear and tear. Pay particular attention to the stitching, especially where the girth tabs (billets) are joined to the saddle.

3 Don't forget to clean the underside of the saddle as this can get sweaty even if a numnah or saddle cloth has been used.

4 Allow the leather to dry slightly before applying the saddle soap. Use a fresh sponge and work the saddle soap into the leather with a circular rubbing motion. Cover the entire surface of the saddle, including under the saddle flaps.

SADDLING UP

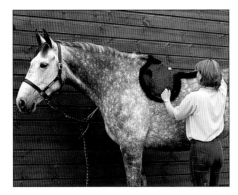

1 Place a numnah or saddle cloth on the horse's back, making sure it is positioned sufficiently high up the horse's withers.

2 Lift the saddle over the horse's back and carefully lower it into position on top of the numnah or saddle cloth. Ensure both saddle flaps are lying flat against the horse's sides.

3 Pull the numnah or saddle cloth up into the gullet of the saddle so that it is clear of the horse's withers.

4 Numnahs usually have straps to anchor them to the saddle and stop them from slipping. Attach the top straps to the saddle's girth tabs (billets) through which the girth is fitted above the girth guard before doing up the girth.

5 Buckle the girth to the off side (right) of the saddle first and pass it through the bottom strap on the numnah. Move back to the near side (left) of the horse, reach underneath him and take hold of the girth.

6 Pass the girth through the retaining strap on the numnah before buckling to the saddle girth tabs on the near side.

5 Remove dirt and grease from the stirrup leathers with a sponge. Apply the saddle soap and check the stitching for wear. Check that the leathers have not stretched: because we mount from the near side, one leather will become longer than the other if they are not switched regularly.

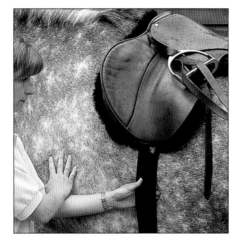

7 Tighten up the girth gradually (it should be equal on both sides) until there is just room to fit the flat of your hand between the girth and the horse's side. Picking up the horse's feet, one at a time, and pulling them forward will also help you to judge if the girth is comfortable for the horse.

8 Once the girth has been tightened, slide the buckle guard down over the girth buckles to prevent them from rubbing against and damaging the saddle flaps. Slide your hand round the horse's belly under the girth to ensure that there are no wrinkles in the horse's skin.

Bridles and Bits

Along with the saddle, the bridle and bit are the most
important pieces of equipment for the ridden horse. Combined
with the rider's legs, voice and body position, the bridle and
bit provide that important line of communication which allows
you to control the horse.

Bridles are traditionally made of leather. However, synthetic
bridles, which come in a choice of vivid colors, are becoming
much more popular, especially in the sports of flat racing and
endurance riding.

The variety of bits available can be bewildering, and choosing
the right bit for a horse is almost a science in itself. To simplify
matters, bits are divided into five groups which are categorized
by their action, based on the area of the horse's head to which
pressure is applied. The five groups are: snaffles, doubles,
pelhams, gag snaffles and bitless bridles. It is important to make
an accurate judgment over your choice of bit: a bit that is too weak
will result in the rider having no control over the horse, while one
that is too severe will encourage the horse to fight against it.

▌ OPPOSITE
A correctly "put up"
bridle, with the throat
latch fastened in a
figure-of-eight.

▌ LEFT
A Rugby pelham fitted
with a curb chain.

Snaffle Bridle

The snaffle bridle is a simple, basic bridle which is suitable for most types of riding. In particular it is the appropriate bridle for horses in the early stages of training. The noseband is not essential and need not be fitted; however, many horses, especially those with longer heads, tend to look better with the noseband in place. By changing the bit or fitting a different type of noseband, the action of the bridle can be made stronger, so that the rider has greater control over the horse and the way in which he carries his head.

headpiece (crownpiece)

browband

throatlatch

cheekpieces

noseband

eggbutt snaffle

reins

▮ RIGHT
The snaffle bridle is the standard type of bridle used with all single bits.

Double Bridle

The double bridle is basically the same in design as the snaffle bridle, although the addition of an extra bridoon sliphead means that two bits can be used simultaneously with two sets of reins. Unlike the snaffle bridle, which can be used with a variety of nosebands, the double bridle should only be fitted with a basic cavesson noseband so that the action of the curb is not interfered with.

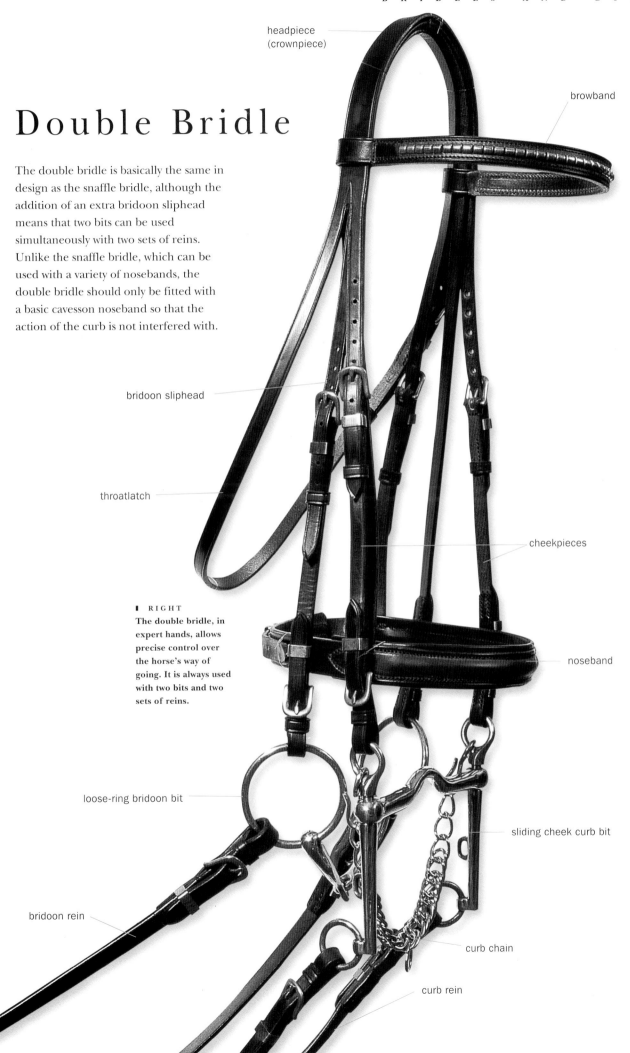

headpiece
(crownpiece)

browband

bridoon sliphead

throatlatch

cheekpieces

▌ RIGHT
The double bridle, in expert hands, allows precise control over the horse's way of going. It is always used with two bits and two sets of reins.

noseband

loose-ring bridoon bit

sliding cheek curb bit

bridoon rein

curb chain

curb rein

Western Bridle

The traditional Western bridle is fastened with narrow leather thongs, which enabled the cowboy to carry out running repairs on any items of broken tack himself when he was miles from the nearest saddler. Western bridles are referred to as either "one-ear" or "split-ear". The headpiece (crownpiece) of a split-ear bridle is made from a single piece of leather which has slits cut into it to fit over each ear. This is to prevent the bridle from being pulled off accidentally. The one-ear bridle incorporates a definite loop which fits over one of the horse's ear. The reins of the Western bridle are not joined at the end. This is to avoid the risk of the horse getting a foot caught in the reins if they trail on the ground.

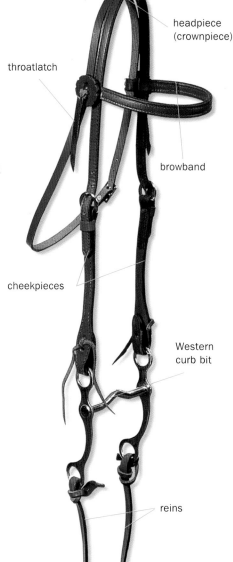

headpiece (crownpiece)

throatlatch

browband

cheekpieces

Western curb bit

reins

■ RIGHT
split-ear Western bridle

■ BELOW
one-ear Western bridle

Endurance 2-in-1 Bridle

The endurance bridle is a combination of a headcollar (crownpiece) and a standard bridle. The cheekpieces and reins can be quickly unclipped to leave just the headcollar in place. The headcollar can also be ridden as a Scawbrig, a type of bitless bridle, by attaching the reins to the noseband. The endurance bridle (also known as the combination bridle) has proved popular with endurance riders because of its practical design: the bit can be removed quickly to give the horse a drink during competition, while the reins very usefully double as a lead rope.

■ RIGHT
endurance 2-in-1 bridle

THE MAIN POINTS OF CONTROL

Bits, bitless bridles and certain types of nosebands will all act on specific parts of the horse's head.

The poll – the headpiece (crownpiece) of the bridle applies pressure here when a gag or curb bit is used.

The nose – bitless bridles and specific types of nosebands affect the nose.

The mouthcorners – snaffle bits bring pressure on the corners of the horse's mouth and lips.

Side of the face – bits with full cheeks, D rings or large racing rings affect this area.

Curb groove – the curb chain fitted with a pelham or Weymouth bit affects the curb groove.

Roof of the mouth – bits with ported mouthpieces affect this area.

Tongue – all bits apply pressure to the tongue.

Bars – all bits affect the bars, a sensitive part of the horse's mouth between the incisors and premolar teeth.

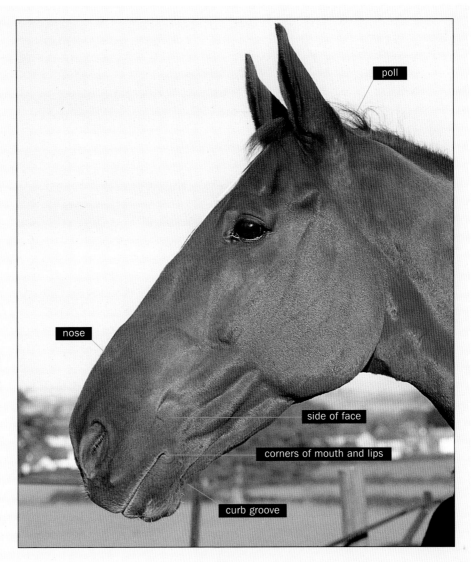

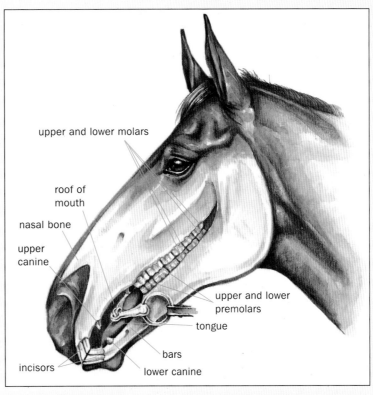

Snaffle Bits

The snaffle bit is the largest of the five bit groups. It contains a wide variety of different types of bit which vary in strength of action from very mild to severe. Snaffle bits act on the tongue, the bars and the corners of the mouth; some also act on the roof of the mouth. Snaffle bits encourage the horse to raise his head and bring it back towards your hands for greater control. In its basic form the snaffle is the most commonly used bit for horses in the early stages of schooling. Any well-schooled horse should go happily in a snaffle bit.

While all snaffles have the same basic action, different cheek- and mouthpieces will affect the action and severity of the bit. The single-jointed **eggbutt snaffle** has rounded edges where the rings join the mouthpiece to prevent the lips being pinched. The fixed cheek rings keep the bit relatively still in the horse's mouth.

The rings of the **loose-ring snaffle** allow the bit to move more freely in the horse's mouth, which some horses prefer. This type should be fitted slightly wider than the eggbutt snaffle, and can have rubber bit guards fitted over the rings to prevent it from pinching the horse's lips.

The **full-cheek snaffle** has extended cheekpieces which prevent the bit from sliding through the horse's mouth, and help to steer the horse by bringing pressure against the side of his face. This type of bit should be fitted with leather **fulmer keepers** attached to the cheekpieces of the bridle, to hold the bit still in the mouth and to prevent a cheekpiece from accidentally getting stuck up the horse's nostril. The **fulmer snaffle** is similar to the full-cheek but has loose, rather than fixed, bit rings.

The **half-spoon cheek snaffle** has spoon-shaped cheeks which extend downwards to put pressure on the outside of the lower jaw, helping with steering. The **D-ring snaffle** is often used on racehorses in preference to a fulmer

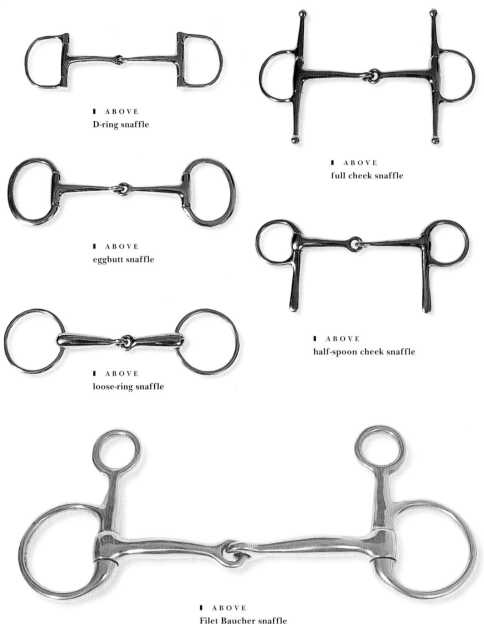

■ ABOVE
D-ring snaffle

■ ABOVE
full cheek snaffle

■ ABOVE
eggbutt snaffle

■ ABOVE
half-spoon cheek snaffle

■ ABOVE
loose-ring snaffle

■ ABOVE
Filet Baucher snaffle

snaffle. Like the fulmer, the shape of the cheekpieces prevents the bit being pulled through the mouth. By bringing pressure on the sides of the horse's face it can also help to steer the horse.

The **Filet Baucher** or **hanging cheek snaffle** has separate rings to which the cheekpieces of the bridle are attached so that the bit is suspended in the horse's mouth. Unlike other snaffles, the cheekpieces will exert some pressure on the horse's poll.

■ ABOVE
fulmer keepers

TYPES OF MOUTHPIECE

Snaffle bits come with a variety of mouthpieces which vary in the severity of their action.

The **straight bar mouthpiece** usually comes with non-riding bits such as stallion-showing bits or in-hand bits, and acts primarily on the tongue and lips.

The **mullen mouth** is a mild, simple unjointed mouthpiece, more curved than the straight bar. The mullen mouth rests on the bars of the mouth, exerting less pressure on the corners of the mouth and a more uniform pressure on the tongue.

When pressure is applied to the reins, the **single-jointed bit** squeezes the corners of the mouth in a nutcracker action, as well as applying pressure to the bars, the tongue and the roof of the mouth. Single-jointed snaffles have either a narrow, solid mouthpiece or fatter hollow mouthpiece (this latter type is known as the German snaffle). As a general rule of thumb, the fatter the mouthpiece, the milder its action.

Double-jointed mouthpieces feature a central link, which comes in different shapes and sizes. The nutcracker action is less severe than with single-jointed bits. However, these bits still act on the bars and corners of the horse's mouth.

The **French link** has a kidney-shaped link in the middle of the mouthpiece. It increases the flexibility of the bit, stops the horse from leaning and encourages him to soften his mouth.

The **Dr Bristol** incorporates a flat plate link which is much more severe in action than the French link. It is used in vigorous competition events such as jumping or cross-country. The plate applies strong pressure on the horse's tongue unless the head is carried in the position needed for the rider to control him. No small amount of pain will be inflicted on the horse if the bit is misused and it should only be used by experienced riders on particularly boisterous horses.

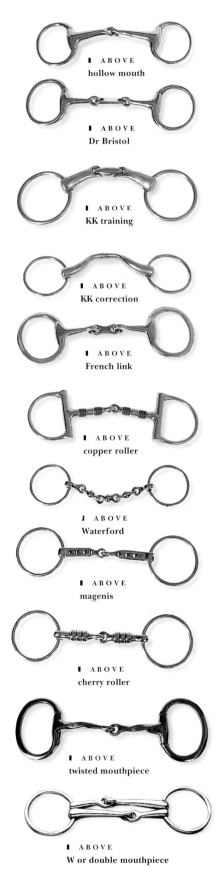

■ **ABOVE**
hollow mouth

■ **ABOVE**
Dr Bristol

■ **ABOVE**
KK training

■ **ABOVE**
KK correction

■ **ABOVE**
French link

■ **ABOVE**
copper roller

⌡ **ABOVE**
Waterford

■ **ABOVE**
magenis

■ **ABOVE**
cherry roller

■ **ABOVE**
twisted mouthpiece

■ **ABOVE**
W or double mouthpiece

The **KK training bit** has a central lozenge-shaped link which is designed to shift pressure away from the lips and corners towards the center of the horse's mouth to give a milder bit action.

The **Waterford bit** has a multi-jointed mouthpiece made up of a series of bulbous links. Because of the number of links, this mouthpiece is extremely flexible, which discourages the horse from leaning on it.

Roller mouthpieces feature a series of rollers in either steel or steel and copper. Because of the movement, these mouthpieces are used to discourage the horse from leaning on the rider's hands. There are two main types of roller mouthpieces: the **magenis** is a strong bit which features small rollers set into a squared-off mouthpiece; the **cherry roller** has rollers across the length of the mouthpiece and will encourage the horse to play with the bit, keeping his mouth relaxed. The more rounded shape of the mouthpiece means it has a kinder action than the magenis. Another roller mouthpiece, the **copper roller**, is similar to the cherry roller except that the rollers alternate between copper and steel. The copper is included to encourage the horse to salivate and relax his jaw.

The **twisted mouthpiece** is very severe, putting sharp pressure on the horse's tongue and the corners of his mouth.

Ported mouthpieces allow more room for the horse's tongue than other types of mouthpiece, while placing more contact on the bars. Bits with a high port will also act on the roof of the horse's mouth, causing the horse to raise his head.

The **KK correction bit** is a training bit made from Aurigan (a copper alloy) and is designed for strong, pulling horses.

The **W** or **double mouthpiece** has two thin, single-jointed mouthpieces attached to a set of bit rings. Strong bits like this are best left to expert riders because of the damage they can do to the horse's mouth.

Double Bits

Double bits are a combination of two bits: the **bridoon** (a snaffle bit) and a **curb bit**, also known as a **Weymouth**, which is fitted with a curb chain. The bridoon acts in exactly the same way as the snaffle, raising the horse's head, while the curb bit acts on the horse's poll and curb groove. Combining these two bits in one bridle enables you to fine tune your horse's head and neck carriage. A double bridle is used on horses who are already well schooled, particularly for dressage. It is also considered the correct bridle for the show ring. The curb bit comes with a mullen or ported mouthpiece. The length of the cheekpieces on curb bits varies but in general, the longer the cheekpieces, the greater the poll pressure.

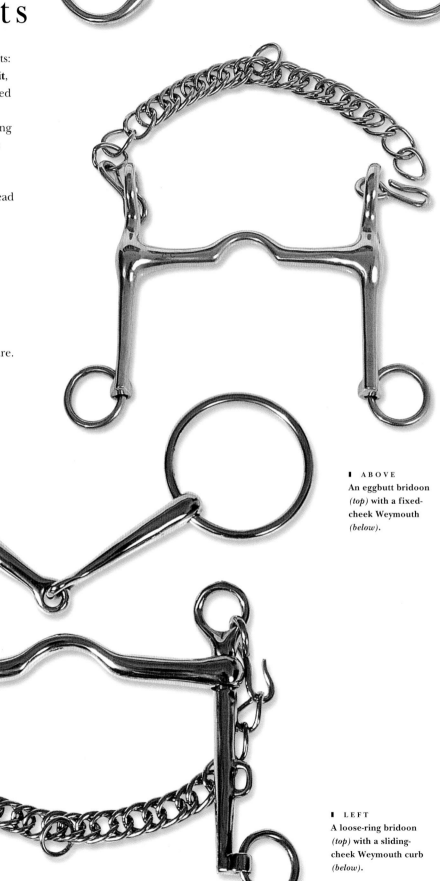

▌ **ABOVE**
An eggbutt bridoon
(top) **with a fixed-cheek Weymouth**
(below).

▌ **LEFT**
A loose-ring bridoon
(top) **with a sliding-cheek Weymouth curb**
(below).

Pelham Bits

The pelham is a compromise between a snaffle and a double bridle, combining the actions of both. As well as exerting pressure on the horse's mouth, pelhams also act on the poll and curb groove. Unlike the double bridle, it has only one mouthpiece and can be ridden with pelham roundings, the short pieces of leather linking the top and bottom rings, so that only one set of reins is needed (although it is more correct to ride with two). It is ideal for a show horse whose mouth is too small for a double bridle.

The **mullen-mouthed pelham** is the most popular pelham mouthpiece and also the mildest in action. The **jointed pelham** is very strong, the jointed mouthpiece having a direct action on the horse's tongue. The **Rugby pelham** has a loose-ring link for the bridoon rein, and as a consequence it brings greater pressure on the horse's curb and poll. The **Scamperdale pelham** is ideal for horses with fleshy lips. The mouthpiece is shaped so that it bends back at either end. This helps to keep the cheekpieces of the bit away from the horse's lips to prevent chafing. Unlike most other pelhams, the **globe pelham** is fitted with only one set of reins, which are attached to the lower rings.

The **kimblewick**, also known as the **Kimberwicke** or **Spanish jumping bit**, comes into the category of pelhams although it has less leverage action than a pelham and is ridden with only one set of reins. The **slotted-cheek kimblewick** (shown here with a hinged, copper, quarter-moon mouthpiece) enables you to choose at what height to attach the reins. The lower they are fitted, the greater the curb action of the bit. The **rounded-cheek kimblewick** has a similar action to a snaffle bit when the rider's hands are held high: lowering the hands emphasizes the curb action.

■ ABOVE
jointed pelham

■ ABOVE
Scamperdale pelham

■ ABOVE
Uxeter hinged copper kimblewick

■ ABOVE
mullen-mouthed
pelham

■ RIGHT
globe pelham

■ ABOVE
Cambridge mouth kimblewick

■ ABOVE
Rugby pelham

■ ABOVE
pelham roundings

■ ABOVE
slotted-cheek kimblewick

Gag Snaffles

This group of bits encourages the horse to raise his head by raising the bit in his mouth, as well as acting on the corners of the mouth and the poll. Gag snaffles are popular bits for strong, fit horses ridden across country and for those who like to put their heads down and gallop off. Like the pelham, the gag snaffle should be fitted with two sets of reins (although they can be used with only one set, attached to the roundings). One set is attached to the bit ring like a snaffle, the second set to the roundings which pass from the cheekpieces through the bit rings. This enables the rider to utilize the strong gag action only when it is actually needed.

The **Balding gag** has loose-ring cheekpieces through which gag roundings pass. The **Cheltenham gag** is similar in design but features eggbutt bit rings. With both types of gag, the larger the bit ring, the more severe the bit's action.

The **half-ring**, or **Duncan gag**, is a particularly strong type of gag as it can only be used with one set of reins, which is fitted to the gag roundings.

The **Dutch gag**, also called the **continental** or **three-ring gag**, can be used with one or two sets of reins. The bridle cheekpieces are attached to the top rings to produce poll pressure. The reins can be fitted to any of the three lower rings: the

lower the reins are fitted, the stronger the leverage action on the horse's mouth.

The **American gag** should also be used with two sets of reins (one set fitted to the central rings and the other fitted to the lower rings). As the gag (lower) rein is used, the mouthpiece slides up the cheekpieces, encouraging the horse to raise his head.

Gag roundings, or **running cheeks**, are leather or nylon straps which are attached to the cheekpieces of the bridle and then passed through the bit rings and attached directly to the reins. As the rider takes a contact on the reins, the bit slides up the roundings and the horse's head is raised.

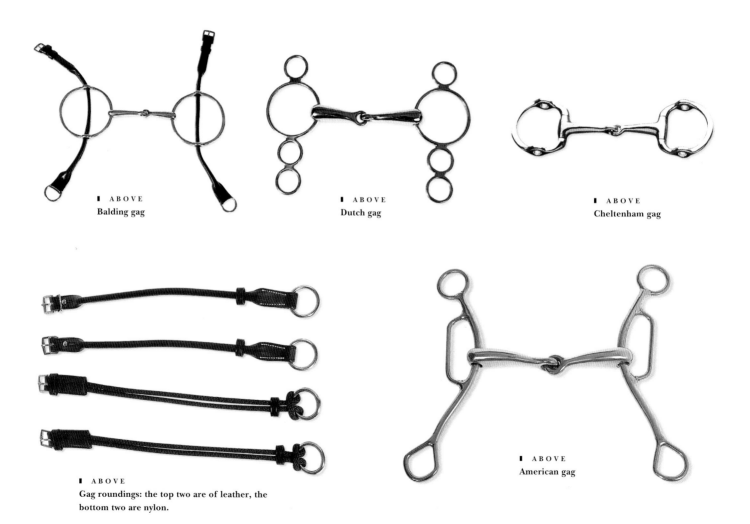

▌ ABOVE
Balding gag

▌ ABOVE
Dutch gag

▌ ABOVE
Cheltenham gag

▌ ABOVE
Gag roundings: the top two are of leather, the bottom two are nylon.

▌ ABOVE
American gag

The Bitless Bridle

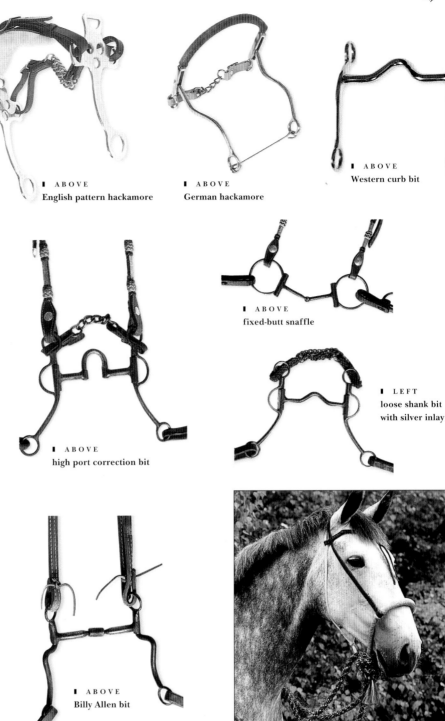

■ ABOVE
English pattern hackamore

■ ABOVE
German hackamore

■ ABOVE
Western curb bit

■ ABOVE
fixed-butt snaffle

■ ABOVE
high port correction bit

■ LEFT
loose shank bit
with silver inlay

■ ABOVE
Billy Allen bit

■ RIGHT
The bosal in use.

Although not a bit at all, bitless bridles, also known as hackamores, make up the fifth bit group. Instead of acting on the horse's mouth, bitless bridles apply pressure to the horse's nose as well as to the poll and curb groove. They can be used on horses who have injured their mouths but need to be kept in ridden work. Although bitless bridles have no influence on the horse's mouth, they can still be severe in inexperienced hands.

The **English pattern** or **Blair hackamore** has a padded noseband, metal cheeks and a leather curb strap (which is fitted slightly higher than a normal curb chain). Take care when fitting the English hackamore: if it is too high, the cheekpieces may rub the horse's cheeks; if it is too low, it can interfere with his breathing.

The **German hackamore** has a rubber-covered metal noseband, often worn padded with sheepskin, and a curb chain . The longer cheekpieces of the German hackamore have a stronger leverage action than the English pattern. Both types of hackamore can be used in conjunction with a bit by simply adding an extra sliphead to the bridle.

The **bosal** forms an integral part of Western training and riding. It is usually made from plaited (braided) rawhide and is used with a normal or one-ear bridle. The reins are attached directly to the "heel" knot at the back of the bridle.

WESTERN BITS

With their long cheekpieces and ported mouthpieces **Western curb bits** can appear severe, but in practice the Western horse is ridden with such a light contact that this is not the case. The horse is systematically trained, first using a bosal, then a combination of bosal and bit, and finally a bit alone. Western riders traditionally ride with just the weight of the rein itself maintaining the contact. Western bits are usually made out of sweet iron. This is "warmer" than stainless steel, and the rusting that naturally occurs encourages the horse to salivate.

The **high port correction bit** has loose shanks which allow the cheekpieces to swivel at the butt of the mouthpiece. The high port acts on the roof of the horse's mouth when a contact is taken.

The **low port bit** has silver inlay, a chain and a plaited (braided) nylon curb strap. The angle of the shank on the bit determines the severity of the leverage action, with a more angled shank giving a milder leverage action.

The **Billy Allen bit** has a jointed mouthpiece with a central roller, which lessens the nutcracker action of the mouthpiece. It is used as a transitional bit between the shank snaffle and a curb bit.

The **fixed-butt snaffle** is similar in action to an English eggbutt snaffle – the fixed butt keeps the bit still in the horse's mouth while the single joint has a nutcracker action on the horse's tongue.

Unusual Bits

There will always be bits that do not fit neatly into specific categories or those which have evolved with a specific sport in mind. Here are a few examples.

The **citation bit** forms part of a combination bit and bridling system called a Norton bridle. It has two mouthpieces, the thinner of which is attached directly to the noseband via the links on the bit rings. This is a highly specialized bit and bridle and is strictly for experienced hands only.

The **scourier** or **Cornish bit** has two sets of bit rings, one of which passes through holes in the mouthpiece. The inside rings are attached to the bridle while the outer rings are attached to the reins. This, combined with a grooved mouthpiece, results in a very severe bit.

The **Wilson snaffle**, like the scourier, has two pairs of bit rings. This bit is used for driving. Its action is similar to that of the scourier – pressure applied to the reins causes the bit rings to squeeze on the sides of the horse's mouth.

The **wind-sucking bridoon** or **flute bit** has a wide, hollow mouthpiece pierced with a series of small holes. It is designed to stop the horse from gulping down air when crib biting or wind-sucking.

The **tongue bit** incorporates a flat metal plate which prevents the horse from evading the bit by getting his tongue over the mouthpiece.

The **butterfly bit** is not a bit as such, but an attachment which clips on to the mouthpiece of an existing bit to increase the severity of its action.

The **loose-ring racing snaffle** has much larger bit rings than normal snaffles. The larger rings prevent the bit from being pulled through the horse's mouth. They can also help to steer the horse in a chosen direction by bringing pressure on the side of the face.

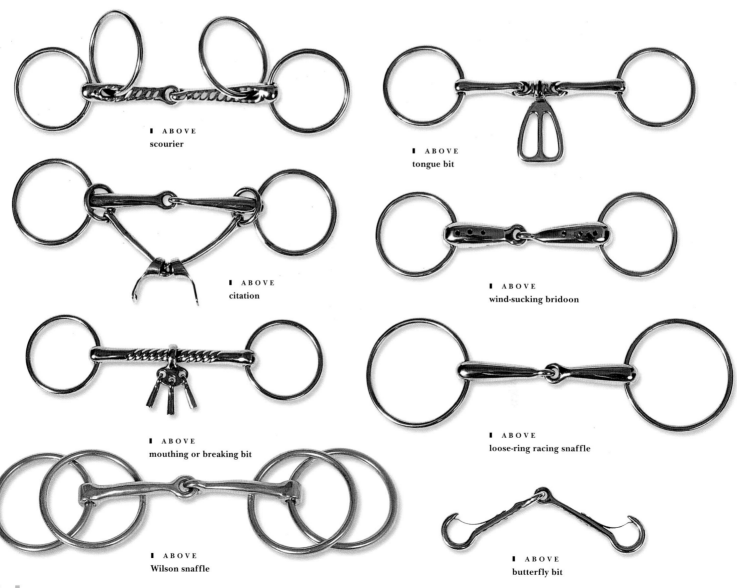

▎ ABOVE
scourier

▎ ABOVE
tongue bit

▎ ABOVE
citation

▎ ABOVE
wind-sucking bridoon

▎ ABOVE
mouthing or breaking bit

▎ ABOVE
loose-ring racing snaffle

▎ ABOVE
Wilson snaffle

▎ ABOVE
butterfly bit

Training and Showing Bits

Some bits are specifically designed for training young horses and for leading and showing horses in-hand.

The **chifney**, also known as an **anti-rearing bit**, consists of a ring which sits in the horse's mouth and is attached to a separate headstall. It is often used when leading stallions and racehorses in the parade ring.

The **Tattersall ring bit**, similar to the chifney, is useful for leading boisterous youngsters. The bit is held in place by a headstall which is attached to the two metal loops on either side. The lead rope is attached to the rear of the ring.

Mouthing or **breaking bits** are designed to encourage young horses to play with the mouthpiece. They can have a single or unjointed mouthpiece and feature small metal "keys" in the center of the mouthpiece with which the young horse plays.

The **horseshoe stallion bridoon**, which looks similar to the **overcheck bridoon**, is designed for showing stallions in-hand.

■ ABOVE
A Thoroughbred yearling with a Tattersall ring bit fitted to a leather headcollar.

■ RIGHT
Top to bottom: chifney; Tattersall ring bit; horseshoe stallion bridoon; overcheck bridoon

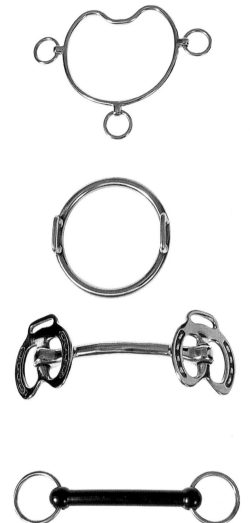

BIT MATERIALS

Bits are available in a wide variety of metals, alloys and synthetic materials. The following materials are listed in order of common usage.

Stainless steel is strong and easy to clean. Steel is the most popular choice of bit material. One of the disadvantages of steel is that it is a "cold" metal which does not encourage salivation.

Rubber is used to cover metal bits to soften their action. However, rubber is not particularly hardwearing and is easily chewed.

Vulcanite or vulcanized rubber is harder wearing than rubber but heavier and not as flexible.

Polyurethane and **nylon** bits are flexible if unjointed. These materials are also used to cover jointed metal bits. A mouthpiece using polyurethane or nylon can be very mild in action and often has an

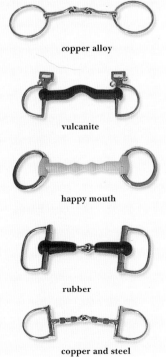

copper alloy

vulcanite

happy mouth

rubber

copper and steel

apple scent to make it more appealing to horses.

Copper mouthpieces warm up to the horse's body temperature more quickly than steel but are less hardwearing. They are designed to encourage horses with dry mouths to salivate.

Copper alloy bits are designed to combine the qualities of copper with the strength of stainless steel. Manufacturers claim that they improve the contact between the rider's hands and the horse.

Brass alloy bits are claimed to have the same qualities as copper. They are a combination of brass with silicon and aluminum.

Sweet iron mouthpieces rust very quickly when allowed to get wet, thereby encouraging the horse to salivate.

nathe

stainless steel

brass alloy

sweet iron

Curb Chains and Lip Straps

Curb bits and pelhams should always be fitted with a curb chain or strap. The curb chain brings pressure on the horse's curb groove. The chain or strap itself should be fitted so that it is brought into action when the shank of the curb bit is at an angle of 45 degrees.

The **Western leather curb strap** is used with a Western curb bit. The **single-link curb chain** is light in weight but, because of its design, can pinch the horse's skin; the **double-link curb chain** is preferable to the single-link type as it is less likely to do this. A **leather curb chain** is designed to be fitted to an English curb bit. The **elasticized curb chain**, like the leather curb chain, has a milder action than the metal type. The **rubber-covered chain** is more comfortable for the horse than an uncovered curb chain, and has a milder action on the curb groove.

All English curb straps or chains should be fitted with a fly ring through which a **lip strap** passes. The strap, attached to either side of the curb bit or pelham, helps to keep the curb chain in place.

Fulmer keepers are small leather straps which are fitted to the cheekpieces of a snaffle bridle. They are used to prevent the upper cheekpiece of a full-cheek snaffle from tipping forward. They also help to keep the bit raised in the horse's mouth, preventing the horse from getting his tongue over the bit.

Leather pelham roundings can be fitted to pelhams and certain types of gag bit when only one set of reins is used.

❚ ABOVE
Western curb strap

❚ ABOVE
double-link chain

❚ ABOVE
single-link chain

❚ ABOVE
leather curb chain

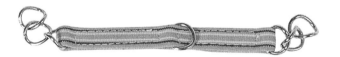
❚ ABOVE
elasticized curb chain

❚ ABOVE
rubber-covered chain

❚ RIGHT
Lip strap fitted to a Weymouth bit.

Nosebands

Nosebands are available in a variety of designs, from those chosen purely for aesthetic reasons, to corrective nosebands which offer more control, acting in conjunction with the bit to increase the strength of the bit action or to prevent the horse evading it.

The **cavesson** is the simplest noseband design available. It is the only type of noseband to use with a double bridle and can also be used with a standing martingale. When fitted correctly, it should have little or no action on the horse's head. The cavesson should be fitted loosely enough to allow room for two fingers under the noseband.

Rope cavessons are much more severe in action than leather ones and are more commonly seen on polo ponies or strong show jumpers. The **continental** or **cinchback cavesson** is designed to be fitted

LEFT
cavesson noseband

BELOW
continental cavesson

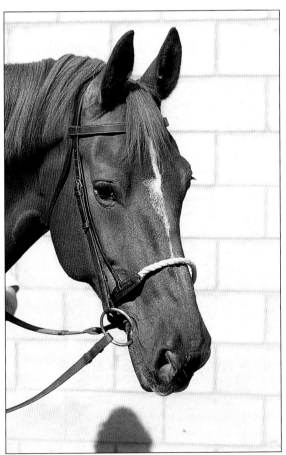

LEFT
rope cavesson
noseband

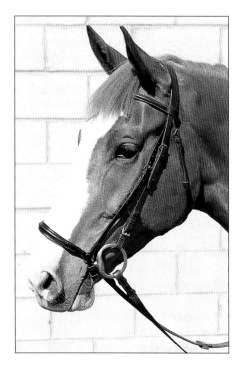

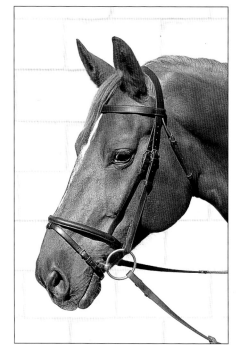

more tightly than a traditional cavesson to discourage the horse from opening his mouth. It can be used with a double bridle and for this reason is often used for dressage or showing.

The **dropped noseband** is fitted with the back strap passing below the bit. It is designed to prevent the horse from opening his mouth and evading the bit. The dropped noseband (when fitted correctly) can increase pressure on the horse's poll as well as on the nose and lower jaw. The dropped noseband should not be used if a standing martingale is fitted. Take care not to fit it below the base of the nasal bone as this can restrict the horse's breathing.

The **flash** is based on the cavesson noseband but has an additional strap which is fitted below the bit. It was originally developed for riders who wanted a noseband which closed the mouth like a dropped noseband, but which could be used alongside a standing martingale. The flash noseband is fitted slightly higher and tighter than the cavesson. Attachments are available which can transform an ordinary cavesson into a flash noseband.

The **Grakle** or **figure-of-eight** takes its name from the eponymous winner of the British 1931 Grand National steeplechase. The Grakle should be fitted snugly so that the top strap goes around the horse's jaws above the bit (resting just below the facial

bone) while the lower strap passes below the bit, keeping the mouth closed. The Grakle puts pressure on the horse's nose (where the straps cross) and helps to stop the horse from crossing his jaws.

Take care that the central point does not lie below the nasal bone as this will cause discomfort to the horse. There should be a short strap fitted at the back of the noseband to keep the straps in place.

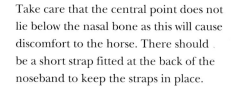

▌ A B O V E
Left to right:
**dropped noseband;
flash noseband;
Grakle or figure-of-eight noseband**

▌ L E F T
Mexican Grakle

BELOW
Australian cheeker

RIGHT
sheepskin noseband

The **Mexican** or **high-ring Grakle** is fitted higher than a normal Grakle, above the cheek bones. It sits higher up the face and is thought to be more effective at preventing the horse crossing his jaws.

The **Kineton** or **Puckle noseband** is a severe noseband which derives its name from its designer, a Mr Puckle of Kineton. Metal loops pass under the bit so that when a contact is taken up, strong pressure is brought to bear on both the nose and the bit, encouraging the horse to lower his head. As with the dropped noseband, take care not to fit it too low.

The **sheepskin noseband**, often used on racehorses, is basically a cavesson noseband covered with a sheepskin sleeve. It encourages the horse to lower his head, which he must do if he is to see over the noseband.

The **Australian cheeker** is a rubber attachment which fastens to the headstall of the bridle and either side of a snaffle bit. It helps to keep the bit raised in the mouth, preventing the horse from getting his tongue over it. It is thought that being able to see the central strap encourages the horse to back off the bit.

The **controller** or **combination noseband** combines the action of a dropped and a Grakle noseband. The two straps help to keep the horse's mouth closed and discourage him from opening his mouth. The front strap is adjustable and is fitted like a dropped noseband. For very strong horses, the front strap can be reinforced with a strip of metal.

BELOW LEFT
Kineton noseband

BELOW RIGHT
controller noseband

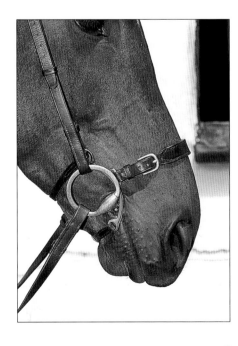

Reins

The reins provide the vital line of communication between your hands and the bit in the horse's mouth.

Plain leather reins are very smart and make an ideal choice for showing. They are often used with double bridles as they are not bulky. A thicker rein is fitted to the bridoon with a thinner rein used for the curb. A disadvantage of plain leather reins is that they can be slippery, especially if allowed to get wet. **Plain leather dressage reins** incorporate small leather "stops" which help to improve grip.

Laced leather reins have thin strips of leather laced through them to improve grip. **Plaited (braided) leather reins** are easy to grip but are more expensive than laced reins and with use they will stretch.

Rubber-covered reins are the popular choice for everyday riding because of their durability. They are very easy to grip, even when wet, and for this reason are often used for racing, eventing and general riding. **Half-rubber reins** are less slippery than plain leather ones, and are more attractive and less cumbersome than rubber-covered reins. **Continental reins** are made of webbing with leather stops to improve grip. **Rubberized webbing reins** are lightweight and incorporate rubber for improved grip.

Plaited (braided) cotton reins are light in weight and reasonably easy to grip. **Plaited (braided) nylon reins** are slightly cheaper than plaited cotton reins, but can be very slippery and will stretch easily. **Western reins** are traditionally ridden split, without being secured at the end with a buckle, to prevent the horse catching his foot if the reins trail on the ground once the rider has dismounted.

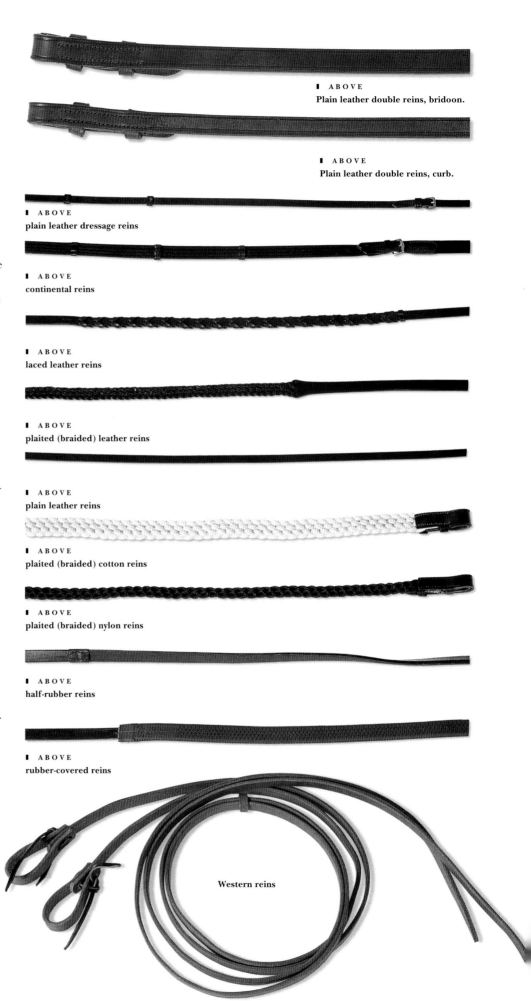

▐ ABOVE
Plain leather double reins, bridoon.

▐ ABOVE
Plain leather double reins, curb.

▐ ABOVE
plain leather dressage reins

▐ ABOVE
continental reins

▐ ABOVE
laced leather reins

▐ ABOVE
plaited (braided) leather reins

▐ ABOVE
plain leather reins

▐ ABOVE
plaited (braided) cotton reins

▐ ABOVE
plaited (braided) nylon reins

▐ ABOVE
half-rubber reins

▐ ABOVE
rubber-covered reins

Western reins

Rein Attachments

There are a number of ways in which reins can be attached to the bridle, depending on the reason the horse is being tacked up. For instance in showing classes, where appearance is of the utmost importance, reins will often be stitched on to the bit.

Although this makes changing the bit difficult, it does look much neater than billets (stud hooks) or buckles.

Billets are small metal hooks which fasten into a small hole in the rein to attach it to the bridle. The billet and billet

hole should be checked regularly for wear and tear. **Buckles** are a secure way of attaching reins but can look bulky. Western reins are attached to the bit by **hide thongs**. **Loops** are a less secure method of fastening reins than buckles.

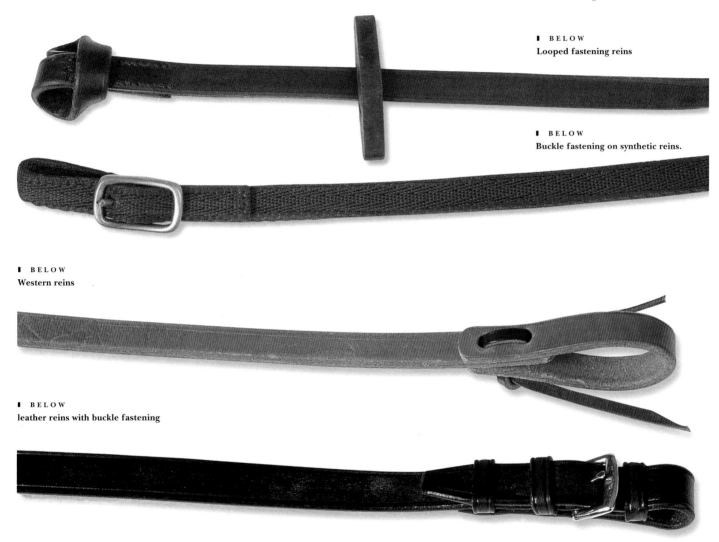

■ BELOW
Looped fastening reins

■ BELOW
Buckle fastening on synthetic reins.

■ BELOW
Western reins

■ BELOW
leather reins with buckle fastening

Browbands

The browband helps to keep the bridle in position on the horse's head. It is very important that the browband is fitted correctly as a browband fitted too loosely looks untidy and may not be effective in preventing the bridle from slipping back. If fitted too tightly, the browband can pinch the horse's ears, thereby forcing him to shake his head. Available in a wide range of designs, browbands are always highly decorative.

The **plain browband** is ideal for horses with heavier, coarser heads. **Padded browbands** feature a raised central section, which suits larger warmblood heads. A raised strip of colored **plaited (braided) leather** can add contrast to an otherwise plain bridle. **Velvet-covered browbands** are available in a wide choice of colors and can be selected to match your outfit. They are popular for showing hacks and children's ponies. A delicate browband, the **plaited (braided) Arab**, is specially designed to suit the finer features of the Arab horse. **Clincher browbands** have studs (clinchers) in silver or brass. They come in all sorts of decorative designs which feature metal bobbles and small, mirrored strips. **Diamanté browbands** are popular for horses competing indoors where the light catches the stones. The **chain browband** is best suited to horses or ponies with extremely fine heads. The **bit motif browband** incorporates a gilt snaffle design. **Western browbands** can be very simple in design, with little or no ornamentation, although highly decorative browbands with silver detailing are often used for showing or parades. Not all Western bridles feature browbands: the one ear and split ear bridles do not require a browband to keep them in place.

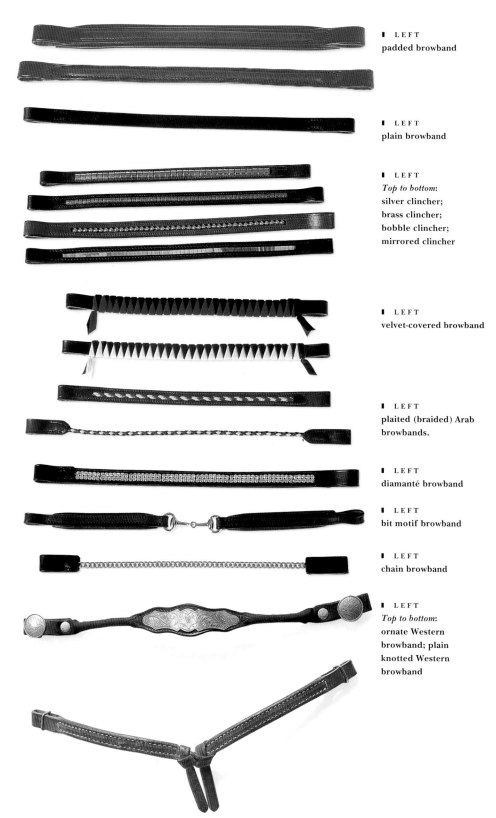

■ LEFT
padded browband

■ LEFT
plain browband

■ LEFT
Top to bottom:
silver clincher;
brass clincher;
bobble clincher;
mirrored clincher

■ LEFT
velvet-covered browband

■ LEFT
plaited (braided) Arab
browbands.

■ LEFT
diamanté browband

■ LEFT
bit motif browband

■ LEFT
chain browband

■ LEFT
Top to bottom:
ornate Western
browband; plain
knotted Western
browband

Bridle Accessories

There is a range of items which can be fitted to the horse's bridle or halter. Many of these pieces are corrective items designed to discourage the horse from a bad habit, while some are aids to improve his comfort.

▌ RIGHT
Bit guards are rubber disks which can be fitted to loose-ring bits to prevent them from pinching the horse's lips. They also help to keep the bit positioned centrally in the horse's mouth.

▌ BELOW
The pricker pad is a leather pad with sharp bristles. It is fitted to one side of the bit against the side of the horse's face to discourage the horse from leaning to one side.

▌ ABOVE
A face net is a fine mesh net which is fitted over the horse's head. It can help protect the horse from flies when he is turned out in the field.

▌ ABOVE
Rein stops should always be fitted when a martingale is used. They stop the martingale rings slipping down towards the bit and getting stuck.

▌ ABOVE
Blinkers are mainly used on racehorses. They block the horse's view to either side, helping him to concentrate and thus improve his racing performance.

▌ RIGHT
Martingale stops are fitted to running and standing martingales to stop the central strap slipping through the chestpiece.

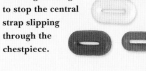

▌ RIGHT
The tongue guard is a rubber attachment which fastens to the bit. It is used to prevent the horse getting his tongue over the bit.

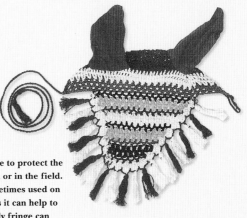

▌ ABOVE AND RIGHT
Fly fringes are attached to the bridle to protect the horse's face from flies when ridden or in the field. The type with earpieces is also sometimes used on show jumpers competing indoors as it can help to muffle spectator noise. A simpler fly fringe can be fitted to the horse's headcollar to protect him from flies when turned out in the field.

Putting on a Bridle

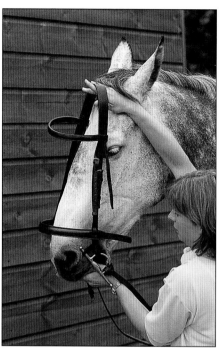

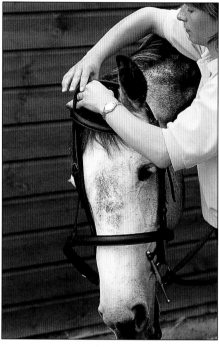

1 Stand on the near (left) side of the horse and hold the headpiece (crownpiece) of the bridle in your right hand. Place your left hand (holding the bit) under the horse's muzzle.

2 Press your thumb firmly but gently against the bars of the horse's mouth to encourage him to open his mouth.

3 Guide the bit gently into the horse's mouth, taking care not to bang it against his teeth. Draw the bridle up with the right hand and, using the left hand, guide the left and then the right ear under the headpiece of the bridle.

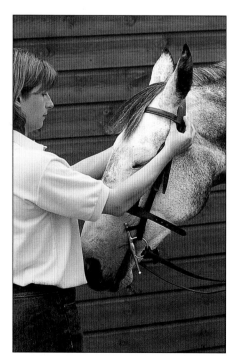

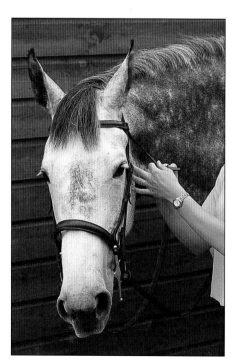

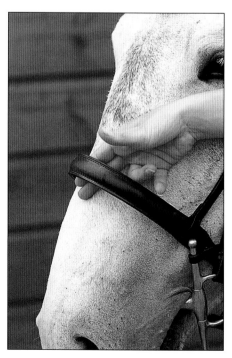

4 Separate the mane under the headpiece (a small section of mane, called a bridle path, can be clipped from this area) and bring the forelock out over the browband.

5 Fasten the throatlatch. It should be loose enough to allow you to fit four fingers between the throatlatch and the horse's cheeks.

6 Fasten the noseband (in this case a cavesson) so that it passes underneath the cheekpieces of the bridle. It should be loose enough to allow you to place two fingers underneath the noseband.

CLEANING THE BRIDLE

Bridle Care

A leather bridle should be cleaned regularly to keep it in top condition and to prolong its life. Remove sweat and grime every time the bridle is used and once a week dismantle it completely for a thorough cleaning. A synthetic bridle can be simply wiped down with a damp cloth or immersed in water. Check the stitching and billets (stud hooks) regularly, paying particular attention to where the bit is attached to the bridle at the reins and the cheekpieces.

1 Hang the bridle from a suitable hook, undoing all the straps from their keepers.

2 Wipe the bridle down with a damp sponge to remove dirt and grease.

3 Use a clean sponge to rub in lightly moistened saddle soap.

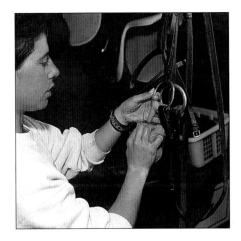

4 Wipe the bit, or rinse it under running water. Do this each time it has been used to prevent a build-up of saliva and food.

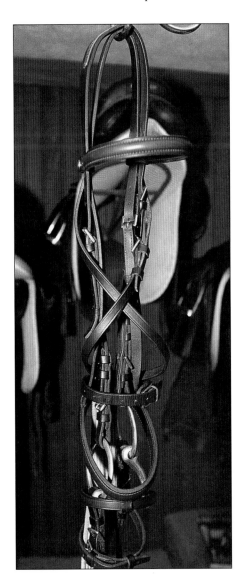

A correctly put up bridle. Cross the throatlatch over the front of the bridle, loop up the reins and fasten the noseband around it.

▌ LEFT
Jockeys will often tie a knot at the end of the reins. This is a safety measure in case the buckle joining the reins were to break during the race.

Training Aids and Gadgets

There is a saying that gadgets and training aids are fine in the hands of experts but that experts have no need for them. This may apply in an ideal world but every horseman or woman, however expert, will encounter problems when schooling and training horses and may occasionally need additional help in the form of an aid or a gadget.

A training aid is a piece of equipment used to develop a well-schooled, obedient horse to improve his performance, while a gadget is a piece of equipment which prevents or restrains an aspect of the horse's behavior which makes him dangerous or difficult to ride.

A degree of skill is required when using training aids or gadgets. The equipment must be fitted correctly, and you must be aware of its strength and severity. Only use it when it is specifically required, never as a matter of course. Training aids and gadgets in the wrong hands can damage the horse physically and psychologically.

▌ OPPOSITE
A rider schooling on
the flat to encourage
obedience and
suppleness.

▌ LEFT
A leather lunging
cavesson.

Martingales

Martingales are designed to assist the bridle in controlling the horse. They prevent the horse from raising his head beyond the point at which the rider can control him.

The **running martingale** consists of a neck strap and a second strap which is attached to the girth and passes between the horse's front legs before dividing into two pieces. At the end of each of these straps is a small metal ring through which the reins pass. **Rein stops** should be fitted to the reins, below the bit, to prevent the martingale rings from getting caught on the bit. When the horse carries his head in the correct position no pressure is felt. However, when he raises his head above a certain point, the martingale restricts the movement of the reins which in turn causes the bit to bear down on the bars of the horse's mouth. The running martingale should be fitted so that the rings are in line with the withers to prevent it putting any pressure on the

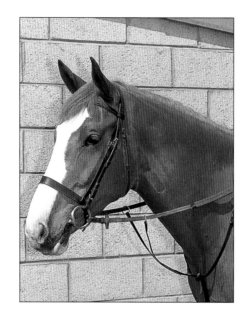

▌ ABOVE
running martingale

▌ BELOW LEFT
combined breastplate and martingale

▌ BELOW RIGHT
bib martingale

reins when the horse's head is held in the correct position. It should not be used in conjunction with a curb bit.

The **bib martingale** is a variation on the running martingale. The two straps of the martingale are joined by a triangle of leather. This is to prevent an excitable horse from getting caught up in the straps; the design is often used on racehorses.

The **combined breastplate and martingale** is a traditional heavyweight hunting-style breastplate used to stop the saddle from slipping back. The breastplate has a central ring to which a running martingale attachment is fixed.

The **standing martingale** has a single strap which is attached to the girth, passes between the horse's front legs and is fixed to the back of the noseband (a cavesson or the cavesson part of a flash noseband). Like the running martingale, it has a neck strap. When correctly fitted it should be possible to push the martingale strap up into the horse's gullet.

■ LEFT
standing martingale

■ LEFT AND
BELOW
The Irish
martingale is
used to prevent
the reins being
thrown over the
horse's head in
the event of
a fall. It is
often used on
racehorses, as
shown here on
Desert Orchid.

A **rubber martingale stop** should
always be fitted to running and standing
martingales to stop the martingale from
slipping through the neck strap, which
could result in the horse getting a foot
caught in the straps.

The **Market Harborough** consists of a
leather strap attached to the girth, which
passes between the horse's front legs
before dividing into two straps with a clip
at each end. These straps pass through the
bit rings and are clipped on to one of a
series of rings on the side of the reins.
Like the running martingale, the Market
Harborough will only put pressure on the
bit (and as a consequence on the bars of
the horse's mouth) if the horse brings his
head up beyond a certain point. The
Market Harborough should only be used
with an ordinary snaffle.

The **Irish martingale**, unlike other
martingales, has no direct action on the
horse's head carriage. It consists of a short
piece of leather with a ring at either end

through which the reins pass. The Irish
martingale is used to prevent the reins
from being pulled over the horse's head
in the event of a fall. It can also be used
for horses who have a habit of suddenly
tossing their heads in the air – "star
gazers" – resulting in the reins being
thrown over their heads.

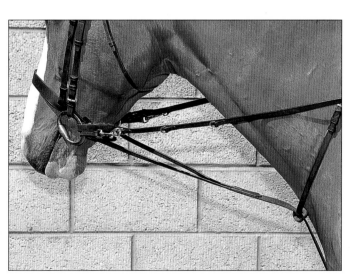

■ LEFT
Market Harborough
martingale

Training Reins

Training reins are used when schooling the horse to help him develop the correct musculature for ridden work, or as a corrective aid to encourage the horse to carry himself well.

Running reins, also known as **draw reins**, are long pieces of leather or webbing with a loop at each end which fit around either side of the girth; the reins pass through the bit rings (from the inside to the outside) and up to the rider's hands. Running reins encourage the horse to lower his head, bringing it towards the vertical to promote the correct development of his back muscles. Running reins should only be used with an ordinary snaffle bridle to which an independent set of reins is also attached, and the rider must be quick to release the pressure on the running reins when the horse lowers his head. It is important that the horse is ridden forwards or there is a danger that he will become over-bent (with his head held behind the vertical).

A more severe method of fitting running reins is to attach them to the

Running reins attached to either side of the girth.

Attach running reins at the chest for more control.

girth at the chest before passing them through the front legs up to the bit and back to the rider's hands. Fitted in this way the running reins (more correctly referred to as draw reins) impart a stronger leverage action on the horse's head.

An **overcheck rein** has a center buckle and passes over the horse's poll, through the bit rings to the rider's hands. Overcheck reins will encourage the horse to raise his head by raising the bit in his mouth, rather like a gag snaffle.

The **De Gogue schooling system** is used for ridden work or lunging. A strap from the girth passes between the horse's legs and divides into two cord straps. A piece of leather with pulleys on either side is fixed to the headpiece of the bridle. The cord straps go over the pulleys and down to the bit. For ridden work, short reins can be attached to the straps (with a second independent set of reins also fitted). For lunging, the cords pass through the bit rings and clip on to the chest strap.

The De Gogue schooling system for lunging or ridden work.

The Chambon system for lunging or loose schooling only.

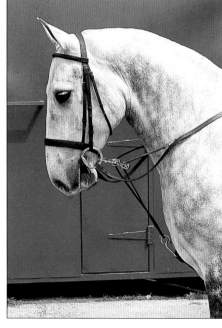

The Abbot Davies balancing rein.

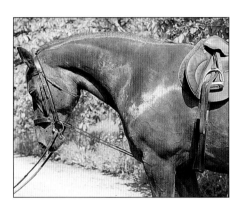

▌ LEFT
Two ways of attaching the
elastic training rein.

▌ BELOW
The Pessoa training
system.

The **Chambon** is a schooling system consisting of a poll pad fitted over the top of the horse's head, to which pulleys are attached on either side. A strap is attached to the lunging roller which passes up between the horse's front legs before dividing into two cords. The two cords fit over the pulleys and are clipped on to the bit rings. The Chambon encourages the horse to lower his head and neck and round his back, which in turn encourages engagement of the hindquarters. The Chambon can be used on horses which are being loose-schooled but is not designed to be ridden in.

The **Abbot Davies balancing rein** encourages the horse to develop the muscles of his back and hindquarters by raising his neck at its base. A combined system of pulleys and straps will prevent the horse leaning. It can be fitted from tail to mouth but more commonly, or in the latter stages of training, it is fitted from girth to mouth or mouth to ears.

The **Harbridge** aims to encourage the horse to work correctly by discouraging leaning, enhancing self-carriage and generally stimulating softness in the horse's back. It is not dissimilar in appearance to a running martingale. A strap attached to the girth passes through the horse's front legs and divides

into two pieces of elastic which are clipped on to the bit rings. It should be used for flat work only, and is not suitable for schooling over jumps.

The **Schoolmasta training aid** is designed for horses which lean on the bit or have a tendency to over-bend and carry their heads behind the vertical. The system works independently of the rider's hands: straps clipped on to either side of the bit are attached to a pulley fitted to a special numnah, and this helps to correct the horse's posture.

The **elastic training rein** fits over the horse's poll, passes through the rings and clips on to the girth at the side or at the chest. The rein is designed to promote self-carriage without putting pressure on the horse's mouth.

The **Pessoa training system** aims to give the horse a rounded outline. It consists of a roller and pulleys attached from the roller to the bit rings, and to a strap passed round the hindquarters. As with all training equipment, skill and experience are needed for it to be used successfully.

The Harbridge has two elasticized
straps that clip on to the bit.

The Schoolmasta training aid is used in conjunction with a specially
adapted numnah.

Lunging and Long Reining

Lunging is a method of exercising or training the horse from a single long rein. The horse is worked in a circle, at a distance of 20m/66ft from the handler, in both directions and in walk, trot and canter.

The **lunge cavesson** is an essential piece of lunging equipment. It is fitted over a bridle if side reins are to be used. A lunge line is attached to the central ring on the noseband. The cavesson should fit snugly so that it does not slip when in use.

Lunging and **breaking rollers** are necessary when side reins or long lines are used. In the examples shown here, the top roller has large rings through which long-reining lines are fitted. Side reins can be attached to the smaller D rings. A crupper prevents the roller slipping forward; a breastgirth keeps it from slipping back. Lunging the horse with side reins fitted

LEFT AND BELOW
Shown here are two examples of a lunge cavesson, in leather (*left*) and webbing (*below*).

BELOW
Top to bottom: **Leather breaking roller, leather lunge roller and web lunge roller.**

enables the handler to influence the horse's outline and general way of going by containing impulsion. Working the horse on long lines enables the trainer to teach the young horse to respond to the feel of reins before a rider is introduced.

The **Elwyn Hartley-Edwards breaking roller** is a webbing and leather roller designed specifically for training the young horse. It features a built-in crupper to prevent the roller from being pulled forwards as the horse is worked.

Side reins are attached to the roller and clip on to the bit rings to encourage the horse to work in a correct outline. There is some debate as to whether elasticized or non-elasticized types are better. Some trainers feel that a rein that "gives" is better than a fixed type, while others suggest that elasticized reins can encourage the horse to evade the contact of the reins.

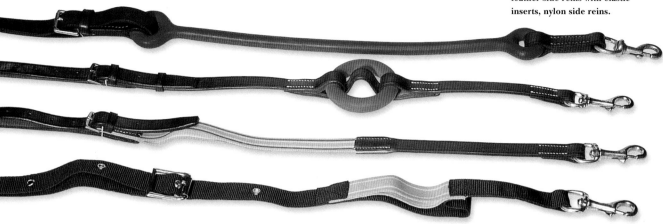

Continental pattern side reins in leather have rubber inserts which allow the reins to "give" as the horse moves. **Leather side reins** are available, many with elastic inserts. Leather side reins can be costly but if well cared for they will last longer than synthetic ones. **Nylon side reins**, with or without elastic inserts, are a cheaper alternative.

The **lunge line**, available in cord or webbing, is attached to the central ring on the lunge cavesson by means of a spring clip or a buckled strap. The lunge line enables the handler to control and guide the horse around a circle.

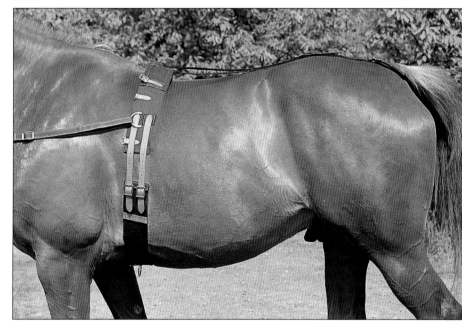

■ ABOVE
The Elwyn Hartley-Edwards breaking roller shown fitted with side reins and a crupper.

■ LEFT
lunge lines

LUNGING CAVESSON FITTED OVER A BRIDLE

The cavesson has been fitted over a bridle with the noseband removed. The reins have been twisted and looped through the throatlatch to prevent the horse accidentally getting caught in them. The side reins are attached to the bit rings: these should only be attached when the horse is being lunged. Start with the side reins fitted loosely and adjust them as the horse warms up.

HORSE TACKED UP FOR LUNGING

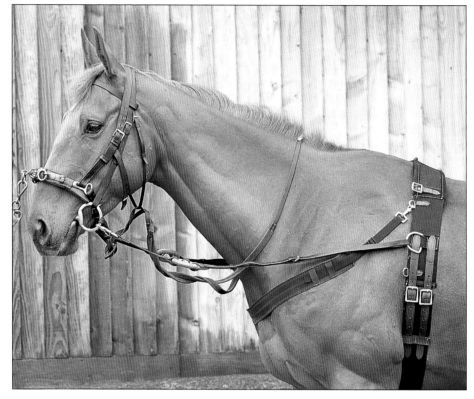

Lunging roller fitted with a breastplate.

USING A SADDLE INSTEAD OF A ROLLER

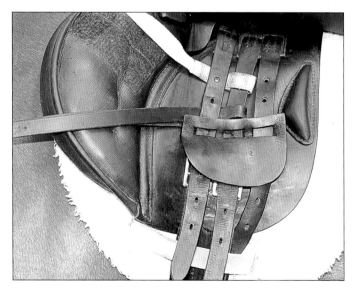

1 Side reins can be fitted to the girth straps on a saddle instead of the roller. They are useful if you plan to ride the horse after it has been lunged or if the horse is being lunged with a rider on board. The side reins pass round the second girth strap and under the first. This will prevent them from slipping down.

2 The stirrups can be removed from the saddle or, if the horse is to be ridden, they can be held securely in place by looping the stirrup leather around the stirrup and securing it with the spare end.

Lead Reins and Ropes

Lead reins and ropes are essential items of equipment when handling horses.

Lead ropes are inexpensive and sturdy, and are the practical choice for everyday use. They are clipped on to the horse's headcollar or halter so that he can be secured when travelling, or when being groomed or tacked up. Cotton and plaited (braided) nylon lead ropes come in a variety of colors: choose one to match your horse's headcollar.

When securing a horse with a lead rope, always use a quick release knot to allow the horse to be untied quickly in an emergency. Tying a horse directly to a fixed object, such as a gate or metal tie ring, can risk injuring him if he decides to pull back suddenly. Instead, attach the rope to the fixed object with a loop of bailing twine. If the horse pulls back suddenly, the twine will break and the horse will be released unhurt.

Leather and **webbing lead reins** are very smart and are commonly used for showing horses in-hand. The leather type has a double chain attachment called a **Newmarket chain**, which clips on to either bit ring and gives the handler greater control over the horse. The webbing lead rein is popular for showing and attaches directly to the headcollar or halter.

▮ BELOW
plaited (braided) nylon lead rope

▮ BELOW
cotton lead rope

▮ BELOW
webbing (*top*) and leather lead reins

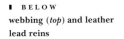
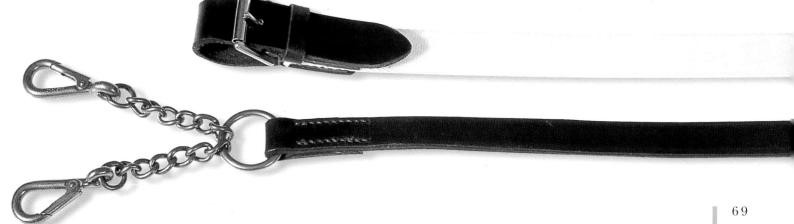

Headcollars and Halters

Headcollars and halters are indispensable items of tack which are used to lead horses in-hand or to secure them when travelling or in the stable. Some are also designed to control or restrain horses.

The best-quality **leather headcollars** are made from English leather and, like all good-quality leather tack, they will last for years if well cared for. As an extra feature, you can attach a brass plate engraved with your horse's name.

Synthetic headcollars are ideal for everyday use. They are extremely strong, although this can be a problem – if the horse is turned out in one and gets caught on a branch, gate or fence, the synthetic headcollar will not break easily. The **synthetic rope halter** is made of strong nylon cord and fastens simply by tying. **Rope halters** are commonly used for showing young stock in-hand.

The **Controller headcollar** can be used for horses with a tendency to pull when led in-hand. The headcollar is designed to apply pressure on the nose when the horse pulls against the handler.

The **"Be-Nice"** halter, popularized by the American trainer, Monty Roberts, will train the horse to be led in-hand. The halter tightens around the horse's head and applies pressure to the poll when the horse resists being led. It should never be used to secure the horse.

The decorative **Western show halter** is made from leather with engraved silver detailing. The **in-hand bridle** is halfway between a bridle and a headcollar. It has short leather straps to which a bit is fitted and is used, as its name implies, for showing horses in-hand. The **rolled Arab slip** is a delicate halter which will enhance the fineness of the Arab head in in-hand showing classes. The **foal slip** is designed as a first headcollar for young foals. The short strap which hangs down is used instead of a separate lead rope.

A leather headcollar makes a very smart piece of equipment. A brass plate engraved with the horse's name can be fitted as an extra feature.

The synthetic headcollar is strong, durable and easy to care for. It is available in many colors and is a popular choice for children's ponies.

The unusual design of the synthetic rope halter means that it can be fastened without buckles.

The simple rope halter is popular for showing young horses in-hand.

▮ **ABOVE LEFT**
controller headcollar

▮ **ABOVE MIDDLE**
"Be Nice" halter

▮ **ABOVE RIGHT**
Western show halter

▮ **LEFT AND RIGHT**
foal slip

▮ **ABOVE LEFT**
in-hand bridle

▮ **BELOW LEFT**
rolled Arab slip

Clothing and Equipment

The ridden horse needs a variety of clothing and equipment to keep him warm, clean and dry, and to protect him from injury. Rugs are a necessity for clipped horses and for fine-skinned, hot-blooded types such as Thoroughbreds. Modern rugs are lighter in weight than their predecessors, making them more comfortable for horses to wear and easier to clean. They are also more effective at keeping the horse warm, dry, cool or clean.

There is always a risk that a horse may be injured during exercise or when he is competing or travelling to and from shows. To minimize the risk there is a range of equipment and clothing available to protect him literally from top to tail. Grooming equipment is an essential part of the horse owner's kit. Whether your horse lives out or is stabled, regular grooming will help maintain his health by encouraging good circulation, removing dirt and dead skin and generally improving his appearance. Keeping the horse's coat clean will also help to keep the tack itself clean.

❙ OPPOSITE
Horses need extra
protection from the
potential hazards
of road travel.

❙ LEFT
felt covering boots

Turnout and Stable Rugs

TURNOUT RUGS

Turnout rugs are used to keep the horse warm and dry when turned out in the field. Turnout rugs are made from tough synthetic fabrics. Modern turnout rugs incorporate state-of-the-art breathable materials which are highly water- and windproof but still allow moisture to pass from the horse's body through the rug, preventing the horse from getting overheated.

The **New Zealand turnout rug** is a heavyweight canvas turnout rug, so-called because it was first developed in New Zealand. The self-righting type has breast and leg straps which help the rug to stay in place, whatever the horse gets up to.

The **Wug** and **Gladiator turnout rugs** are made from synthetic material. Both feature an extended neck which helps to keep the horse warm and dry.

▌ LEFT
The Wug turnout rug, with its extended neck, is made from a tough yet lightweight material.

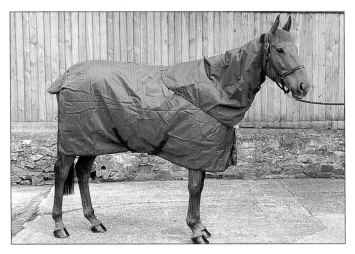

▌ LEFT
The Gladiator turnout rug features a useful neck cover.

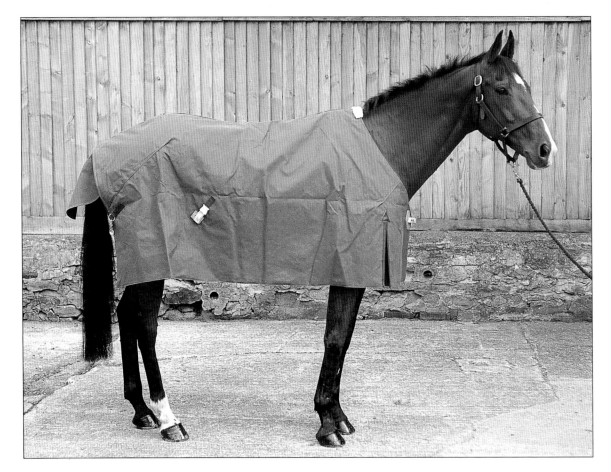

▌ LEFT
The New Zealand rug is a heavyweight proofed canvas turnout rug.

▌ BELOW
The stable synthetic
rug can be used as a
day or night rug.

▌ RIGHT
quilted foal rug

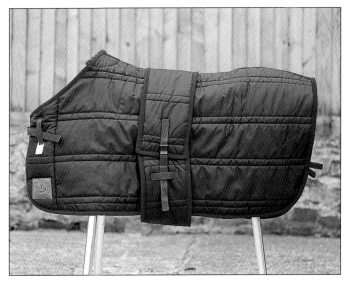

STABLE RUGS

Stable rugs keep the horse clean and
warm in the stable. The models available
range from lightweight cotton rugs for
summer to thick quilted rugs for winter.

Melton day rugs are made of wool
and are available in a range of colors.
A woolen rug will keep the horse warm
but it can be heavy and less breathable
than modern fabrics, and is more
difficult to clean. Woolen rugs can be
personalized with the owner's initials or
a sponsor's logo.

The **synthetic stable rug** is a modern
alternative to the traditional woolen rug.
New fabric technology means that stable
rugs can be both lightweight and warm,
allowing any sweat from the horse's body
to pass through the fabric. Because they
are easy to wash, synthetic stable rugs also
work well as night rugs.

Under rugs (blanket liners), available
in different thicknesses, are designed to
be fitted under a horse's stable rug to
provide extra warmth during the cold
winter months. Extra warmth may also
be provided by a **horse blanket** fitted
under a stable or night rug.

Jute rugs, traditionally used as night
rugs, have a natural fiber outer layer and
a blanket lining. Their main disadvantage
is that they are very heavy.

▌ RIGHT
The woollen Melton
day rug is effective
at keeping the horse
warm, but is heavier
than rugs made from
synthetic fabrics.

▌ BELOW
The Jute rug is a
natural fiber rug
traditionally used
as a night rug.

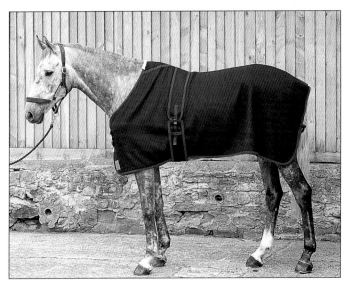

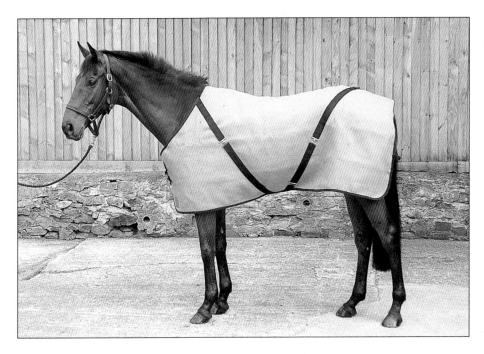

Sheets and Coolers

BELOW
A linen summer (stable) sheet can be used to keep
the stabled horse clean during warmer weather.

SHEETS

Sheets are made from lighter materials
than turnout or stable rugs. A sheet can
be used either in the summer months
when the temperatures are higher, or
immediately before or after exercise.

Summer (stable) sheets, made from
linen or cotton, are lightweight rugs used
to help keep the stabled horse clean.

Paddock sheets are shaped rugs in
cotton or wool, so-called because they are
used to keep racehorses warm while being
paraded in the paddock before the race.
The paddock rug is held in place with a
surcingle and breastgirth. It can double as
an exercise sheet, also called a half-sheet
or quarter-sheet, to keep the racehorse's
hindquarters warm during early morning
exercise on the gallops.

Many exercise sheets are designed to
keep the horse warm and dry while active,
and are particularly useful for clipped
horses. The synthetic polypropylene fabric
used for the **wicking exercise sheet** will
only allow moisture to pass through if
the horse begins to sweat. This type of
exercise sheet is worn under the saddle.

BELOW
paddock sheet

COOLERS

Coolers are multi-purpose rugs, often
incorporating the latest developments in
fabric technology. They allow the horse
to dry off quickly after exercise or bathing
without the risk of catching a chill because
of a wicking effect which allows moisture
to pass from the horse's body through the
fabric. Cooler rugs are ideal for those
horses with a tendency to sweat profusely
when travelling.

The non-absorbent breathable fabric
of the **Coolmasta rug** makes it suitable
for use as an anti-sweat rug, a travelling
rug or a stable rug. The polypropylene
fabric of the **Universal wicking rug** allows
dampness from the horse's body to pass
through the rug to prevent chills, as does
the **fleece rug**. The **Combi sweat (anti-
sweat) rug and fly sheet (scrim)** is a fine-
mesh rug. The knit of the cotton fabric
creates air pockets which help the horse
to dry off quickly. These rugs can be used
on a stabled horse under a lightweight
summer sheet to speed up the drying
process after exercise.

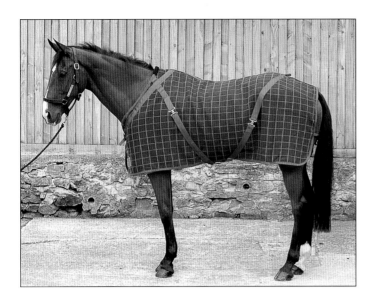

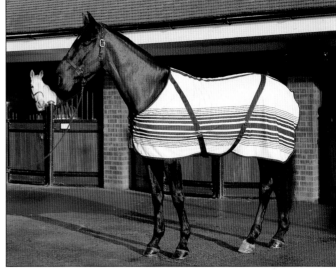

ABOVE LEFT
Universal wicking rug. A multi-purpose rug which lets body moisture through the fabric to prevent the horse catching a chill.

ABOVE RIGHT
Coolmasta synthetic rug. A cooler which is versatile enough to be used as summer (stable) sheet, anti-sweat rug, travel or day rug.

RIGHT
Fleece rug. While moisture evaporates away through the rug, the fleece fabric ensures that the horse's body temperature does not drop.

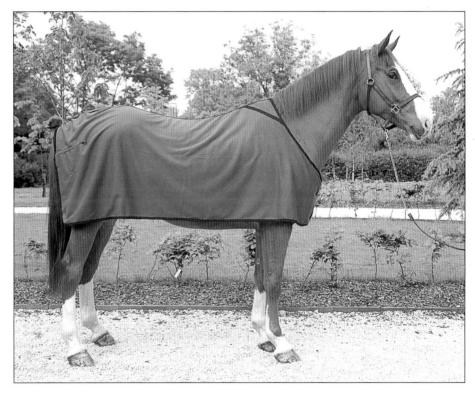

BELOW
Combi sweat (anti-sweat) rug and fly sheet (scrim). A fine mesh rug which can be used under a summer sheet to speed up drying.

BELOW RIGHT
Rain sheet. This waterproof rug (cover) will keep the horse dry at shows and competitions.

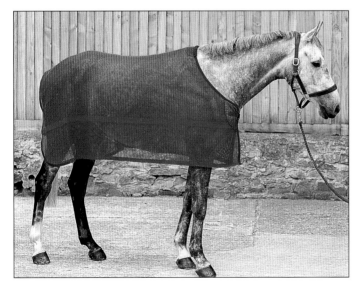

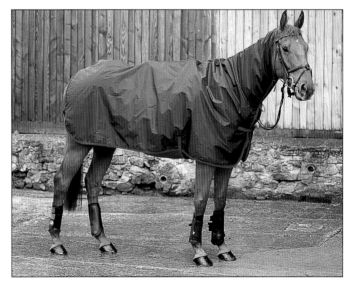

Specialist Sheets and Rugs

■ BELOW
Continental waterproof exercise sheet

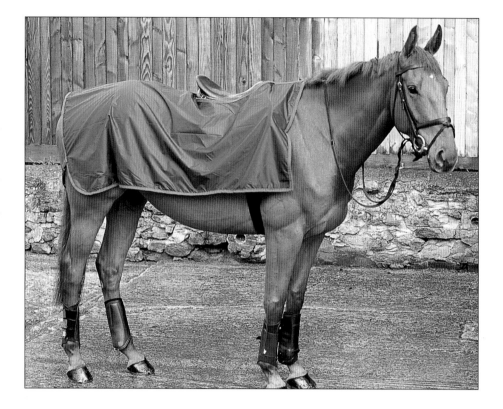

Besides the basic types of rug, an increasing number of rug products are available for more specific needs.

Exercise sheets will keep thin-skinned horses warm and dry during exercise sessions. The **continental waterproof exercise sheet** has a lightweight outer shell with a twill lining and can be fitted over the saddle in wet weather. The **fluorescent exercise sheet** ensures that both horse and rider are easily seen by other road users, and is especially useful for anyone who has to ride on roads at times of poor visibility.

The **rain sheet** is a lightweight synthetic sheet which covers the horse from ears to tail. The sheet will keep the horse dry at competitions and shows but should not be used on horses turned out in the field.

New born foals do not normally require rugs. However, the **quilted foal rug** can be very useful in helping to keep a sickly foal warm in the stable.

The **rug bib (blanket bib)** is fitted under the rug to prevent it from rubbing the horse's shoulders, leading to sores and bare patches in his coat.

Hoods can be fitted to rugs to provide extra warmth and to help keep the horse clean. The **outdoor hood**, made from a synthetic material, can be fitted to a turnout rug. The **lycra hood** is used in the stable to keep the horse clean.

Chest extenders are panels of fabric with straps which can be buckled on to the horse's existing rug to provide a better fit.

■ BELOW LEFT
fluorescent exercise sheet

■ BELOW RIGHT
wicking exercise sheet

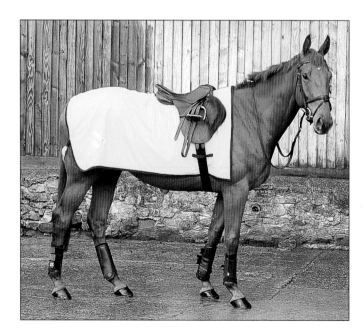

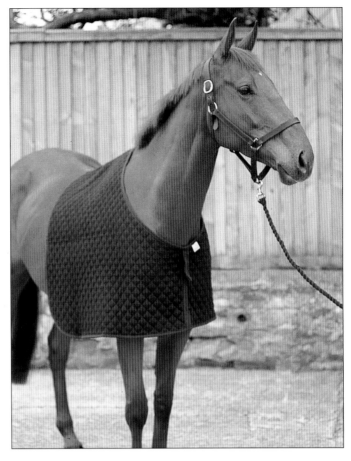

■ ABOVE
A rug bib is fitted
under the rug to
prevent the rug
from rubbing.

■ ABOVE
golden stripe horse blanket

■ BELOW
lycra hood

■ BELOW
under rug

HOW TO PUT ON A RUG

Fitting a Rug

Whatever type of rug you use, it is important that it is fitted correctly. Rugs are often left on for long periods of time and an ill-fitting rug can cause rubbing and discomfort. Rugs are sized according to their length, with the measurement based on the length of the horse taken from the center of the chest to the tail.

HOW TO REMOVE A RUG

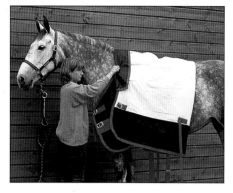

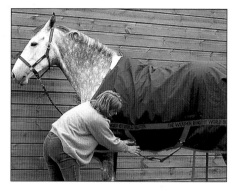

1 Stand on the near (left) side of the horse. Fold the blanket in half widthways and place it over the horse's neck. Fold the rug back over the horse's hindquarters.

2 Fasten the cross surcingles, but not too tightly: there should be room for the width of a hand between the horse's belly and the straps. These straps should be fastened first so that there is no risk of the rug ending up hanging around the horse's neck, or worse still, his legs.

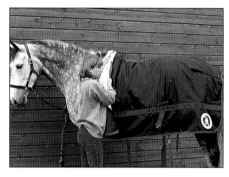

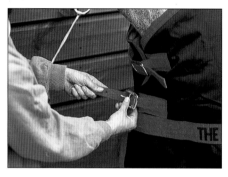

To remove the rug, undo the leg straps first, then the chest straps and finally the cross surcingles. Fold the front of the rug over the horse's hindquarters and slide off carefully.

3 Next fasten the chest straps: there should be room for a hand's width at the chest.

4 Finally, fasten the leg straps. Fitted correctly, the straps should hang clear of the horse's legs so that they do not rub, but should not be loose enough for the horse to get his leg caught.

▌ RIGHT
Modern turnout rugs allow horses to spend time out in their field whatever the weather. It is important to remember that turned out horses should have their rugs checked at least once a day, as the rug can slip and become uncomfortable for the horse.

Rug Rollers and Surcingles

Most modern stable rugs have surcingles already fitted but separate rollers and surcingles can be used to keep in place those rugs which do not incorporate their own. A separate roller or surcingle is also necessary when more than one rug at a time is worn, to keep them both in place.

Rollers and surcingles should be fitted snugly enough to secure the rug, but they should not be so tight as to be uncomfortable for the horse after long periods of time. Correctly tightened, there should be just enough room to allow four fingers between the roller or surcingle and the rug.

Surcingles used to secure rugs differ significantly from surcingles used to secure saddles, since the needs of the turned out horse and the ridden horse are not the same. The **rug surcingle** is designed for comfort. It is wrapped in protective padding and replaces the buckles and clasps of the saddle surcingle with thick rounded straps, to allow the horse the freedom to sit or roll.

The **elasticized surcingle** fits around the horse's girth. If you are using one of these, it is a good idea to fit a pad over the withers to prevent pressure sores. The **elasticized roller** has padding built in to the area in contact with the withers, as does the **jute surcingle**, which fastens with strong leather straps.

The **anti-cast roller**, made from webbing and leather, has a large metal hoop on the top which prevents the horse from getting cast or wedged when rolling in his stable (stall).

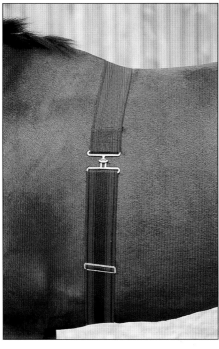

Elasticized surcingle. This type should be used with a pad over the withers to prevent pressure sores.

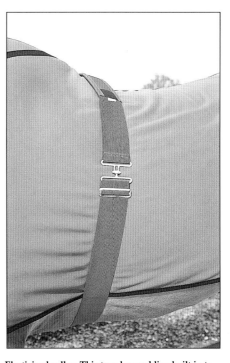

Elasticized roller. This type has padding built in to protect the withers.

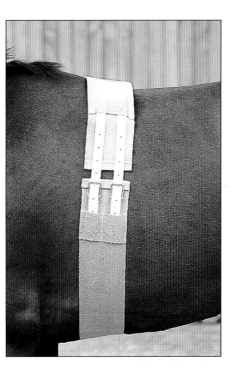

Jute surcingle. This type has built-in padding and fastens with strong leather straps.

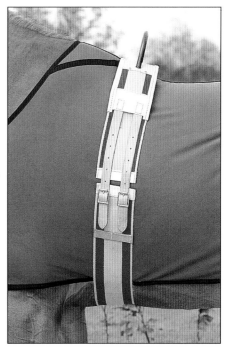

Webbing anti-cast roller. The large metal hoop on the top prevents the horse from getting cast.

Boots

Boots are designed to protect the horse's legs when travelling, turned out or being ridden, and a wide choice is available. Many equestrian activities place extreme demands on the horse's legs and protection is needed to prevent injury. Some horses are also predisposed conformationally to striking themselves accidentally while being exercised.

Brushing boots, also referred to as **splint boots**, have a reinforced pad along the inside of the boot to prevent injuries caused when one leg knocks against the other. The boot should start just below the knee and finish just below the fetlock (or ankle) joint. **Hind brushing boots** are longer than **fore brushing boots** to protect the hind cannon bone. **Leather brushing boots** have buckle and strap fastenings. They are tougher than synthetic boots but must be looked after to maintain their condition. **Synthetic brushing boots** are held in place with Velcro straps. They are lightweight and easily washed.

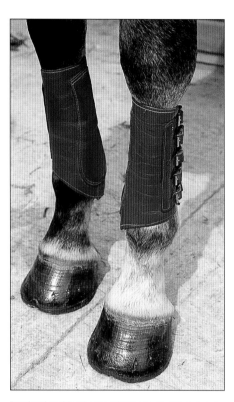

Leather brushing boots. These are used to prevent injuries inflicted as the horse is being brushed.

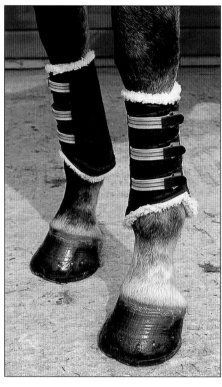

Synthetic brushing boots. These particular boots are fleece lined to prevent rubbing.

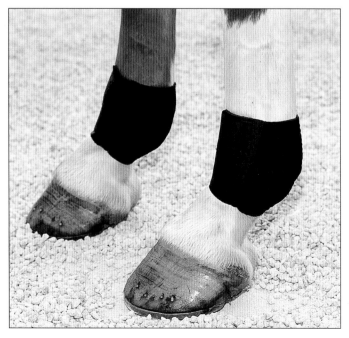

Sesamoid boots. These boots protect the base of the horse's fetlock.

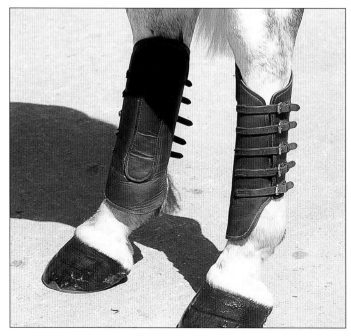

Speedicut boots. These are fitted to the hind legs to prevent injuries if the horse were to accidentally kick himself while galloping.

Speedicut boots are fitted to the hind legs and are designed to protect against injuries that occur when one leg strikes another during fast work. When the horse is travelling at high speed, the vulnerable area is the upper part of the leg, hence the boot's extra length.

Tendon boots are designed to protect the tendons which run down the back of the horse's lower foreleg, so are normally open-fronted. The boots should start high enough to protect the tendon and extend low enough to protect the fetlock joint. **Leather tendon boots** have buckle and strap fastenings and may be lined with sheepskin to prevent rubbing. **Synthetic tendon boots** usually have strap and clip fastenings.

Open-fronted boots are popular with show jumpers because they protect the vulnerable part of the horse's leg while still allowing him to feel the poles of the jump.

Sesamoid boots protect the base of the fetlock joint and are often used on

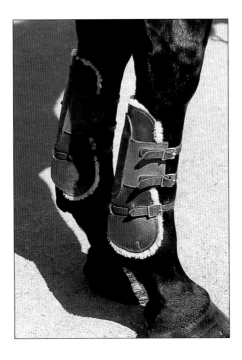

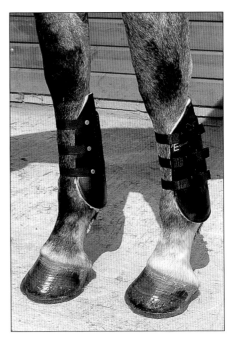

racehorses that are trained or run on all-weather or dirt tracks. The base of the fetlock would be damaged if unprotected as it touches the ground as the result of the forces exerted when galloping.

Fetlock boots are shortened versions of brushing boots, fitted to the hind legs. **Skid boots** are used for Western riding. They prevent fetlock injuries which can occur when the horse makes sliding halts.

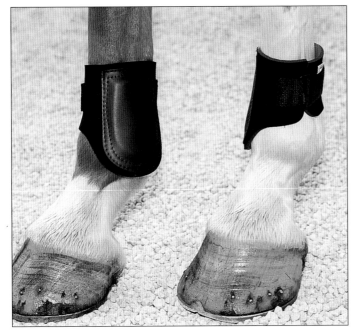

Fetlock boots. These are a shortened version of the brushing boot, and are normally fitted to the hind legs only.

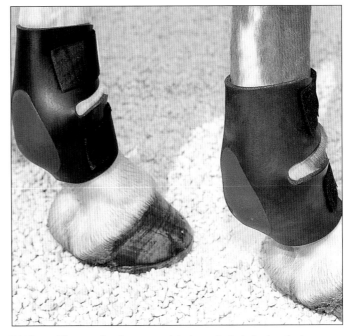

Skid boots. These are fitted to prevent injuries to the fetlock when the horse comes to a sliding halt.

Free knee boots prevent damage to the horse's knees when jumping. Because of their design – they can flip up – they are not suitable for road work or travelling. **Skeleton knee boots** have a lower strap fitted which prevents the pad from flipping up in the event of the horse falling. They are not suitable for jumping as there is a risk that the horse could get a hoof caught in the back strap.

The **coronet ring**, also called an anti-brushing ring, is fitted to one of a pair of legs to prevent brushing injuries. A **sausage boot**, also referred to as a **shoe-boil boot**, is used on stabled horses to prevent injury to the elbow when the horse lies down.

Overreach boots, or **bell boots**, prevent overreach injuries. An overreach is caused by the toe of the hind foot striking into the heel or coronet of the front foot. **Pull-on rubber overreach boots** can be difficult to get on but, once on, stay in place well. A disadvantage of this type of overreach boot is that it can flip up, in which case it will not protect the heel and coronet. **Velcro-fastened rubber overreach boots** are easier to put on and take off. **Petal boots** are less likely to flip up because of their segmented design. They are made up of a series of tough plastic segments or petals which are attached to a strap fitted around the coronet.

Covering boots are felt shoes which fit over the mare's hind feet. They are used on mares being covered, to avoid risking injury to the stallion should the mare try to kick him.

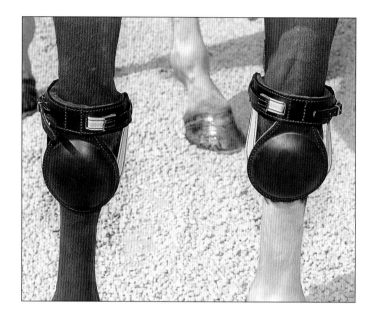

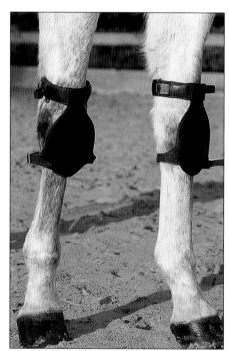

▌ ABOVE
Skeleton knee boots. These have a lower strap fitted which prevents the pad flipping up.

▌ RIGHT
Sausage boot. These are used on stabled horses to prevent injuries to the elbow.

▌ LEFT
Free knee boots. Because of their design, these boots are not suitable for roadwork or travelling.

▌ ABOVE
Coronet ring. This is fitted to one leg to prevent brushing injuries.

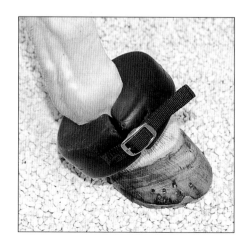

▌ L E F T
Protection is necessary to guard against the hazards encountered during the cross-country phase of a one-day event. Because the horse is jumping fixed objects, it is vital that his legs are protected with boots or bandages.

▌ A B O V E
Mare's covering boots. These felt shoes are fitted over the mare's hind feet to protect the stallion should she lash out at him.

▌ A B O V E
Velcro-fastened rubber overreach boots. This type is easier to put on and take off than the pull-on variety of overreach boot.

▌ R I G H T
Pull-on rubber overreach boots. These molded boots will sit securely on the hoof, but they do flip up easily and can offer no protection when this happens.

▌ L E F T
Petal boots are made up of a series of tough plastic segments which are attached to a strap.

EXERCISE BOOTS

Exercise boots, such as brushing boots, are much more convenient to use than exercise bandages (polo wraps) as they are quicker and easier to put on.

▌ BELOW
Skid boots are worn by reining horses to protect the base of the fetlock joint from injury as he comes to a sliding halt.

FITTING BRUSHING BOOTS

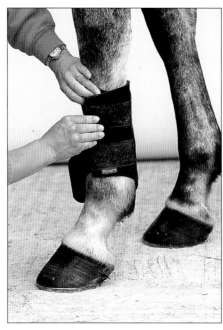

1 Never kneel down when putting on or taking off boots – always crouch so that you can get out of the way quickly should the horse suddenly move. When fitting boots with two straps, fasten the top strap first.

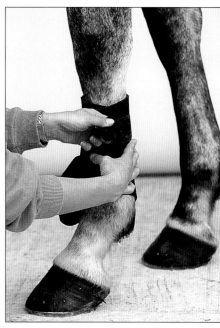

2 On most boots, straps fasten from the front to the back. For boots with more than two straps, fasten the middle strap first, then the top strap and finally the bottom strap or straps.

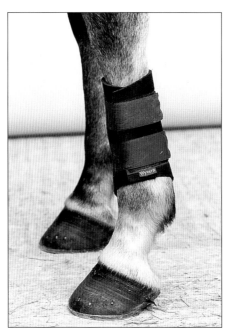

3 Be careful not to over-tighten boots as this is uncomfortable for the horse and can damage the tendons in his lower legs.

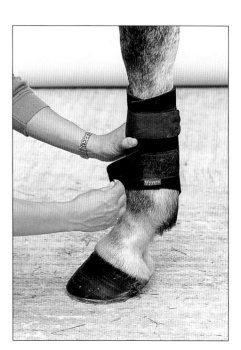

4 When removing boots, undo the bottom strap before unfastening the top one.

THERAPY BOOTS

These boots are designed to keep in place poultices, which are used to draw out dirt from a wound, and otherwise to assist in the treatment of injuries.

Rubber over-shoes fit over the horse's foot. One of these can be used to cover a foot bandage or poultice, or to protect the unshod hoof during ridden work. The **Tenderfoot sox** is used to hold a foot poultice in place.

A **tendon-hosing boot** fitted to the horse's lower leg allows cold water to be trickled down the leg to help reduce swelling caused by stresses, strains or injuries. If something more than a trickle is needed **aqua boots**, covering the entire lower leg and foot, are attached to a compressor which forces water to move around inside, massaging the lower leg.

Magnetic therapy boots are available in various designs. They incorporate thin, flexible magnetic pads which, when placed over the injured area, are said to assist in the repair of muscle, tendon or bone damage.

▌ LEFT
rubber over-shoe

▌ LEFT
magnetic therapy
boots

▌ BELOW LEFT
tendon-hosing boot

▌ BELOW RIGHT
aqua boots.

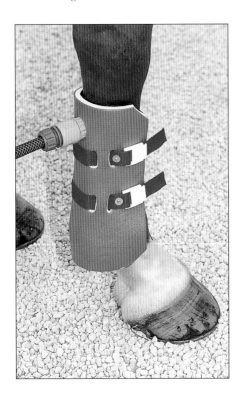

Bandages and Pads

BANDAGES

Like boots, bandages can be used to protect the horse's legs during exercise or travelling as well as for first-aid purposes.

Travelling or **stable bandages** are non-stretch bandages usually made of wool or acrylic and used for warmth and protection. To prevent pressure sores developing on the leg, they should always be used with padding underneath.

Exercise or **tail bandages** are lighter in weight than stable bandages. They are usually slightly elasticized and are held in place with ties. When used to protect the leg during competitions, in particular horse trials, they can be stitched in place. They will help to smooth the tail hair down as well as protecting the tail while the horse is travelling to the competition.

Polo wraps are made from strong, shock-absorbent felt. Unlike traditional bandages, polo wraps do not require padding underneath.

A **cohesive bandage** is a stretchy bandage which sticks to itself. It can be used as an alternative to an exercise bandage or for holding dressings and poultices in place.

PADS

Bandages should never be applied directly to the leg (except for polo bandages) but should be used with bandage pads to help reduce the risk of pressure sores developing on the legs.

Felt pads are hardwearing and shock absorbent, but they do not mold easily to the shape of the horse's leg. **Cotton quilted pads** are easily washable and hardwearing but, like felt, do not mold easily to the horse's leg. **Porter boots** are hard-shelled leg protectors which mold to the shape of the horse's leg and are held in place with an exercise bandage. They are used instead of pads to protect the leg from injury during competitions.

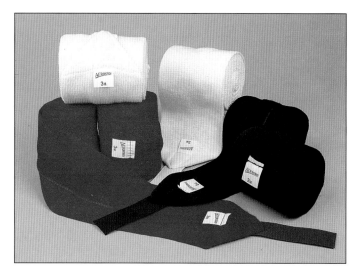

■ **LEFT**
travelling or stable bandages

■ **BELOW LEFT**
exercise or tail bandage

■ **BELOW RIGHT**
polo wraps

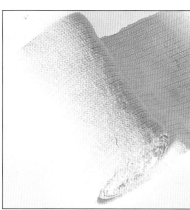

■ **ABOVE LEFT**
stable bandages

■ **ABOVE RIGHT**
Porter protector

■ **LEFT**
cohesive bandage

PUTTING ON AN EXERCISE BANDAGE

EXERCISE BANDAGES

Exercise bandages and polo wraps are used to protect the horse's legs during exercise or work. A great deal of skill is required to apply bandages which are neither too tight (which can lead to damaged tendons), nor too loose (when they can unravel and cause the horse to fall). Exercise bandages must always be applied over some sort of padding, such as a Gamgee, Fybagee or Porter boot.

1 Place the padding around the leg, making sure that the edge of the pad lies between the tendons, on the outside of the leg. The padding should start just below the knee or hock and finish just below the fetlock joint. Wrap the pad around the leg firmly, from front to back, making sure that there are no lumps or wrinkles.

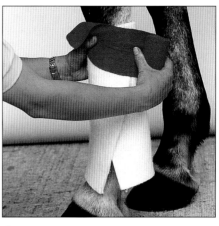

2 Bandage in the same direction as the padding and start just below the padding at the top.

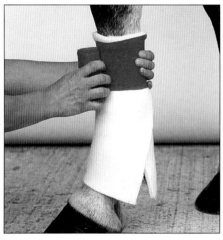

3 Do one complete turn with the bandage around the top of the padding before working down the leg. Exercise bandages are elasticized so be careful not to pull the bandage in too tightly.

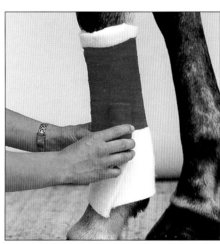

4 Make sure that the bandage stays smooth and that the tension is even.

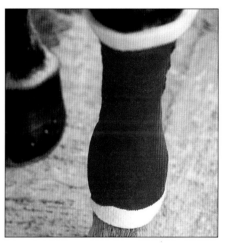

5 At the bottom of the leg the bandage should follow the same angle as the fetlock joint so that it forms a V at the front of the leg. This will ensure that the movement of the fetlock is not restricted.

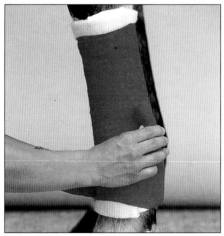

6 Continue to wrap the bandage around the leg, working back up to the top of the padding.

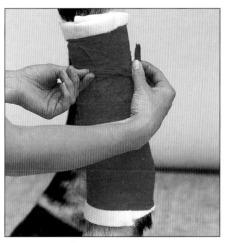

7 Secure the bandage by fastening the ties with a simple knot. The knot should be flat and sit on the outside of the leg. For competitions, stitch the bandage to ensure that it stays in place. Cover the stitched end with insulating tape.

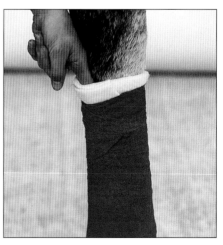

8 The bandage should be firm enough not to slide down but not so tight that it could damage the tendons. You should just be able to slide your finger inside the bandage.

Travelling Equipment

Special clothing can be used to protect the horse from injuries incurred during transportation in a horse truck or trailer.

A **tail guard** prevents the horse from rubbing his tail when travelling. Linen and cotton tail guards are secured with strips tied to the surcingle. The padded tail guard is fitted with Velcro fastenings.

Shaped travel boots can be used instead of travelling bandages to protect the front and hindlegs, from the coronet up to the knee and hock. **Travel boots** are simple square wraps which give protection to the lower leg.

Hock boots, made from leather and felt, are fitted over the top of travel bandages to protect the hock from injury, in the same way that **knee pads** are used to protect the knees. **Felt travel pads** under travel bandages will do the same job.

A **poll guard**, made from leather with a felt lining, provides protection for the sensitive poll area of the horse's head. It is attached to the headcollar or halter.

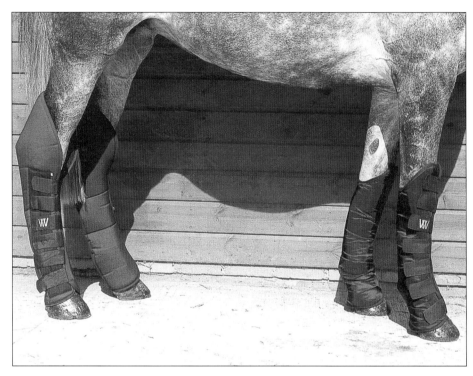

Shaped travel boots. These are designed for front or hind legs to protect them from the coronet right up to the knee or hock.

Travel boots. These simple square padded wraps are effective in protecting the lower leg.

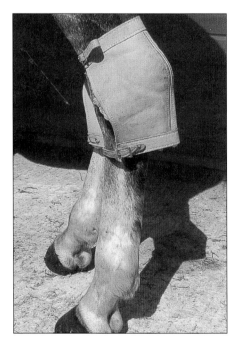

Hock boots. These are fitted to protect the hock joint from injury during transit.

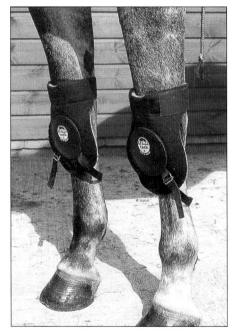

Knee pads. These can be used with travel bandages to protect the knees from damage.

HORSE DRESSED FOR TRAVELLING

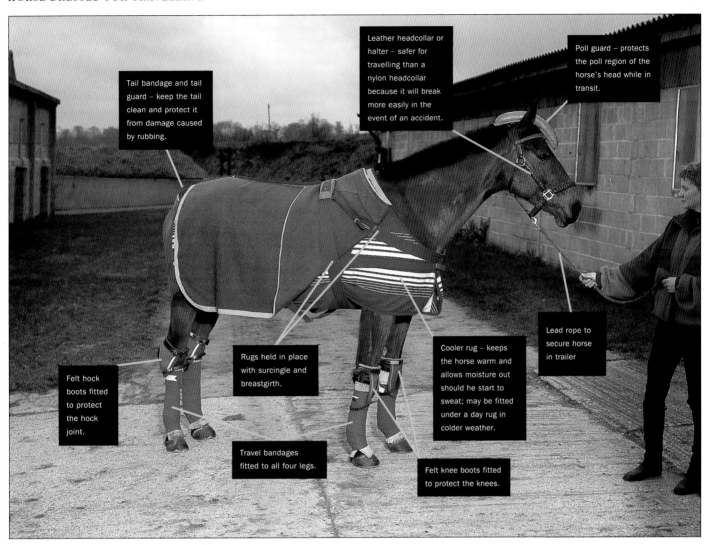

Tail bandage and tail guard – keep the tail clean and protect it from damage caused by rubbing.

Leather headcollar or halter – safer for travelling than a nylon headcollar because it will break more easily in the event of an accident.

Poll guard – protects the poll region of the horse's head while in transit.

Felt hock boots fitted to protect the hock joint.

Rugs held in place with surcingle and breastgirth.

Cooler rug – keeps the horse warm and allows moisture out should he start to sweat; may be fitted under a day rug in colder weather.

Lead rope to secure horse in trailer

Travel bandages fitted to all four legs.

Felt knee boots fitted to protect the knees.

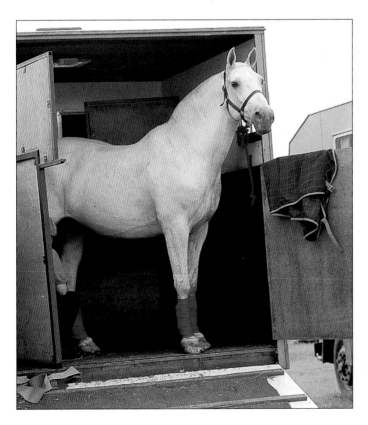

■ LEFT
Horses are very vulnerable to minor injuries when travelling on the roads. While a complete set of travelling equipment is not always necessary, your horse should be fitted with leg protection and a rug. Regular safety checks should also be made on the trailer itself.

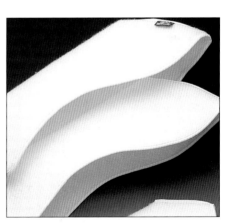

Shaped travel pads can be used in conjunction with travel bandages to protect specific parts of the legs when the horse is in transit.

Corrective Equipment

The following pieces of equipment may be used on the horse to discourage or prevent bad habits when he is stabled or turned out to grass.

A **plastic muzzle** may be used on a horse who is on a strict diet but needs to be turned out. The muzzle prevents him from eating large amounts of food, while the holes in the design allow him to breathe and drink. Plastic muzzles are also useful for horses who bite, chew their rugs or eat their bedding. The design of the **leather muzzle**, made of thick strips, allows the horse to breathe and drink but, like the plastic muzzle, it prevents him from nibbling his rug and biting.

A **bib** is attached to the headcollar and sits below the horse's chin. Like the muzzle, it is fitted to prevent the horse from chewing his rugs or bandages. A much more restrictive item is the **neck cradle**, which should be used only as a last resort to stop a horse from chewing.

A **cribbing collar** is a strong leather strap which is fitted tightly around the horse's throat to prevent him from crib biting and wind-sucking. The collar will not cure the condition, but will stop him doing it while it is fitted.

The design of the leather muzzle allows the horse to breathe and drink but will not allow him to bite and chew.

A plastic muzzle may be used on a horse on a diet who nonetheless needs to be turned out.

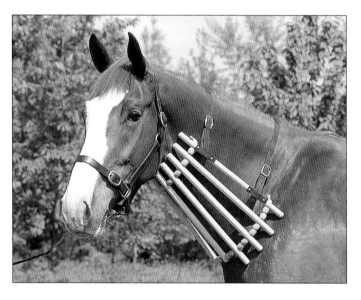

▌ LEFT
The neck cradle offers a last ditch attempt to stop a horse chewing rugs or bandages.

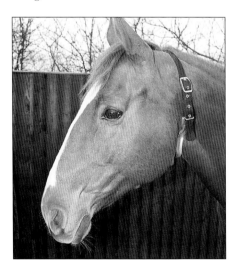

Cribbing collar. This is fitted around the horse's throat to prevent crib biting and wind-sucking.

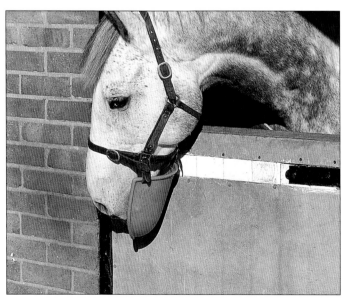

▌ LEFT
The plastic bib is a mildly restrictive piece of equipment which will help to dissuade the horse from chewing his clothing.

Grooming Equipment

Regular grooming is an essential part of good horse management. Besides making the horse look smart, it will help to keep him healthy. By removing accumulated dust, dead skin and hair, the pores of his skin are kept open, and the system for the regulation of body temperature – sweating – is able to function properly. While the stabled horse needs daily grooming, both before and after exercise, the grass-kept horse requires far less attention.

Brushing the horse cleans his coat, and will serve as a massage to improve muscle tone and circulation. The **dandy brush** has long, stiff bristles for removing dried mud or sweat from grass-kept horses, but it can be harsh on finer-coated stabled horses and should be used only on their legs. The **cactus cloth** is ideal for loosening dirt from areas too sensitive for a dandy brush.

The **body brush** has short, fine bristles designed to remove dirt and dead skin from the horse's coat. Use the brush in conjunction with a **metal curry comb**: draw it across the metal curry comb every two or three strokes to remove dirt and grease. The body brush will remove the natural oils from the horse's coat – oils which help to maintain the water-repelling properties of the coat – and is not recommended for horses who live out.

A **face brush** is smaller than a body brush and has softer bristles, making it ideal for grooming the horse's head.

The **water brush** has softer bristles than a dandy brush. Use it to dampen down an unruly mane and tail, and for washing muddy hooves.

ABOVE
Dandy brushes with synthetic bristles (*left*) and natural bristles are ideal for field-kept horses.

LEFT
Synthetic (*far left*) and leather body (*left*) brushes. These should only be used on stabled horses.

LEFT
metal curry comb

BELOW
A water brush can be used to dampen the horse's mane and tail.

BELOW
Plastic curry combs, including one with a hose attachment (*left*).

BELOW
rubber curry comb

BELOW
A rubber washing mitt will have a pleasant massaging effect on the horse's skin.

RIGHT
A face brush is a small soft brush used to groom the horse's head.

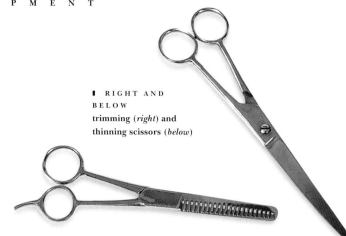

■ RIGHT AND
BELOW
trimming (*right*) and
thinning scissors (*below*)

A **plastic curry comb** will remove dried
mud from the horse's coat, but take care
when using it on very sensitive or ticklish
horses. Some combs can be fixed to a hose
for washing down dirty or sweaty horses.
The softer **rubber curry comb** is used in a
circular motion to remove dried mud and
loose hairs, and to massage the horse's skin.

Drawing a **rubber washing mitt** over the
horse's body when washing him will have
a massaging effect as well as helping to
remove dirt and sweat from his coat. A
sweat scraper can be drawn across the
horse's body, following the lie of the coat,
to remove excess water after washing.

A **massage pad**, made from padded
bridle leather, can be used to rub the
neck, shoulders and hindquarters to
improve tone and circulation. To give
the coat a final polish after grooming,
dampen a **stable rubber**, which is a cotton
cloth or terry towel, and draw it over the
horse following the lie of the coat.

The **hoof pick** is used to remove mud,
stones and soiled bedding from the feet;
a folding version can be safely carried in
a pocket for use on rides. The **hoof-oil
brush** is used to apply hoof-oil or dressing
to the horse's feet, to stop them drying out
and becoming cracked.

Every grooming kit should contain two
sponges, one for cleaning the eyes and
nostrils and one for cleaning the dock.

■ BELOW
Plaiting tubes are
small rigid tubes
used to hold mane
plaits in place.

A **mane comb** is used to remove knots
from the mane before plaiting (braiding).
Use a **pulling comb** to pull manes and
tails. The **Solo mane comb** trims and thins
the mane without pulling out the hairs.

Mane thinning scissors have grooved
blades and will thin the mane for a smarter
appearance. **Trimming scissors** have
curved blades to prevent accidental injury
to the horse. Use them to trim the fetlocks
and heels, as well as the bridle path (the
part on the horse's crest where the
headpiece of the bridle sits).

Use **quarter markers** to produce smart
patterns on the hindquarters. Lay a plastic
sheet over the hindquarter and draw a
body brush over the top to produce an
attractive pattern on the horse's coat.

The traditional method of fixing mane
and tail plaits (braids) for shows and
competitions is with a **plaiting needle** and
thread, but elasticated **plaiting bands** are
also available. Sewn plaits require more
skill than bands but the finished look is
smarter. Easy-to-use **plaiting tubes** are
often used on dressage horses.

■ LEFT
Mane combs
(*far left*), plaiting
bands (*center*)
and a pulling
comb (*below*).

■ BELOW
A sponge and a sweat
scraper are used when
bathing horses.

▍ RIGHT
Use a body brush to groom a stable-kept horse. Used with a metal curry comb it will effectively remove dirt and grease from the horse's coat.

▍ BELOW
Plaiting (braiding) needle and thread. This is the traditional method of fixing mane and tail plaits.

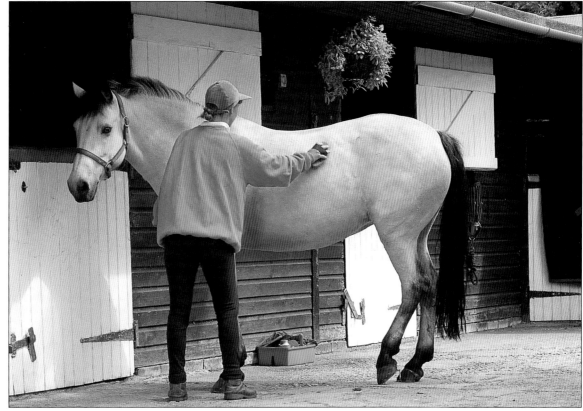

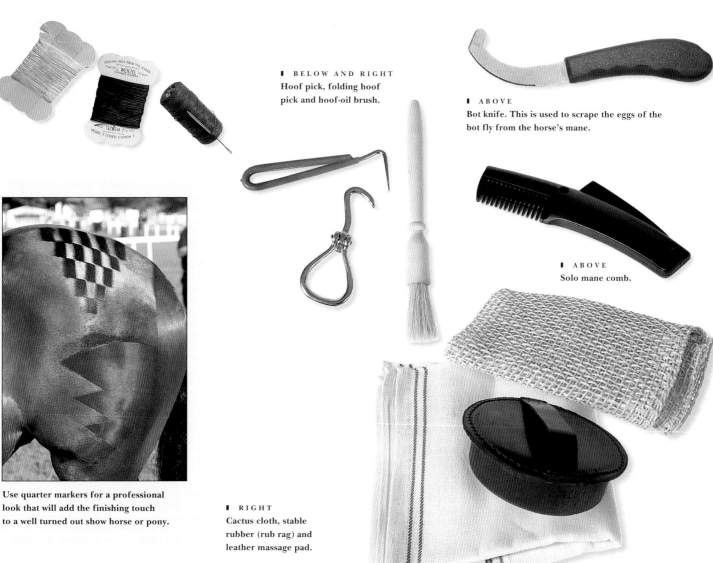

▍ BELOW AND RIGHT
Hoof pick, folding hoof pick and hoof-oil brush.

▍ ABOVE
Bot knife. This is used to scrape the eggs of the bot fly from the horse's mane.

▍ ABOVE
Solo mane comb.

Use quarter markers for a professional look that will add the finishing touch to a well turned out show horse or pony.

▍ RIGHT
Cactus cloth, stable rubber (rub rag) and leather massage pad.

Clothes

When working with horses, whether you are on the ground or riding, safety is the keynote. Horses are big, strong animals and there is always an element of danger, however calm and placid they might normally be. Therefore care should be taken even when choosing clothes for mundane, everyday chores such as mucking out.

Neat clothing which is well fitting without being too tight is the easiest to move around in. A long-sleeved shirt with a sweatshirt or sweater, depending on the weather, and a pair of comfortable trousers, jeans or jodhpurs are ideal for stable work. Avoid overtight trousers as they make bending down difficult. Dark colors will stay looking smart longer. Long sleeves are preferable to short ones since they give some protection from nips from equine teeth. Sleeveless suntops and vests should definitely be avoided.

Footwear is of great importance since a misplaced hoof can do a great deal of damage to a human foot. Sneakers give little protection, so do most rubber boots, though sturdy Wellingtons are as good as anything for mucking out, particularly if you wear thick walking-boot socks inside. At other times a pair of leather jodhpur boots will probably afford the best protection and will certainly enable you to move more quickly than when wearing Wellingtons. Some boots are now fitted with protective toecaps.

Coats and body warmers, when worn, should be kept fastened – a flapping coat can frighten a nervous horse and there is also the danger that it might become caught up on some "foreign body". Some horses are nervous of noisy waterproof fabrics, so avoid wearing them around the stables.

Long hair should be tied up, again to avoid the possibility of scaring a horse or becoming caught up. This is particularly important in windy weather. Avoid wearing jewelry: rings, earrings, nose rings

and the like can all cause nasty injuries if they become caught up.

Most well-trained horses are safe to lead about, in and out of their stables, down to the paddock, etc. But if you have any doubts whatsoever about a horse's good behavior (when handling a young horse, for example) take precautions: wear a hard hat, correctly fastened, in case he rears up and strikes out, boots to protect your feet and a pair of gloves.

▌ **ABOVE**
A sweatshirt, breeches, boots and a hard hat make a suitable outfit for everyday exercise.

▌ **LEFT**
Neat, workmanlike clothes enable you to carry out daily chores in comfort and safety.

Safety Gear

Riding has always been and always will be a risk sport. But modern safety equipment is constantly improving and everyone who rides should ensure that they wear the best available protective gear, which includes hat, body protector and boots.

The most vulnerable part of the rider is the head and it is irresponsible to get on to a horse, or to lunge or long rein or otherwise handle an unpredictable young

■ LEFT
Fluorescent clothing is a wise safety precaution when riding on the roads. The message on the tabard helps to alert drivers.

SAFETY CHECKLIST

☞ Wear a correctly fitting hard hat with the chin strap fastened at all times when mounted.

☞ Replace a hat that has been subjected to impact in a fall – it may not give sufficient protection next time.

☞ Always ride in your own hat – a borrowed hat is unlikely to fit you correctly.

☞ Wear safe footwear at all times when mounted.

☞ Always use the correct stirrup iron size – about 1 inch (2.5cm) wider than your boot – to prevent your foot becoming stuck.

☞ Wear fluorescent garments – hat cover, tabard/body warmer etc – fitted with retro-reflective strips when riding on the roads and fit your horse with similar high visibility leg bands.

☞ Avoid riding on the roads in poor visibility and after dark.

☞ Never ride in jewelry.

☞ Always fasten tiepins horizontally or at an angle, never vertically.

☞ Always ride with your coat fastened.

☞ Never take off a coat or sweater while mounted – while you are taking your arms out of the sleeves you will have no control over the horse should he make an unexpected move.

☞ If you have less than perfect eyesight, wear soft contact lenses if possible. If not, seek your optician's advice on the safest type of spectacles.

horse, without wearing a **hard hat** securely fastened with a **chin strap**. Your country's national federation (for example in Britain the British Horse Society, in the United States the American Horse Shows Association) will advise on the most up-to-date safety standards. The **jockey skull**, or **crash hat**, is generally considered to give maximum protection and is therefore recommended (and obligatory under the rules of most sports) for all riding which involves fast work or jumping. The **chin harness** must be correctly adjusted and fastened at all times. It may be worn on the point of the chin, with a chin cup, or under the chin, whichever is most comfortable. The alternative is the traditional **hunting cap** which must have a soft peak (a hard peak can cause facial, head or neck injuries in a fall). All riding

hats should be correctly fitted (many retailers are trained in hat fitting).

Body protectors are designed to protect the torso and the shoulders in the event of a fall. They should fit well, feel comfortable and not restrict the rider's movement.

Riding boots and **jodhpur boots** are designed to prevent the foot from sliding right through the stirrup iron or otherwise becoming caught up in the iron in the event of a fall – a potentially fatal situation. They have smooth soles and a clearly defined heel. Leather boots afford the best protection from knocks, for example when riding across country, but rubber ones fashioned in the same style are suitable for everyday riding. Wellington boots, trainers and other boots or shoes with ridged soles and little or no heel should never be worn for riding.

■ LEFT
A jockey skull or "crash hat", with a correctly adjusted chin harness, gives the head maximum protection. It is fitted with a silk cover.

■ LEFT
A body protector should be worn when jumping fixed fences and by people needing special protection (for example, an older person with more brittle bones).

Riding Clothes

By and large all riding clothes are designed for comfort and protection. Only with the odd item of equipment (such as the top hat for dressage) is clothing dictated by fashion.

Most riding clothes are based on hunting attire, which evolved over a long period and led to the design of an entire outfit which would give protection from wet, cold and the many knocks experienced when travelling at speed across country. Long leather boots keep the feet and lower legs dry and give maximum protection from painful encounters with gateposts or other fixed objects. Breeches keep the upper legs warm and dry and protect the insides of the knees from chafing against the saddle. A well-fitting jacket made of a good stout tweed or twill gives warmth and a certain amount of waterproofing while at the same time affording complete freedom of movement – essential for all riding, but particularly for jumping and riding at speed. Gloves keep the hands warm and dry and give a secure grip on the reins. A hunting tie or stock helps protect the neck in the event of a fall. A hard hat, correctly secured with a chin harness, protects the most vulnerable part of all, the head.

For everyday riding there is a wealth of suitable clothing to choose from which is both cheaper than more formal attire and suited to frequent immersion in the washing machine. **Jodhpurs**, which extend down the leg to the ankle, and are usually worn with short, elastic-sided leather jodhpur boots, are cooler in summer than breeches and long boots. They come in a range of materials, from lightweight cotton suitable for hot climates to thermal material for wear in extremes of cold. Instead of jodhpur boots, jodhpurs may be worn with **half-chaps**, which cover the leg from below the knee to the foot, or with full **chaps**, which extend up to the thigh.

Close-fitting **riding trousers** are also suitable for everyday wear. Like jodhpurs,

■ LEFT
Everyday riding clothes should be neat and safe. Dark colors are more practical than the light shades worn with traditional hunting dress.

■ BELOW LEFT
Chaps are a good alternative to boots. This rider is prepared for roadwork – note the fluorescent tabard and the horse's protective boots.

they come with "strappings" – reinforcements at the knee and thigh. Some garments are also fitted with an inset seat panel made in an extra-grip material.

Rubber **riding boots** are a cheaper alternative to leather ones, though they can be cold in winter, when an inner sole

or an extra pair of socks may be required.

Casual **riding coats** such as waxed or quilted jackets, blousons and body warmers are fine for everyday riding and may be worn with a shirt and/or sweatshirt or sweater. Modern waterproof materials are light and comfortable to wear and the more expensive ones have the advantage of being "breathable". Waterproofs come in a range of lengths and may have added features such as storm collar and cuffs, fleecy lining and pommel flap. Noisy waterproof materials should be avoided as horses tend to be frightened of them, particularly on a windy day.

There are **gloves** for every occasion, specially designed for the rider. Special features include reinforced rein fingers, pimple palm grips and lycra inserts for extra flexibility.

Clothes for Competition

For most forms of competitive riding it is usual to wear a riding coat with breeches and boots, a shirt with a collar and tie or collarless shirt with a hunting tie or stock. The rules of some sports also stipulate the wearing of spurs. A hat is obligatory and although the bowler hat (derby) is still seen in show classes and the top hat in dressage, the trend is more and more to the safer type of hunting cap and, even more so, the jockey skull. The latter is usually worn with a dark-coloured silk cover.

For cross-country riding the jacket is replaced by a sweater or shirt, according to the weather, which may be in the rider's own colours, as may the hat silk.

Endurance riding is one area where tradition holds less sway, partly because the sport is of fairly recent origin (at least in an organized competitive way) and also because at the higher echelons riders are not only in the saddle for very long periods but also spend some of the time on their feet, running alongside their horses to give them a breather. Breeches and boots would be too hot and uncomfortable so this is the one sport where running shoes are permitted. However, as a safety precaution, riders are required to use enclosed-type stirrup irons to prevent their feet slipping right through.

LEFT
Correct dress for top-level dressage includes a top hat, tail coat and waistcoat.

BELOW
Most riding gear, for women as well as men, is based on clothes developed for the hunting field.

BOTTOM LEFT
The clothes worn for endurance riding are less formal than in other competitive sports.

Whips and Spurs

Whips and spurs (referred to as artificial aids) can be used by the rider to reinforce the leg aids.

The rider uses a whip just behind his or her leg if the horse does not respond to a command from the leg. Whips should only be used in these circumstances and not as an alternative to the leg, or as a punishment.

Shorter, thicker whips are used for show jumping and cross country. Longer, finer whips are ideal for schooling horses on the flat, because they can be used to give a gentle flick without the rider having to take his or her hands off the reins.

Hunting whips are not used on the horse, but are traditionally carried out hunting. They usually have a bent top which is very useful for pulling gates shut,

■ LEFT
This cross-country rider is carrying a short, thick whip, only to be used if the horse does not respond to a command from the leg.

and a plaited leather thong and cord lash which is carried looped round. For showing horses, a simple malacca or leather-covered cane is often carried.

Spurs can be worn to emphasize the rider's leg aids. The most common type of spur used for English riding is called a Prince of Wales spur. It has a short blunt-ended neck which, when fitted, points downward. The spur fits snugly around the back of the rider's boot and is held in place with a strap. Spurs are also available with rowels (small metal discs fitted to the tip of the spurs) which give them a much sharper action. Spurs should only be used by experienced riders who have an independent seat and can maintain control when the spur is applied to the horse.

■ LEFT
A dressage whip is longer and allows the rider to use the whip without letting go of the reins.

▌ LEFT
The hunting whip is not used on the horse, but is carried as a hunting tradition, and is sometimes used for pulling gates shut. It is much longer than the show-jumping or cross-country whip.

▌ ABOVE
Spurs, like whips, can be used to emphasize the rider's leg aids. They should only be used by experienced riders.

▌ RIGHT
A show-jumping whip, used for encouraging the horse to move forward if he doesn't respond to the rider's leg aids.

101

Learning to Ride

Before Climbing Aboard

There are few more enviable sights in the world than a horse and rider enjoying a happy, trusting partnership. To be able to harness the spirit and beauty of an animal as majestic as the horse so that he is happy to work with you, and willing to do all that you ask of him, has to be one of life's greatest pleasures. A horse and rider in harmony appear to move by magic, but although the spectator may appreciate the words of Robert Surtees—"there is no closer secret than that between a rider and his horse"—anyone who has experienced some of the setbacks that can occur while trying to acquire the art of horsemanship may wonder whether these words were spoken with admiration, envy or in sheer frustration!

For some, horse riding is an occasional pastime, for others it is a lifelong passion—either way it should be a pleasure for both horse and rider. Learning to ride involves two living creatures—the rider relies on the horse's generosity and cooperation, the horse, in return, deserves fair and sensitive treatment from his rider.

▌ OPPOSITE
A happy partnership
leads to good
horsemanship.

▌ LEFT
Whatever your
ambition, or lack
of it, riding should
be enjoyable.

If You Have Never Sat on a Horse...

If you have never so much as sat on a horse or pony, there will be a great deal to take in to start with. It will help to have an overall idea in your mind of what it is you are trying to achieve.

Once you have mounted, the means of communication with the horse are through the use of the legs, seat, hands and voice. Anything that you ask the horse to do—from simply walking forward to performing an intricate dressage movement to jumping a huge fence—is achieved by using a combination of leg, seat, hand and, sometimes, the voice. The art of riding lies in learning to feel what the horse is doing underneath you, and understanding how to influence what he does and how well he performs by mastering this subtle combination of leg, seat and hand. These means of communicating with the horse are called aids. Leg, hand and seat aids, as well as your voice, are called natural aids and they can be backed up by the artificial aids, which are the spur and whip. The spur is a short stump of blunt metal that is worn over the rider's boot just above the heel; the whip is either a short stick or a longer schooling whip.

Ultimately, riding a horse should have the same smooth feeling of power and control as driving a high-performance sports car or a speed boat. Just as a powerful car responds instantly to a light touch on the accelerator pedal, a horse should move forward the instant he feels a light squeeze from the rider's leg. The feeling of lightness and control that power steering in a car gives you is the same feeling that a well-schooled horse should give you through the reins. Just an inclination of your hand to guide the horse in one direction or another, or a slight squeeze and hold of the rein to help gather up all his energy and power, is all that should be needed. It takes a long period of careful training for a horse to become as responsive as this, and it takes

time and practice for a rider to get to the stage of being able to provide that training.

In the beginning, as a general rule of thumb, the novice rider should appreciate that it is the legs that are used first and foremost to instruct the horse to do something. The legs create the power, while the hands gently guide the horse in the right direction.

As a beginner, you will usually find yourself riding in a circle around an instructor. The hand and leg on the inside of the circle, i.e. the hand and leg nearest the instructor, are referred to as the inside hand and leg. The hand and leg on the outside of the circle are known as the outside hand and leg. If your inside hand is your left hand, i.e. you are going in a counter-clockwise direction, you are said to be riding on the left rein. If you are told to change the rein, this involves turning

the horse around and circling in the opposite direction, so that the inside hand is now your right hand, which means you are now riding on the right rein.

Your arms and hands are linked via the reins to the bit in the horse's mouth. This line of contact is all part of your communication with the horse, and to make life comfortable for him you must aim to relax your arms, so that as the horse's head and neck move you follow that movement. Ideally this is done while still maintaining a consistent but soft contact with the horse's mouth. The idea is not to let the reins keep going slack and then tight, but to relax your arms enough to follow what the horse's head and neck are doing while keeping a constant feel on the reins. The feel that you have down the reins to the horse's mouth is known as the contact, and the ultimate aim is to ride

AN INDEPENDENT SEAT

The key to all successful riding is to attain what is commonly known as "an independent seat." The means of communication with the horse are through your seat, legs, hands and voice—they are six different things and on some occasions you may have to do something different with each of them at the same time! To do this you must be able to sit securely and centrally in the saddle, while leaving your legs and hands free to communicate with the horse. This means being able to keep your balance without gripping with your legs, or hanging on by the reins, at all the gaits. Only then can your legs, seat and hands be used independently of each other to ask the horse to perform some of the more elaborate and enjoyable movements that he can offer you.

In an ideal world, any would-be horseman would first gain this independent seat by riding a horse or pony that is being lunged. To begin with you might hold on to the front of the saddle or to a neck strap to help you keep your balance, but as your body and muscles gradually become used to the movement of the horse underneath you, it becomes easier to remain relaxed and balanced. Various exercises without reins or stirrups will help reinforce the balance and security of your

■ **LEFT**
Learning to ride on the lunge is one of the best ways to acquire the feel and balance that are needed to develop an independent seat. Once this is achieved, you can start to ride properly and really influence the horse.

seat until you have attained true independence of hands, seat and legs at all gaits. Lunging can be a tiring and time-consuming operation, besides which, most potential riders are in a rush to enjoy more of the thrill and excitement of horse riding. But if you really want to master the art of riding, it

is time well spent, and this will be repaid when you discover how much more effective and sensitive a rider you are when you do progress to more exciting things. Remember—patience and practice are the keys to becoming a successful rider.

with a very light contact. It sometimes helps to imagine that the rein is an extension of your arm and that your hands are attached directly to the bit in the horse's mouth. As the horse's head moves, your arms will have to move with him.

However ambitious or casual you may be, by persevering and mastering the correct techniques of horse riding, your satisfaction and enjoyment of your hobby or sport will be greatly enhanced. You may have no desire to reach the dizzy heights

of the competition world—perhaps a simple ride through the countryside is your idea of paradise—but either way, life will be more enjoyable for both you and your horse if you at least attempt to master the art of horsemanship.

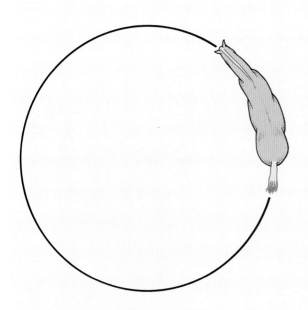

Riding on the left rein, or tracking left.

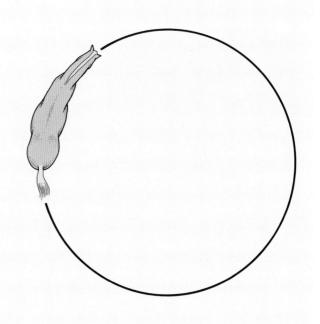

Riding on the right rein, or tracking right.

Understanding Horses and Ponies

The first thing that any would-be rider must appreciate is the sheer strength and bulk that a horse or pony represents. Common sense should tell even the most inexperienced person that the relationship between horse and rider cannot possibly be based on force—if it were, the horse would win every time. As a rider, you are totally dependent on the horse's cooperation, and so the partnership between horse and rider is one of mutual respect.

Much of the secret behind the successful handling of a horse or pony, either from the ground or from the saddle, is based on the human being in the partnership appearing both calm and confident. So before considering actually riding a horse or pony, it is well worth spending time just getting used to working with them. Most riding establishments

Spending time grooming and preparing the horse you are going to ride is all part of building up a good partnership.

would be more than happy to accept an offer of help around the yard, and this is a good opportunity to learn how to feel comfortable around horses.

A horse is happiest if he is handled confidently and positively. He is far more likely to become nervous and unsure if his handler is jittery and tentative. A horse or pony should always be handled firmly, but fairly, so that he learns what is expected of him. It is the rider's job to teach the horse

Spending time helping to care for and handle horses helps beginners to feel at ease with them.

what is acceptable and what is not. The training of a horse has the same basis as the training of any other animal—when the horse does what is required he is rewarded, when he does not he is quietly reprimanded. It is vital that the handler is consistent in what he or she asks. It is not fair to drape yourself around your pony's neck, hugging and kissing him, only to turn around and strike him when he shifts his position and accidentally steps on your toe! It is wrong to punish the horse when it was you, the handler, who put yourself in a position where you could get hurt. Although you may think it at the time, the horse would not step on you on purpose if he could avoid doing so!

Your voice is the most valuable form of communication you can have with a horse or pony. He will know from the tone of your voice whether you are pleased with him or otherwise. So it is your voice which should be used to tell the horse when he is behaving well and when he isn't. Your commands should be kept clear and

simple—if the horse does something wrong, then a stern "No" is often all it takes to let him know. A long, angry tirade will only confuse him and wear you out. Keep it simple—"No" when he is wrong, and "Good boy" or "Good girl" when things are going well. Far too many people forget to tell the horse when they are pleased with him.

Horses, like people, have different temperaments and characters, and not every horse will get along in the same way with every person. A very tense, jittery horse probably won't feel comfortable with an equally nervous person—he is more likely to respond to a quieter character. An energetic person can sometimes inspire confidence and coax a little more effort out of a horse with a more laid-back character.

NEAR SIDE, OFF SIDE

Some of the first things to learn in order to avoid confusion all around are the terms used to describe each side of the horse. If you stand facing the same direction as the horse, his left-hand side is known as the near side, and his right-hand side is known as the off side. The horse is led from the near side; you mount and dismount from the near side. The same terms are used to describe each of the horse's limbs—if a horse is said to be lame on his off fore, this refers to the front leg on the right-hand side.

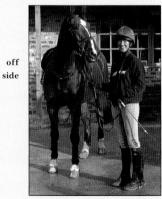

off side   near side

Where to Learn

Some children are lucky enough to be put on a pony before they can even walk—long before they are in a position to control their ponies off the leadline, they will have developed a natural seat. This is because someone else has been in charge of the pony—all the rider has had to worry about is staying on board. It is the same principle as being lunged.

For those who haven't had that lucky start, if time and money allow, the best investment is in a course of lunge lessons at an equestrian center with a good reputation. The advantages of this are that you will be receiving individual attention and, most importantly, you will start to acquire a deep, balanced but relaxed seat in the saddle. Lunging will also give you the opportunity to concentrate on trying to feel how the horse is actually moving underneath you.

There is the danger of the first riding lesson being a miserable experience. Avoid any establishment where novices are put on badly schooled, bored mounts and stuck in a class with any number of other potential riders, and where inexperienced or simply incompetent instructors swagger around shouting instructions or criticism. The poor riders are expected to master

All too often a lack of communication and understanding between horse and rider leads to a lack of cooperation.

the correct riding position, keep their balance in the saddle, and maneuver unresponsive creatures around the arena. These new riders will either give up or become insensitive riders, uneducated in the value of true horsemanship.

Lunge lessons will help the rider to develop a good seat, from which he or she will be able to communicate effectively with the horse. For any rider unable to enjoy such an opportunity, the next best thing is to opt for private lessons, rather than group lessons. Once you have mastered the basics, riding in a group can be a positive and enjoyable experience, but if you are just learning to ride, you will benefit most from private lessons right at the beginning. This may either be at a commercial riding school or equestrian center, or with an individual who may give lessons using their own horses and facilities.

Always ensure that the instructor of your choice has a good reputation both for teaching ability and for being safe and responsible. In most countries there is some form of recognized teaching body and a structured system of examinations for instructors; if you have nobody to advise you, always opt for a registered and approved instructor. But if someone is highly recommended to you by more experienced riders, do not be afraid to try them even if teaching is not their profession—some people are naturally gifted teachers.

With a willing helper to lead the way, the world is yours to explore. It is a great advantage to learn to ride at such an early age. There are classes for young riders on leadlines at most equestrian centers.

Group riding lessons are beneficial and fun once the potential rider has had a chance to master some of the basics.

Sitting Comfortably

Before you even get as far as sitting on a horse there is quite
a lot of groundwork to master, such as tacking up and
mounting. Riding schools vary in their approach to tacking
up for beginners. Some have the horse ready and waiting
for his rider; others feel that tacking up is all part of the
learning process and that it will give you a few minutes of
unpressured time in which to start to get to know your horse.
If a friend is teaching you, it is all part of the fun to help get
the horse ready.

▌ OPPOSITE
Learning to ride
correctly will give
you great confidence
—it is never too early
to start.

▌ LEFT
Once you feel
confident and
comfortable on the
horse's back, you can
begin to learn how to
ask the horse to do
things for you.

Tacking Up

The order in which the horse is tacked up varies, but any form of boots should be put on first, once the horse's legs have been checked for signs of heat or swelling. This should have been done while the horse was being groomed, but it is good practice to double check when putting on the boots—there is no point tacking up and then discovering that the horse is lame!

Whether the saddle or bridle is put on next is a matter for discussion. Some riders like to put the bridle on first, so that they have better control of the horse should he pull back and break free from his halter. Others like to put the saddle on first so that, having removed the horse's blanket, the saddle goes straight onto a warm back and the horse's muscles will remain warm underneath the saddle. On a cold day, a blanket should be kept over the horse's back and quarters while he is being tacked up.

PUTTING ON BOOTS

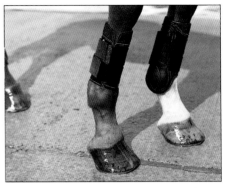

Protective boots reduce the risk of injury. Hold the boot securely in place and fasten the first strap. Then fasten the second strap firmly enough to prevent the boot from slipping. Tighten the first strap if it seems looser than the second strap. These boots protect the tendon area of the legs as well as the inside of the fetlocks. Many horses are prone to knocking one leg against the inside of the opposite leg—this is called brushing—and boots prevent the horse from injuring himself as a result.

PUTTING ON THE BRIDLE

1 While being tacked up or groomed, the horse is usually secured by a halter. Before removing the halter put the reins over the horse's head so that you have a means of holding him.

2 Remove the halter by lifting the crownpiece forward and then gently over the horse's ears.

3 With one hand holding the horse's nose to keep his head steady, bring the bridle up in front of his face.

4 Use your right hand to hold the bridle, lay the bit over the palm of your left hand and gently lift it up into the horse's mouth. Use your thumb to press his gum in the gap where his teeth end which will encourage him to open his mouth.

5 Once the bit is in place, keep some tension on each side of the bridle to hold it there while you bring the crownpiece of the bridle up and over the horse's ears. Do not allow the bit to bang against his teeth, as this will make him wary next time.

6 With the crownpiece in place, separate the hair of the forelock from the rest of the mane (to let the bridle sit comfortably, cut a small section out of the mane where the crownpiece sits). Bring the forelock forward and lift it clear of the browband.

7 Keep your hand looped through the rein so that you have a contact with the horse, and therefore control over him, and then do up the throatlatch.

8 It should not be fastened too tightly—make sure you can still get four fingers of your hand between the horse's cheek and the throatlatch.

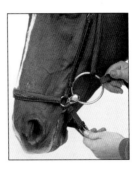

9 Fasten the noseband—in this case a drop noseband that fastens below the bit rings. A cavesson noseband, used for lunging, sits higher up the horse's nose and fastens above the bit rings.

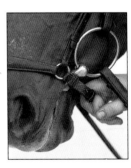

10 You should be able to place one finger between the horse's chin and the noseband.

SADDLING UP

1 Place a soft, clean saddlepad on the horse's back. This acts as a cushion between the horse and the saddle and can relieve pressure points and reduce the risk of rubbing. It is also a warmer layer to have against the horse's skin than the leather of the saddle.

2 Keeping the saddle well clear of the horse's back, lift it so that it is poised in the right position to be lowered onto the back. Lower the saddle into place, making sure that the saddle flap on the off side is lying flat.

3 Use your left hand to lift the pad so that it is not pulled tight over the horse's withers. It should be tucked up to lie snugly under the pommel of the saddle, clear of the withers.

4 Most saddle pads have two straps that hold them in position under the saddle. The first one is usually attached to the billets, so pull it over the knee roll of the saddle and put it on the billet before you fasten the girth.

5 Position the strap above the buckle guard; otherwise you will not be able to pull this down into the correct position. Pull the billet out from the buckle guard, thread through the strap, then put the strap back through the buckle guard.

6 Buckle the girth to the saddle on the off side. Return to the near side, and reach under the horse's belly to catch the girth. Thread the girth buckles through the second securing strap of the saddle pad and fasten them, one at a time, to each billet.

7 Gently tighten the girth, one buckle at a time, until you can just squeeze the flat of your hand between the horse's belly and the girth. Fasten the girth equally on each side.

8 Pull the buckle guard down so that it covers the buckles—otherwise they will gradually wear a hole through the saddle flap.

9 Smooth down under the girth so that there are no wrinkles of skin caught up which might rub. Slide your hand under the girth just clear of the saddle flap and run it down under the horse's belly, taking particular care to smooth any wrinkles in the horse's elbow area.

10 A correctly fitted jumping saddle, with the girth tightened and the stirrups run up so that they don't swing and bang against the horse's sides. A jumping saddle has forward-cut flaps and knee rolls to allow the rider to keep his or her leg on the saddle even when riding with shorter stirrups.

PUTTING ON A DRESSAGE SADDLE

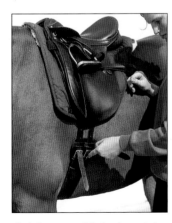

1 A dressage saddle has long girth straps that fasten below the saddle flap. The girth must still be tightened gradually, one buckle at a time, and the skin and hair smoothed down underneath it.

2 Dressage saddles allow your legs to hang much longer and closer to the horse's sides. This gives the best possible position for you to communicate with the horse through your legs and seat.

LEADING A TACKED-UP HORSE

▌ LEFT
When leading a tacked-up horse, stand on his near side and bring the reins over his head. The stirrups should be run up so that they do not swing or bang against the horse's sides. Carry the excess loop of rein and your stick in your left hand. Have the stick pointing backward so you can give the horse a tap behind the girth if he refuses to walk on. You should always wear a helmet whenever you lead a horse.

MOUNTING FROM THE GROUND

Mounting

So now it is time to step aboard. It is essential to learn how to mount correctly from the ground but, as a general rule, it is far less stressful on the horse's back to use a mounting block or be given a leg-up. Either of these methods is also a lot safer than mounting from the ground. Many accidents occur when riders are trying to get on their horses. If you do mount from the ground, ideally an assistant should stand on the far side of the horse and, by putting his or her hand in the stirrup iron, should use some of his or her own weight to counteract your weight swinging up from the other side. This helps to reduce the amount of twisting and pulling on the horse's spine.

1 Before attempting to get on your horse you will need to put the reins back over his head, and let down the stirrups.

2 As you pull the stirrup irons down, keep them away from the horse's sides so that they don't bump him. When they are fully down, place them gently back against his sides.

3 Stand on the near side of the horse, facing his tail and put both reins in your left hand. It also helps to loop a finger through the neck strap and hold on to a little piece of the mane.

4 Take the stirrup iron in your right hand and turn it to face you. The stirrup should be turned clockwise, so that once you are mounted the stirrup leather lies correctly against your leg.

5 Lift your left leg and place your foot in the stirrup iron. Put your right hand on the seat of the saddle.

6 Push with your right leg to spring off the ground and, at the same time, reach to the back of the saddle with your right hand.

Voilà! You are now mounted on your horse. Put your right foot in the stirrup and then take up a rein in each hand.

7 Once you are high enough off the ground, you will be able to grip the back of the saddle with your right hand and this will help you to balance. Keep bringing your right leg up until it is clear of the horse's back and hindquarters.

8 At this point start to swing your right leg over the back of the horse. Bring your right hand back to the front of the saddle and rest it on either the pommel or the horse's neck to help you support and balance your upper body.

9 As your right leg starts to come down over the off side of the horse, take your weight on your hands and arms so that you don't flop down in the saddle. Lower your seat gently into the saddle.

GETTING A LEG-UP

1 If someone is going to give you a leg-up onto your horse, you should stand on the near side facing the saddle. Take both reins and your stick in your left hand—making sure you carry the stick down over the off-side shoulder of the horse; otherwise you will hit your helper in the face with it as you mount up! Rest your left hand on the horse's neck or on the pommel of the saddle, and reach up with your right hand so that it is resting near the back of the saddle.

USING A MOUNTING BLOCK

It is far less stressful for both horse and rider if you are able to get aboard by using a mounting block. The horse is led alongside the mounting block so that his near side is parallel to the block. Use the stirrup to mount in the normal way. Now that you are that much higher off the ground, there is less strain on the horse's back when you step up into the stirrup.

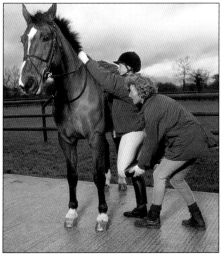

2 Bend your left leg up from the knee so that your helper can take hold of it with both hands.

3 Sink your weight down into your right leg and when your helper gives the command be ready to spring up in the air off your right leg.

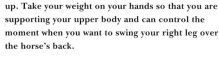

4 As you spring up off your right leg, your helper will also lift your weight by lifting your left leg up. Take your weight on your hands so that you are supporting your upper body and can control the moment when you want to swing your right leg over the horse's back.

5 As you swing your right leg over the horse's back you will need to transfer your right hand from the back of the saddle to either the pommel or the top of the saddle flap on the off side. Make sure you continue to support your upper body on both your arms.

6 With your weight on your arms you can lower your seat down gently into the saddle.

Adjusting Tack

Having learned how to tack up and mount your horse, there are one or two other small adjustments you will need to make once you are on board. The first thing you must do is tighten the girth. Although this is tightened from the ground before you mount, your weight pushing the saddle down onto the horse's back will cause the girth to need retightening. Also, many horses push their stomachs out against the pressure of the girth, and only relax again once their riders are in the saddle.

It is only once you are sitting on your horse that you can feel if your stirrups are set at a comfortable length for you; they may need adjusting. When you change from riding on the flat to jumping you will also want to shorten your stirrups while still sitting on the horse.

TIGHTENING THE GIRTH

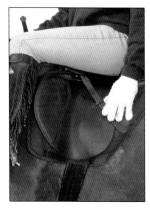

1 To retighten the girth, put both reins and your stick in your right hand and bring your left leg clear of the saddle flap.

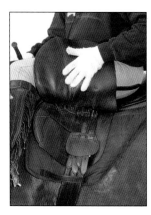

2 Reach down and lift up the saddle flap so that you have access to the billets.

3 Hold the saddle flap out of the way with your right hand; with your left hand, pull the buckle guard up away from the billets and buckles.

4 Take hold of the first billet and pull it up gently. Use your index finger to press the spike of the buckle through the hole.

5 Do the same to the second billet—make sure each is tightened by the same number of holes.

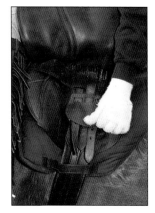

6 Pull the buckle guard back down so that it sits snugly over the billets. Put the saddle flap back down and return your leg to the correct position.

HOLDING THE REINS

1 Hold the reins by allowing them to lie across the palm of your hand. The end that comes from the horse's mouth passes between your third and fourth finger.

2 It rests over the top of your first finger and is held in place by closing your thumb and fingers. You can lengthen the reins by relaxing the tension in your hand and letting them slip through your fingers.

3 This picture shows you how to hold a stick as well as your reins. When your thumb and fingers close back around the rein and stick, they are held safely in place.

ADJUSTING THE STIRRUP LEATHERS

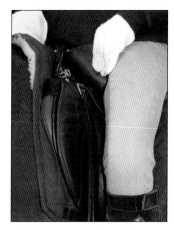

1 Once you are in the saddle you may need to adjust your stirrup leathers in order to sit comfortably and correctly. Put the reins and stick in your right hand, and use your left hand to lift the leather flap that covers the stirrup-leather buckle.

2 Pull the free end of the stirrup leather out of its keeper if necessary, and then pull it upward so that the buckle is released.

3 To shorten your stirrup, pull the stirrup leather upward, as shown. To lengthen your stirrup, put your weight down into the stirrup iron and with your left hand allow the stirrup leather to slide back down through the stirrup bar.

4 When the stirrup is at the required length, push the buckle back through the appropriate hole.

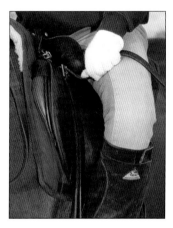

5 Make sure the stirrup-leather buckle slides back into position against the stirrup bar.

6 Push the free end of the stirrup leather back through the keeper.

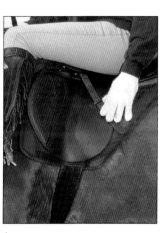

7 Ensure that the leather is lying flat before repeating the procedure for the right stirrup.

POSITIONING THE STIRRUP LEATHER

Each stirrup leather should be turned outward, rather than inward, in order to position the stirrup iron so that your foot can go into it. This allows the stirrup leather to curve smoothly across the inside of your leg. So to put your right foot (off-side foot) in the stirrup iron, give the leather a quarter turn in a clockwise direction. For the near-side foot (left foot), turn the stirrup leather in a counterclockwise direction.

4 You should always hold both your hands at the same height, usually just above the withers and a few inches apart. The basic rule for hand position is that there should be a straight line running from your elbow, down your arm, through the wrist and hand, down the rein to the horse's mouth. It is this rule that dictates the exact position of your hands, which will therefore alter depending on what the horse is doing with his head carriage. This hand and arm position allows you to maintain a soft, elastic but consistent contact with the horse's mouth. (See *The Hands*, which illustrates three different but correct positions.)

Dismounting

Dismounting from the horse should also be done correctly. Do not be tempted to follow the example of countless cowboys and Indians in Wild West movies by flinging your leg over the front of the saddle. If the horse throws his head up you will, at best, be knocked off backward or, at worst, startle the horse so that he either jumps or bolts, leading to even more painful consequences. Always remove both feet from the stirrups, lean forward and swing your right leg up and over behind the saddle. As obvious as it may sound, always check that the ground where you are about to land is safe and free of obstacles before you dismount.

GETTING OFF

1 To prepare to dismount from your horse you should take both feet out of the stirrups and put both reins, and your stick, in your left hand.

2 Rest both hands on the pommel of the saddle or on the horse's neck. Lean your upper body forward.

3 Now swing your right leg up and over the horse's back.

4 Swing your left leg back and out slightly so that it meets your right leg, which has now swung over onto the near side of the horse. Use your hands on the saddle to help support your body.

5 Allow both your legs to drop to the ground together. Bend your knees as you land to absorb the impact.

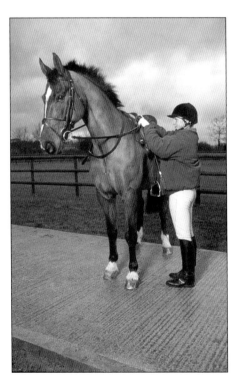

6 Straighten up, and you are ready to run up your stirrups, take the reins over your horse's head, and lead him back to the stable.

The Ideal Position

Once on the horse, you should try to adopt a proud and elegant posture. The ideal, classical position is like that of a person standing with their knees slightly bent, not sitting in an armchair. Your ear, shoulder, hip and heel should all be in line, with equal weight placed on each seat bone so that you are not tipped too far forward or sitting back on your buttocks. Always remember how heavy your head is in relation to the rest of your body—if you look down, or tilt your head to the side, or push it too far forward, it will affect your, and therefore the horse's, balance. Your legs should hang long and loose down the horse's sides. When your foot is balanced in the stirrup, think of allowing your weight to sink down into your heel.

Although it is often frowned upon today by many who consider it unsafe, anyone who was fortunate enough to learn to ride bareback tends to adopt a correct position automatically. Often, it is the addition of the saddle and the stirrups which compromises what was otherwise a near-perfect position.

By practicing the ideal position on the ground, you can start to get a good feel of what you are aiming for, before the added complication of the movement of the horse underneath you enters the equation. Similarly, while sitting on the stationary horse, you can be shown how to follow the movement of his head and neck, so that you do not restrict the horse or harm him by pulling on the reins in an attempt to keep your balance.

Your foot should be balanced centrally in the stirrup, with the stirrup tread positioned under the ball of your foot and your weight lowered gently down into your heel.

If you sit a child on a pony bareback, his or her leg position will automatically be long and low as required for the classical position.

As soon as a saddle is introduced, note how the child adopts an armchair seat. The best way to acquire a natural, classical seat is to learn to ride either bareback or without stirrups.

1 You can practice the classical riding position on the ground. First stand straight, with your legs about 2 feet (0.5 m) apart, and your arms bent at the elbow as if you were holding the horse's reins.

2 Keeping your whole body straight and upright, simply bend your knees slightly—now you are in the classical dressage position. For jumping you simply bend your knees more. Your position on a horse should be as if you were standing with your knees bent, rather than as if you were sitting in a chair.

█ LEFT
Your position in the saddle should be exactly the same as the position you have practiced on the ground. See how this rider appears to be standing with her knees bent rather than sitting on the saddle. Note how there is a straight line through the rider's ear, shoulder, hip and heel. Similarly there is another straight line running from the elbow, down through the wrist and hand to the rein and eventually to the bit.

COMMON FAULTS

How not to sit! You should not allow your weight to fall on to the back of your buttocks as if you were sitting on a chair. Note how, when this happens, the rider's lower leg swings forward and becomes ineffective as a result.

You should not sit with your weight pitched forward. It prevents you from sitting properly and using your legs correctly—and it is painful! Note how this position causes the lower leg to slide back.

PRACTICING A SOFT CONTACT

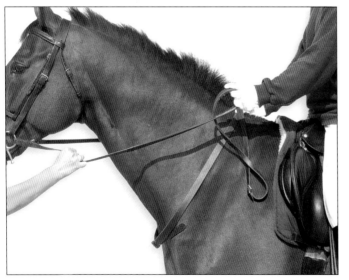

1 One of the secrets of sympathetic and effective riding is to learn how to maintain a soft but constant contact with the horse's mouth, while allowing him to move his head and neck freely. Take up a rein in each hand, and ask a friend to hold the rein further down toward the horse's mouth.

2 Ask your friend to mimic the movement of the horse's head and neck by drawing the rein forward and then releasing it. Concentrate on maintaining the straight line from your elbow, through your wrist and hand down the rein. Keep your elbows and wrists soft and relaxed, and allow your whole arm, from the shoulder down, to be moved by the pull on the reins.

COMMON FAULTS

The Hands

Never forget that your hands are attached directly, via the reins, to a large piece of metal in the horse's mouth. Like your own, the horse's mouth is soft and sensitive, and you must never be harsh or abusive with your hands. One of the most important ideas to grasp is that your hands belong to the horse's mouth. Although a light, consistent contact must be maintained so that you have a line of communication with the horse, that contact should be elastic. Your hands must follow the movement of the horse's head and neck. It should feel as if you are shaking hands politely with someone; there is equal pressure and movement from each party. It is not polite to clasp someone's hand roughly and shake it as violently as a terrier might shake a rat! Nor is it kind to grasp the reins and swing and tug on them. An old Spanish proverb suggests that "you should ride as if with reins of silk." This can only be achieved if the whole arm stays soft and relaxed, right from the shoulder through the elbow to the hand. The elbow opens out softly to allow the hands to go forward as the horse's head moves.

A common fault is to have stiff, straight arms and to turn the wrists and hands outward. You can see from this position how harsh this looks, and how impossible it would be to keep a sympathetic contact with the horse.

A similar error is to carry your hands so that the thumbs are pointing downward—again this prevents you from maintaining a soft, consistent contact with the horse's mouth.

The exact position of the hands, how close they are held to the withers, depends upon the horse's head carriage. There should always be a straight line from the elbow, through the wrist, down the rein to the bit; so, if the horse is working with his head quite low, the hands must be carried a little lower and to either side of the withers in order to keep this straight line.

When the horse is working in a rounder frame, the hands can be carried a little higher, and when you find yourself riding a highly schooled horse who carries his head and neck higher still, your hands should be carried a few inches above the withers. The rule of thumb is to be aware of keeping the straight line from the elbow, through the rein to the horse's mouth.

You must adjust your arm position, following the horse's head and neck, so that you maintain an imaginary straight line from your elbow, through your wrist and hand, down the rein to the bit. This horse is working in a good outline in trot and you can see how the straight line is maintained.

When you encourage the horse to stretch and lower his neck, you must still keep the straight line. This rider has allowed her arms and elbows to be drawn forward and down so that the line is maintained.

Here, the horse is working with more pronounced flexion and bend through his neck. In this case you should raise your lower arms and hands slightly to maintain the line.

The Legs

The most important way that you can communicate with the horse is through the legs and seat. Your legs should hang long and relaxed around the horse's sides, with no tightness in the knee joints in particular. It is the insides of the calves that squeeze against the horse to ask him to move either forward or across to one side or the other. If you run your hand down the inside of your leg just below the knee, you should feel the slight outward bulge of your calf muscle; it is this part of the leg that is used to communicate with the horse.

Check that your stirrup length is correct by allowing each leg to hang long and loose, and free of the stirrup. You should then only need to turn your toe up slightly to find the stirrup. This is the position that you should be aiming for,

Ask a friend to adjust the stirrup leather so that you only need to turn up your toe to find the stirrup iron. It may take some time for you to be able to ride comfortably with a stirrup as long your muscles will need to supple up and stretch, but this is what you are aiming for.

This is the classical position viewed from the front. You can see how the rider's legs would completely encompass the body of the horse; it is this position that allows the leg to support the horse at all times, and from which you can communicate with the horse through your leg aids.

although at first it is likely to produce too much pull down the back of the thigh and calf muscles. Until your muscles have toned, stretched and strengthened sufficiently, it is sensible to ride with the leg in as long a position as is still comfortable. With time, and particularly as you begin to find your balance on the horse and the beginnings of an independent seat, you will gradually find it easier to ride with the leg in a longer position.

Keep your knee joint relaxed and let it fall away from the saddle slightly, which will allow the leg to hang correctly around the horse's side. Contrary to popular belief, you should not grip with the knees, as doing so will effectively push your seat up and out of the saddle. Equally, if you hold your knees tightly against the saddle, you cannot squeeze the horse's sides with your legs. The knee and the toe have to be turned slightly outward to allow the inside of the calf to press against the horse's sides, which you will need to do to apply a leg aid correctly.

A common fault is for the lower leg to be drawn back and upward in order to press against the horse's side, but this is an

To find the correct stirrup length that will allow you to adopt the classical position for flatwork, you should sit deep in the saddle and just allow your legs to hang long and loose without putting them in the stirrups.

LEFT
To apply the leg aids correctly you need to be aware of exactly what your lower leg is doing. When the horse is moving at the pace you wish him to, keep your legs gently in contact with his sides, but do not actively do anything. The lower leg and the knee joint should remain soft and relaxed.

ineffective means of communication. The lower leg must lie close to the girth; it will come into contact with the part of the horse's belly which is fractionally behind the girth. For some movements, such as turning, or when the rider wants to control the horse's hindquarters, the lower leg is used a few inches further back behind the girth. But the leg is always used in the same way—with the weight down in the heel, the knee and toe turned out slightly and with a squeeze or nudge inward, not backward. If you conjure up in your mind a picture of an old-fashioned, bow-legged horseman, you will have a good idea of how the rider's legs are used against the horse's sides, and why some riders end up looking bow-legged!

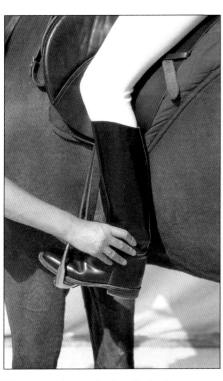

When you wish to apply a leg aid, simply squeeze your lower leg inward. Allow your knee to come slightly away from the saddle so that your lower leg may close in against the horse's side. Your weight remains gently pushed down into your heel. Again you can get a feel for this by asking a friend to push your leg inward against the horse's sides. Having your leg held in the right position will give you a feel for what you are trying to achieve. Until your muscles are used to this movement it will seem difficult, and you will not be able to apply a very strong leg aid. Your thigh and calf muscles will need to stretch and strengthen before your leg aids can be truly effective.

COMMON FAULTS

Picture one shows a bad leg position—see how the lower leg is pushed forward and away from the horse's sides. This is usually a result of the rider adopting an armchair seat in the saddle. It leads to the leg aids being incorrectly applied.

In picture two, instead of squeezing inward this rider has drawn her lower leg back and, as a result, her weight has come out of her heel and her heel is higher than her toe. At this point it is very easy for the stirrup iron to slip off your foot. This type of leg aid is ineffective—the lower leg is simply being brushed backward across the horse's side and is not being applied to the more sensitive area just behind the girth. A horse that is ridden like this will never be able to differentiate between an aid to move forward and an aid to move his quarters, when the rider's lower leg is applied further back behind the girth.

LUNGE LESSONS

Lunging Exercises

One of the best ways to encourage an independent seat is to be lunged. When the horse is lunged, the handler on the ground can control the horse's speed and direction, leaving you free to concentrate fully on your position. Lunge lessons are given at most riding establishments. It is important that the horse you ride is calm and steady on the lunge, and that the person who is lunging you is capable and confident in what they are doing. A lunging cavesson should be used over the horse's usual bridle. This is like a padded halter with a reinforced piece on the noseband that has rings attached to it. These take the lunge line. The handler should maintain a position that allows the lunge line, the lunging whip and the horse to form a triangle.

The voice rather than the lunge whip should be used to ask the horse to move forward. The lunge whip should only be used to back up the voice if the horse does not respond, and then should be moved quietly so that the horse does not suddenly shoot forward. He should be allowed to settle into a steady rhythm; this

The handler keeps a contact with the horse via the lunge line. The lunge whip can be used behind the horse's hindquarters to encourage him to move forward, or it can be flicked toward his shoulder to keep him out on the circle. Both rider and handler should wear a riding hat; the handler should also wear gloves.

will make it easier for you to relax and find your balance. Both horse and rider should be allowed periods of rest during these exercises.

Lunging should only ever take place on a secure surface. If you only have a field and it is hard and rutted, or deep and wet, the horse is likely to injure or strain his tendons if he is made to work on it. Lunge lessons should not last for more than 20–30 minutes, and work should be carried out in both directions. Working on a circle is tiring and stressful to the horse's limbs, and once you are tired or sore you will not be able to do anything more to improve your position. If anything, it will get worse as you tense up with effort. If you are struggling, it is much better to stop than to keep going until you reach the point of exhaustion or frustration.

RIDING WITHOUT STIRRUPS

Although work without stirrups is usually carried out on the lunge, or in an arena, if you have the opportunity to hack out regularly, it is worth making yourself ride for a few minutes each time without stirrups. Normally, the stirrups would be crossed over in front of the saddle so that they don't bang against the horse's sides, but this is not advisable out on a hack in case you need the stirrups back in a hurry. You should only ride without stirrups on a hack at walk. At this gait they should not swing so much that they knock the horse's sides or elbows. Equally, you can quickly slip them back on if necessary. After only a few minutes of riding without stirrups, when you put your feet back in them they often feel too short—that is the time to let the stirrup leathers down a hole so that gradually you can ride at a longer length.

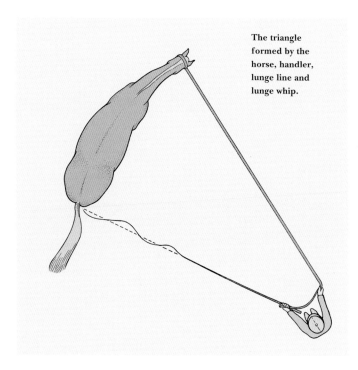

The triangle formed by the horse, handler, lunge line and lunge whip.

To help stretch the thigh muscles, practice this simple exercise. Bring your feet up under your seat and hold them in position with a hand around each ankle. This has the added advantage of helping you to keep your shoulders up and straight, and it automatically puts your seat in the correct position in the saddle. When you take your stirrups back after these exercises, you may feel that you want to lengthen the stirrup leathers. This is a good sign and is the start of the path toward attaining the classical position.

STRENGTHENING EXERCISE

1 Practice riding without stirrups and, to help build up your confidence and balance, spread your arms out to either side.

2 To help strengthen your upper body, twist first round to the left...

3 ...and then back to the right.

HOLDING THE LUNGE LINE

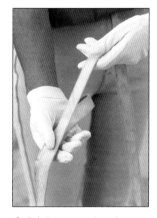

1 It is important that whoever is going to lunge you knows how to do this safely and correctly. One of the biggest risks to the handler is getting his or her hands trapped in the lunge line should the horse panic and try to run away. The safest way to hold the lunge line is not to loop it around your hand but to do the following: Lay the end of the lunge line across the palm of your hand. Do not put your hand through the loop that most lunge lines have on the end.

2 Lay the lunge line, in equal loops, backward and forward across the palm of your hand. Continue to loop the line across your palm until it is the desired length, i.e. you are the distance you want to be away from the horse.

3 Now you can close your hand around the loops and keep a contact with the horse as he moves. If you want to let more lunge line out so that the horse can work on a larger circle, just open your hand and allow one loop to fall away. If the horse did panic and pull away you could close your hand tight around the line and try to stop him. But if he has built up too much speed and is determined to get away, the lunge line will be pulled out of your hand, and you will be free of it. If it is looped around your hand and the horse bolts, the loops will tighten like a noose around your hand. You will either be dragged or have your fingers torn off. Either way the horse will escape if he is determined, so it is better to let him go if you have to and at least remain in one piece and in a position to retrieve him.

"AROUND THE WORLD" EXERCISE

▌ LEFT
The horse or pony you learn to ride on should be a sensible and calm one. This young rider is making the most of her pony's kind nature to have some fun, while also increasing her confidence on horseback. Exercises such as this one—called "Around the World"— should only ever be carried out on a quiet pony and with someone on the ground to hold the pony's head.

Mastering
the Gaits

Having climbed aboard, it is now time to experience some
forward motion! The first thing you will suddenly be aware of
is just how much the horse moves underneath you. The horse
has four legs to operate and, at walk, these move one at a
time. As each shoulder or hindquarter swings the appropriate
leg forward, you will feel it. Each gait that the horse can offer
you—walk, trot, canter and gallop—will give a different
sensation of speed and motion, and you must learn to absorb
it, and to remain balanced on the horse at each gait while still
maintaining the correct, classical position. To the outside eye,
horse and rider should appear to be moving as one.

▍ OPPOSITE
**Mastering the gaits
allows the rider to
enjoy the horse's
power and speed.**

▍ LEFT
**One of the skills the
rider must acquire is
the ability to remain
relaxed on the horse
so that you can absorb
the movement of the
horse's gaits.**

Absorbing the Movement

In an attempt to follow the movement of the horse, many riders end up trying too hard and do too much with their bodies. This, instead of creating a picture of harmony, actually looks completely unco-ordinated; the horse appears to be moving to one beat, and the rider to another. It is also uncomfortable.

The first thing to bear in mind is that your seat belongs to the saddle which, in turn, belongs to the horse's back. The saddle will mimic the movement of the horse's back and you should imagine that your seat is glued to the saddle. Sit deep in the saddle, with your weight distributed equally on each seat bone. When striving for a deep, balanced seat, it sometimes helps to imagine that your legs have been cut off, about halfway down the thigh; therefore it is the top half of the thighs and the seat itself that embrace the saddle. By sitting up straight and keeping the shoulders balanced above the hips, your

weight sinks down into the saddle. This allows the legs to hang long and loose around the horse's sides, with the foot supported softly by the stirrup. The arms follow the movement of the horse's head and neck, and this is achieved by keeping the elbows soft and relaxed with your shoulders remaining still. If your seat is glued to the saddle, and your shoulders, head and neck remain still, the only part of your body that is free to move is the area between your hips and your ribcage. So the hips and stomach are rocked gently forward and back by the movement of the horse. It is by being soft and supple through the hips, the lower back and the stomach that you are able to move as one with the horse. Always remember that it is the horse that moves your body, and so your body must remain relaxed to allow it to be moved by the horse. You should not create any additional movement yourself—this is most likely to happen if your body is tense.

THE WALK

The walk is described as a four-beat gait because the horse moves each leg individually; if you listen to his footfalls you hear four separate hoofbeats. At the trot, the horse moves his legs in diagonal pairs, so this is known as a two-beat gait.

The sequence of footfalls at the walk is as follows: outside hind, outside fore, inside hind, inside fore. The horse should take strides of equal length and he should look energetic and purposeful. If you watch a horse walking you will see that his whole body is in action; the movement flows through the muscles of the hindquarters, up over the back, and through the shoulders and the neck. The horse should look supple, athletic and powerful. Although the walk is the horse's slowest gait, he does use his neck to quite a degree, which means you must be particularly aware of allowing your arms to follow the movement so that you do not restrict the horse.

MOVING WITH THE HORSE

At the walk the rider allows his hips and stomach to be rocked gently forward and back by the push of the horse's hindquarters beneath him. Notice how the rider is maintaining a straight line from the elbow, through the lower arm, and

down the rein to the bit. A light but constant contact is kept with the horse's mouth by allowing the arms to follow the natural movement of the horse's head and neck as he walks.

HALT TO WALK AND WALK TO HALT

Transitions

Changing gaits on a horse, whether it be from halt to walk, or from trot to canter, is known as performing a transition. Like shifting gears in a car, whether you are increasing or decreasing pace, it should appear smooth and effortless.

Transitions are achieved by a subtle balance of the use of the hand and leg. Use your lower leg to activate the horse's hindquarters, which is where his power comes from. You can then use your hands to guide that power in whichever direction you wish.

■ REFINING THE USE OF THE LEGS AND HANDS

To walk forward, squeeze your legs against the horse's sides and allow your hands and arms to be drawn forward. If the horse ignores you, give him a sharper nudge with your heels. If this is ignored, give him a tap with the schooling whip or stick behind your lower leg. If you have to do

COMMON FAULTS

If the rider decides to do nothing with her legs and simply pulls on the reins in an effort to slow down, you can see what happens—the horse resists the request to slow down and throws his head and neck in the air in order to fight the pull of the rider; this is described as the horse hollowing against the rider. The whole picture looks tense and uncomfortable. The rider must first ask with the legs and then only use as much hand as is absolutely necessary to achieve the desired result.

1 At the halt the rider still keeps a light contact with the horse's mouth and lets the legs hang long and loose by the horse's sides. The lower leg is in contact with the horse but is not actively doing anything. Note how a straight line is maintained from the shoulder to the hip to the heel. The position would be better still if the rider kept her chin up—a common fault of many riders is the tendency to look down!

2 To go forward to the walk, the rider squeezes both legs against the horse's sides and, at the same time, allows the hands and arms to go forward to follow the forward movement of the horse's head and neck. Once the horse is walking positively forward the rider allows her legs to relax against the horse's sides. The arms and hands are drawn gently forward and back by the movement of the horse's head and neck. This movement is led by the horse. The rider does not pull back on the reins.

3 To prepare to return to the halt, the rider squeezes her legs inward against the horse's sides and at the same time reduces the degree to which she allows her arms to follow the movement of the horse's head and neck. On a well-schooled horse this very slight blocking of the free forward movement will be enough to halt the horse.

4 On a less responsive horse the rider will have to continue to reduce the degree to which the hands follow the horse's head and neck to the point where they are held still, which will completely block the forward movement. As soon as the horse halts, the rider should soften the hands as much as the horse will allow while still remaining at the halt. Until the horse halts, the rider's legs remain actively against the horse's sides, gently pushing him up into the hands. Once he has halted, the legs relax and remain gently in contact with his sides.

this, you must be very quick to keep the soft forward movement of the hands. The horse may jump forward if he is tapped with the whip, and he must not then be punished by being pulled in the mouth. Remember to reward the horse for obeying and going forward. With practice, he will listen to you and a squeeze with your legs will be sufficient.

To halt the horse, squeeze with the legs but do not allow your hands to be drawn forward so much. The horse will realize that his forward movement is being blocked and will either slow down or

shorten the steps he is taking. Continue to decrease the forward movement of the hands until, if necessary, they are returned to the normal halt position and do not move forward at all. This complete blocking will halt the horse.

As with the leg aids, the long-term aim is to use as light and gentle an aid as possible. To begin with you may have to block completely with your hands but, with practice, the horse will become more attentive until only a slight reduction of the forward movement of the hands is enough to halt him.

Changing Direction

You cannot continue in a straight line forever, so once you are confident with forward movement you must be able to change direction.

When the legs are used together either on or fractionally behind the girth, and the hands are also moving together, the horse is kept in a straight line. To go around a corner, or to turn, the horse has to bend through his body. In order to achieve this, the hands and legs must be used individually. If one leg is allowed to slide further back behind the girth, this will make the horse move his hindquarters away from the leg in question, i.e. if your right leg is used behind the girth, the horse will be encouraged to move his quarters across to the left, and vice versa. So, to make the horse turn, one leg is used in the normal place to encourage him to keep moving forward, and the other leg is used further back behind the girth to control the hindquarters.

The horse should never be turned sharply—any turn should be thought of as part of a circle, so to turn right think about circling away to the right. Then the right hand and leg are referred to as being on the inside, while the left hand and leg are now on the outside.

TURNING RIGHT

1 Horse and rider are about to turn off a straight line and away to the right. The rider has moved the right hand a few inches away from the withers, toward the right. This is called opening the hand, and it invites the horse to turn his head and neck to the right in preparation for the turn.

2 The rider's inside (right) leg is used on the girth to keep the horse moving forward; the outside (left) leg is used behind the girth to prevent his quarters from swinging too far to the left. The left hand and arm soften so that the horse keeps bending to the right. The right hand stays to the right of the withers, inviting the horse to move that way.

3 As soon as the horse has turned as far around to the right as the rider requires, the hands and legs return to their normal position.

4 To turn right, the rider's inside (right) hand is moved a little to the right of the withers—opening the hand; the inside (right) leg remains on the girth, encouraging the horse to move forward.

5 The outside hand is softened so that the horse can bend his head and neck away to the right, while the outside leg is used behind the girth to control the degree to which the hindquarters move.

TURNING LEFT

1 To turn left, the rider opens the inside (left) hand a few inches to the left to invite the horse to turn his head and neck in that direction.

2 The outside (right) hand is softened forward to allow the horse to turn away to the left, while the outside leg is used back behind the girth to control the swing of the hindquarters.

3 As soon as the horse is heading in the required direction, the rider's hands and legs return to the normal position.

4 To turn left the inside (left) hand is opened out to the left to ask the horse to turn his head and neck to the left, while the inside leg is used on the girth.

5 The outside (right) hand must be allowed to soften forward to allow the horse to turn away to the left. The outside leg is used behind the girth in order to control the hindquarters.

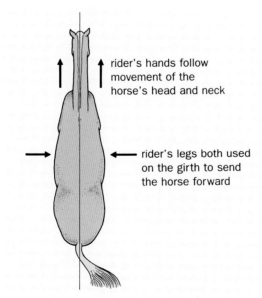

rider's hands follow movement of the horse's head and neck

rider's legs both used on the girth to send the horse forward

▌ **RIGHT**
Riding forward on a straight line.

▌ **FAR RIGHT**
Bending the horse so that he can turn right.

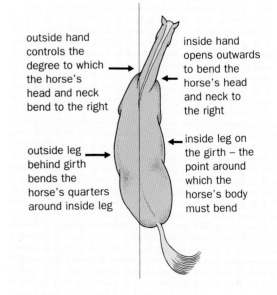

outside hand controls the degree to which the horse's head and neck bend to the right

inside hand opens outwards to bend the horse's head and neck to the right

outside leg behind girth bends the horse's quarters around inside leg

inside leg on the girth – the point around which the horse's body must bend

131

Forward to the Trot

The trot is the next gait that the horse can offer you, and many new riders find this one of the hardest to master. When the horse trots the rider feels a far more powerful force of movement from beneath than is experienced at walk. In order to feel comfortable with this gait, you must try to keep your body relaxed so that it absorbs the movement, rather than tensing up and being bounced around by the horse.

■ THE RISING TROT

When the horse trots you can either sit deep in the saddle the whole time—which is known as the sitting trot—or you can rise out of the saddle with each stride, in time with the beat of the trot. It is far less tiring—and more comfortable—for the new rider to learn the rising trot, than it is to master the sitting trot. Once you feel at ease at this pace, and are able to stay relaxed and balanced, then is the time to practice the sitting trot.

When the horse trots, he is springing from one diagonal pair of legs to the other. To rise to the trot, allow the spring from one pair of legs going forward to lift your seat out of the saddle. The seat returns to the saddle as the other pair of legs springs forward. So as the horse moves each pair of legs in a one-two, one-two, one-two beat, you are sitting and rising to the same beat: up-down, up-down, up-down. This is called posting.

THE TROT

The trot is a two-beat gait—the horse springs from one diagonal pair of legs to the other. If you listen to his hoofbeats, you only hear two footfalls within each complete stride. The outside hind and the inside foreleg move forward together; this is followed by a brief period of suspension, and then the inside hind and outside foreleg move forward as a pair.

PRACTICING THE RISING TROT

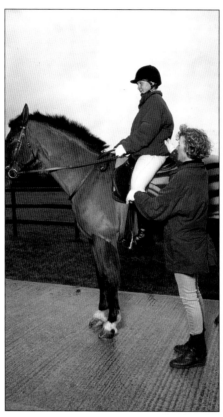

1 Rising to the trot can be practiced when the horse is stationary. The rider sits in the normal classical position, attempting to keep the knee-joints in particular as long and relaxed as possible. Keeping the lower legs as still as possible, the rider should think of just allowing her hips and stomach to swing forward.

■ RISING ON THE CORRECT DIAGONAL

When posting the trot in a circle, the rider is meant to rise in time with a particular diagonal pair of the horse's legs. The easiest way to explain what this entails is for you to look down and watch the horse's outside shoulder for a few minutes once you are trotting. You should be rising out of the saddle as the outside shoulder goes forward. As it comes back, you should sit again.

The reason for bothering to rise on the correct diagonal will become clear later when you are concerned with improving the quality of the horse's work. The horse

2 The seat only comes out of the saddle enough to allow the seat bones to be clear of the saddle. The hips are then allowed to return lightly to the normal sitting position. The shoulders and arms remain still—the rider should think of allowing the hips and stomach to swing forward and up toward her elbows.

will find it easier to balance himself on a turn or circle if the rider is in the saddle when the inside hind leg and the outside foreleg are touching the ground. As the horse uses his legs in diagonal pairs, this is achieved by sitting as the outside shoulder comes back, and rising as it goes forward. When you change the rein and circle in the opposite direction, it follows that you must also change the diagonal, i.e. rise as the new outside shoulder goes forward. Changing the diagonal is achieved by sitting for an extra beat before rising again. So instead of sit-rise, sit-rise, you would sit-rise, sit-sit-rise and this will put you on the correct diagonal.

▌ RIGHT
At the sitting trot the rider retains the correct classical position, allowing her stomach and lower back to absorb the movement of the horse. Note the straight line through the shoulder, hip and heel, as well as the line from the elbow, down along the rein to the bit.

COMMON FAULTS

A common mistake when posting is actively trying to push the body up and down. This causes the shoulders and arms to bob up and down, which is disconcerting and uncomfortable for the horse since his mouth suffers if there is excessive movement of the hands and arms.

Another common mistake when posting is for the rider's shoulders to tip forward. This puts the rider off balance and means the hands are often rested on the horse's neck in an effort to regain balance. If the hands are resting on the neck, they cannot keep a soft but continuous contact with the horse's mouth. The shoulders must stay upright, just as they do when the rider is stationary; only the hips should move forward. If the shoulders remain balanced and in line with the rider's heels, the rider will not be pushed off balance by the movement of the horse.

■ THE SITTING TROT

At the sitting trot you should remain sitting deep in the saddle, maintaining the same classical position as when stationary and at the walk. The movement of the horse is absorbed by the stomach and lower back, so that you remain deep in the saddle without being bounced up and down. As you feel the horse's legs springing forward underneath you, try to think of allowing your ribcage to sink down toward your hips. This means that the stomach and lower back act like an accordion: As the horse springs along at the trot, the stomach and lower back are either contracting or expanding to absorb the movement. You must stay relaxed so that your legs can hang long and loose by the horse's sides, and your arms can still stay soft and maintain a light contact with the horse's mouth. It helps to make a conscious effort to keep breathing—you would be surprised how many riders hold their breath as soon as they concentrate too hard on something. Steady breathing helps you relax.

In sitting trot the knees should be long and loose.

Gripping with the knee makes your seat insecure.

COMMON FAULTS AT THE SITTING TROT

▌ LEFT
Back to the armchair position! How not to sit—the lower leg has slipped forward and the rider is now sitting on the back of her seat. The line from the shoulder through the hip to the heel has been lost.

▌ LEFT
If you fall into the armchair position your body is unable correctly to absorb the movement of the horse. You will be bumped up and down and, as a result, you will find your hands and arms bobbing up and down as well. It's uncomfortable for both horse and rider.

FROM WALK TO TROT TO WALK

1 The horse should be walking forward actively and attentively before the rider asks for the trot. See how the rider is keeping a contact with the horse's mouth without actually pulling or restricting him. The rider's legs are in contact with the horse's sides but are not being used actively. By keeping both the legs and the hands in contact with the horse in this way, you will be keeping open your lines of communication.

2 To ask for the trot, the rider squeezes both legs actively against the horse's sides and softens the hands forward so that the horse feels free to increase the pace and go forward into the trot.

3 Once the horse is trotting on, the rider's legs and hands return to just being in contact with the horse. The leg is there to squeeze the horse forward should he slow down, and the hand is there to guide him.

4 To return to the walk the rider sits deep in the saddle and squeezes the legs against the horse's sides. (If the rider had been at the rising trot, she would return to the sitting trot to achieve this.)

5 Then, instead of softening the hands forward, she keeps the hands still so that the horse's forward movement is blocked, bringing him back to the walk.

6 As soon as the horse walks, the hands and legs relax sufficiently to keep just a light contact.

On into the Canter

It is at the canter that the new rider will first experience the true exhilaration of riding a horse. The feeling of speed and power as the horse eats up the ground with each stride gives a real buzz. But despite the increased speed, the rider generally finds this a very smooth gait.

■ CANTERING ON THE CORRECT LEAD

If you watch a horse cantering in a circle, he should appear to be leading each stride with his inside foreleg. In practice, the inside foreleg is actually the last leg to be moved by the horse within each canter stride, but to the observer it does appear

LEFT
At the canter, the rider sits deeply in the saddle and allows the hips to be rocked forward and back by the movement of the horse. The arms and hands must stay soft and relaxed so that they can follow the movement of the horse's head and neck. Note once more the straight line through the ear, shoulder, hip and heel, and again from the elbow, down the rein to the bit. At all gaits, the correct classical position should be maintained.

THE CANTER

The canter is a three-time pace, with the legs working in the following sequence: outside hind goes forward, then the inside hind and outside fore go forward together, followed by the inside foreleg. There is then a period of suspension when all four feet are off the ground, before the stride pattern is repeated—outside hind, inside hind and outside fore together, then inside fore.

to be leading the stride. When this is the case, the horse is said to be cantering on the correct leg, or the correct lead. So when cantering on the right rein, i.e. circling to the right, the inside (right) foreleg should appear to be leading; and, when cantering on the left rein, the inside (left) foreleg appears to be leading.

To ask the horse to canter forward on the left lead you should use the inside leg

on the girth and the outside leg behind the girth, while opening the left hand slightly to keep the horse bent left, and just keeping a feel on the outside rein to stop the horse from simply accelerating at the trot. To canter on the right lead the aids are reversed; the right leg is used on the girth, the left leg is used behind the girth, and the right hand is opened slightly to bend the horse to the right.

Cantering on the correct lead. This horse and rider are circling on the left rein and you can see how the horse's inside (left) foreleg appears to be leading.

Cantering on the wrong lead. Here you can see that, although the horse is still circling to the left, it is the outside foreleg that appears to be leading the stride.

FROM TROT TO CANTER TO TROT

1 Before asking the horse to canter, the rider must stop posting and be sure that the horse is working forward actively and attentively at the trot.

2 To ask the horse to go forward into a canter on the left rein, i.e. to canter on the left lead, the rider sits deep, presses the inside (left) leg on the girth, but asks more actively with a squeeze or a nudge of the outside leg back behind the girth. This is because it is the horse's outside hindleg that starts off the stride, so the rider activates this leg by using her own outside leg behind the girth. The inside hand is opened out slightly to the left to encourage the horse to keep a bend to the left, but the outside hand may have to keep more of a feel than usual on the outside rein to prevent the horse from simply trotting faster. In this picture the outside hind is just about to take the first step of the canter stride.

3 Once the correct canter is established, with the left leg leading, the rider just keeps her outside leg in place behind the girth to encourage the outside hind to keep initiating the canter stride. The inside leg remains at the girth, so that the horse's body is bent around the rider's inside leg as they progress around the circle.

4 The arms and hands move forward with the movement of the horse's head and neck, and the rider sits deep in the saddle, allowing her hips to be rocked by the horse's stride.

5 In order to return to the trot the rider sits deep in the saddle and closes both legs against the horse's sides.

6 The rider reduces the degree to which she allows her hands and arms to move forward with the horse's head and neck, so that the horse's forward movement is blocked. You may have to keep a slightly stronger feel in the outside hand to help bring the horse back to the trot.

7 As soon as the trot is established the rider softens her hands forward again to follow the movement and allows her legs to hang softly by the horse's sides. She must be ready to squeeze the horse forward again into a more active trot if he tries to slow down anymore.

COMMON FAULT

A common fault when asking the horse to canter is for the rider to tip forward and look down over the inside shoulder. As soon as the rider's shoulders drop forward she is pushed off balance, and then the hands tend to drop down onto the horse looking for support. The rider must stay sitting upright and use her hands and legs independently to ask for a transition to the canter. Leaning forward simply unbalances both horse and rider, and this makes the job harder.

CANTERING IN THE FORWARD SEAT

By taking her weight out of the saddle, the rider can encourage the horse to relax his back and put a little more life and swing into his canter. This is often done out on a hack so that the horse is allowed to move along effortlessly under his rider. In a schooling session, the rider may take his weight out of the saddle to help the horse relax and use his back more. This is often done when the horse is being warmed up before he is asked to jump. It is called riding in the forward seat, and the rider simply lifts his seat bones out of the saddle and allows his weight to sink down into his heels and the stirrups. The rider will need to have gained a good sense of balance to do this, and will also need quite strong leg muscles, as it really stretches the backs of the calves. If you feel you keep leaning back in the saddle, you probably need to bring your shoulders slightly more forward. If you feel you are leaning forward onto the horse's neck, you need to raise your shoulders and check that your lower leg has not slipped backward, which will in turn push your weight forward.

Full Speed Ahead— The Gallop

Riding your horse at the gallop is an invigorating and exciting experience, but for it to be safe and enjoyable for both horse and rider you must develop a well-balanced, secure seat and feel confident about controlling your horse. Balance and security are important because if you lose

THE GALLOP

The gallop is a four-time gait with the legs working in the following sequence: near hind, off hind, near fore, off fore. Because the walk is also a four-time gait it is often said that if a horse has a good walk he will also be a good galloper. Watch race horses walking around at the track and you will appreciate this!

At gallop the horse is at full stretch—he lengthens out his body and neck, and each leg is fully extended as it powers forward over the ground. The rider tucks his upper body in behind the horse's neck so that the outline of the two is as streamlined as possible. The seat is taken out of the saddle, which means the rider's weight is dropped down into the heel and is also pushed further back to allow the rider's upper body to tuck in behind the horse's neck. The rider's arms extend forward as the horse stretches his neck forward within each stride. It is usual to ride with shorter stirrups when galloping, as this makes it easier for the rider's weight to be lifted out of the saddle. The lower leg remains on the girth unless the stirrups are pulled up very short, in which case the lower leg is usually pushed forward in front of the girth with the weight well down in the heel, as demonstrated by any race rider.

your balance at this gait you will either topple off, or end up hanging on to the reins. The horse will fight this pressure on his mouth, and you may find yourself no longer in control. At this pace the horse is at full stretch and, to allow him to use

himself fully, you should bring your weight up out of the saddle, push your seat further back and tuck your upper body in behind the horse's neck, very much like a race jockey but without quite such short stirrups.

STOPPING A HARD-PULLING HORSE

It is often at the faster paces, canter and gallop, that the horse becomes over-excited to the extent that he is less responsive to his rider, particularly when it comes to slowing down again. While in theory it should be possible to stop a horse at any pace by using the subtle balance of hand and leg, in practice the horse's excitement can override his desire to listen to his rider. If you find yourself struggling to slow down a galloping horse, make sure your lower leg is pushed forward while still squeezing both legs against the horse's sides. The slightly forward lower leg position allows you to brace yourself against the stirrup. When a horse gets strong, it is easy to be pulled forward out of the saddle; the lower leg slips back putting the rider in a very vulnerable position. Shorten up the reins as much as you can and put one hand, still holding the rein, tight into the horse's neck. Use the other hand

to keep a strong hold on the other rein and, by gradually giving and taking this rein, the horse will start to listen again and will slow down. If you keep a continuous pull on the rein, the horse will simply lean on the bit and become stronger still—give and take the rein to prevent him doing this. Circling the horse will also cause him to slow down.

HIGH SPIRITS

Most horses enjoy a good gallop and will quite often let their riders know this by popping in a high-spirited leap or buck. If the rider is able to sit this out, it is no more than clean, harmless fun, but it becomes less amusing when it is sufficient to unseat the rider. When cantering or galloping, always keep a contact through the reins with the horse's mouth in order to help balance him. If the horse becomes playful and over-excited in his work, it is even more important to maintain this contact.

Influencing the Horse

There is a subtle difference between learning to ride and actually influencing the horse. The new rider will spend the early period of training simply learning how to sit correctly balanced on the horse, and mastering the basic aids which will enable horse and rider to proceed at the walk, trot and canter, to halt and to circle left or right. Until you achieve this balance and the resulting independent seat, you will be little more than a passenger on the horse. Once you have acquired an independent seat, you can concern yourself with how well or otherwise your horse is performing underneath you. Riding a horse should be a pleasure for both parties—the ultimate aim is to be mounted on a cooperative horse who will respond to your lightest instruction. When this is achieved, those observing you may well marvel at that closest of secrets—the one between a rider and his horse.

▌ OPPOSITE
Having attained an independent seat you can influence how well your horse moves.

▌ LEFT
Once you are able to use each hand and leg independently, without sacrificing your position and balance, you will be able to fully influence the horse's performance. This rider is asking her horse to move sideways in "half-pass."

MOVING TO THE LEFT

Control of the Horse

Use your hands and legs to control and influence the horse's shoulders, hindquarters, head and neck. When making a turn or circling, the horse's shoulders and hindquarters are controlled by the rider's use of the legs. When combined with the hands, this can be taken further still to move the horse in a number of different ways. The rider's leg can be used behind the girth to encourage the horse to move sideways (laterally) away from the leg, or to control the swing and direction of the quarters. The use of the leg at the girth encourages the horse to bend around the leg and allows the rider to control the horse's shoulder.

1 While at a halt, if the rider keeps a light feel on the outside rein (the right rein), opens out the inside rein a few inches and squeezes the horse's side with her inside leg at the girth while the outside leg remains relaxed, the horse will bend his head and neck to the left.

2 If the rider actively presses the outside (right) leg against the horse's side, but blocks the horse's forward movement by not softening her outside hand forward, and just holds her inside leg against the horse's side behind the girth to keep the hindquarters still, the horse will step across to the left. His hindquarters remain still because the feel from the inside leg stops him stepping across with his hind legs, but he will move his shoulders and forelegs across to the left. To straighten up again, the rider presses her left leg against the girth to push the horse's shoulders back over to the right. The left hand prevents the horse from stepping forward, and the right hand is opened out to the right to invite the horse to step over to the right. The left leg stays back behind the girth to keep the horse's hindquarters still.

MOVING TO THE RIGHT

1 Similarly at a halt, if the rider keeps a light feel on the outside (left) rein and opens the inside hand while pressing the inside leg against the girth, the horse will bend his head and neck to the right.

2 If the rider brings her outside (left) leg back behind the girth while blocking any attempt by the horse to move forward with the outside rein, and keeps her inside (right) leg on the girth to keep the horse's shoulders stationary, then as she presses her outside leg against the horse he will swing his quarters over to the right. To straighten the horse up again the aids are then reversed—the right leg is used behind the girth to push the quarters back over to the left, while the right hand prevents the horse from stepping forward. The left leg is used at the girth to make sure the shoulders remain still. Once the horse is straight again, the rider's legs and hands return to the normal position.

The Rider's Goal— To Lighten the Forehand

If you watch a horse showing off loose in a field you will see how proud and active he can look: His neck is high and arched, and he will use his hindquarters powerfully to produce round, elevated strides. As soon as a young or unschooled horse is asked to carry a rider, this picture can change dramatically: the horse's outline becomes flatter and longer, his steps lose their spring and he may lean on the bit by carrying his head and neck low, so that the rider always has a horrible, heavy feel in the hand; alternatively, he may carry his head high in an effort to evade the effect of the rider's hand on the rein and the bit. The rider has to teach the horse how to rebalance himself so that he can comfortably deal with the unbalancing effect of a rider on his back and regain his proud, elegant and light bearing.

An unbalanced horse usually takes advantage of the fact that the rider is holding the reins and will lean on the bit, so the rider is in effect helping to carry the weight of the horse. When this happens the horse is said to be on his forehand, i.e. more of the combined weight of the horse and the rider is carried on the horse's shoulders and forelegs than on the hindquarters and hindlegs. If you piled a lot of heavy weights onto the front of a car it would become heavy to handle, and similarly the horse becomes heavy in the rider's hand and is difficult to steer and control. If the weight is taken off the front of the car and loaded on to the back, suddenly the car is light and maneuverable in front.

The rider's aim is to encourage the horse to carry more of the weight on the hindquarters than on the forehand. In order to do this the horse has to lower his hindquarters and allow his hindlegs to step much further under his body. When he does this, his shoulders, head and neck are automatically raised. This is called lightening the forehand, or transferring the weight from the forehand to the hindquarters.

ENGAGING THE HINDQUARTERS

1 A young or unschooled horse will carry himself in a long, low outline; see how low the head and neck appear to be, and how long and flat the overall picture is as a result.

2 The rider has used her legs and seat to encourage the horse to bring his hind legs further underneath him, and just keeps enough contact on the rein to keep the horse from speeding up. The effect of the rider's legs pushing the horse up into the contact maintained by the hand is that the horse starts to bend and flex his hocks more, so that they can step further underneath the body. This is called engaging the hocks or hindquarters.

3 Various schooling exercises, combined with the horse learning to become more responsive to the leg and seat aids, gradually allow the rider to encourage the horse to use his hindquarters more.

4 The horse's outline is now rounder, and the forehand has been raised slightly higher than the hindquarters so that the horse is carrying more of the weight on the hindquarters and has lightened the forehand. Asking the horse to transfer the weight in this way, from the forehand to the hindquarters, is always brought about by greater use of the rider's legs, not by pulling the horse's head and neck up and in with the reins. The rein contact should remain soft and elastic, only blocking sufficiently to prevent the horse from speeding up when the leg is applied, instead of engaging the hindquarters more as is required.

Control and Motion— Introducing Lateral Work

When first learning to ride, you are concerned primarily with being able to send the horse forward into the walk, trot, canter and gallop, and being able to halt. As your skills develop, you learn how to make the horse move sideways, either by moving his whole body or just his shoulders or hindquarters. This is known as lateral work, and is invaluable for a rider as it teaches him or her to feel and influence the horse's movement. For the horse, it is used as a suppling exercise and to encourage him to work more actively with his hindquarters.

Lateral movements include leg yielding, haunches-in (both described here), shoulder-in and half-pass (see Developing Lateral Work). All horses should be introduced to these exercises as part of their overall training program. Practice them at the walk and, once you have mastered control of the shoulders and hindquarters, you will realize just how maneuverable the horse can be.

■ LEG YIELDING

In this exercise the horse is asked to move forward and sideways at the same time; the inside hind and foreleg cross over in front of the outside hind and foreleg.

■ HAUNCHES-IN

In this exercise the horse continues walking in a straight line but he brings his hind end in to one side. If working on a sand surface, the horse's hoofprints would leave three lines of tracks: the inside line is formed by the inside hind, the middle line is made by the inside fore and the outside hind (which follow each other), and the outside line is made by the outside fore.

■ REIN BACK

The rein back is when the horse is asked, quite literally, to walk backward. It should only ever be performed at the walk, although when frightened, the horse will be quite capable of running backward at a respectable speed!

Although the rein back is not a lateral movement, it is all part of teaching horse and rider the full extent of the control and motion they can achieve.

The horse should step backward, in a straight line, moving his legs clearly and positively in diagonal pairs—inside fore and outside hind together, followed by outside fore and inside hind together.

LEG YIELDING

█ LEFT

To leg yield across to the left, as this rider is doing, she brings her right leg behind the girth which tells the horse to move sideways; her left leg remains on the girth, encouraging the horse to keep moving forward as well as sideways. The right hand is opened a few inches, which encourages the horse to keep a slight right bend through the body; the left hand keeps enough of a feel on the rein to keep the horse from bending too far to the left and, combined with the push from the right leg behind the girth, invites the horse to step sideways. To leg yield away to the right the aids are reversed—the left leg is used behind the girth, the right leg on the girth, the right rein keeps enough contact to invite the horse to step to the right, and the left rein is opened a few inches to encourage the horse to keep a slight bend through his body.

HAUNCHES-IN

▮ RIGHT

In these pictures the horse is being asked to bring his hindquarters to the left while continuing to walk forward in a straight line. The rider uses her outside (right) leg behind the girth to move the quarters across slightly. Her inside leg stays on the girth to encourage the horse to keep moving forward and to prevent the shoulders from moving out of line. The left hand is opened slightly which, combined with the pressure from the left leg on the girth, encourages the horse to keep a bend through his whole body. The outside hand takes up enough of a feel to keep the horse's shoulder moving forward in a straight line.

Haunches-in to the right is achieved by reversing the aids—the left leg is used behind the girth, etc.

REIN BACK

1 The rein back can only be successfully performed if the horse is calm and relaxed when at the halt.

2 The rider squeezes both legs against the horse's sides, but makes sure that she blocks the horse's forward movement by not allowing her hands to move forward. Because the legs are applied actively, the horse knows he has to move somewhere. The rein contact is telling him he cannot go forward and so he goes backward. Some horses, as demonstrated here, understand what is required more easily if you apply both legs behind the girth, and then lift your seat bones off the saddle. This encourages the horse to step back underneath you as required.

3 Having taken one step back with one diagonal pair of legs, the horse proceeds to step back with the remaining diagonal pair. The horse should only be asked to step backward for a limited number of steps. As a reward, allow him to walk forward again while making a fuss over him.

Acceptance of Contact

Right from the start the horse has to learn to accept, without tension or resentment, the fact that the bit in his mouth is attached, via the reins, to the rider's hands, and that there will always be a light but sympathetic contact between the two. It is vital that you achieve a balanced, independent seat so that you are not tempted to hang on to the reins in an effort to balance yourself. Your priority is to learn to follow the movement of the horse's head and neck so that you are able to keep a constant but sympathetic contact with his mouth. In the early stages of training, you should not concern yourself with how the horse is carrying his head and neck, but only with learning to feel,

BASIC PRINCIPLES

Before you can hope to achieve a lightening of the forehand, there are a number of basic principles that you and your horse must master. These form the basis of all horses' training and progression, whether or not you are dealing with a horse who has never been properly schooled, and are as follows:
- Acceptance of the rein contact.
- Free forward movement.
- Maintaining a rhythm.
- Bend and flexion through the body.
- The use of half-halts to engage the hindquarters and rebalance the horse.
Once you have mastered these principles, you will be equipped with the means to ride your horse to the maximum of his potential.

follow and maintain the contact. Once the horse knows that the contact is constant, but kind, he will learn to accept it. Your elbows must remain soft and relaxed so that the contact can be maintained. It may be necessary to open the hands out a little wider than usual so that there is no obstruction—whatever the horse does with his head, you can follow it with your hands.

COMMON FAULTS

How often have you seen a horse dragging along like this? The rider is not keeping a contact with the horse's mouth and, although she is actively using her legs, the horse is completely ignoring the aid and continuing to plod along in a lethargic and disinterested manner.

FOLLOWING THE HORSE'S HEAD AND NECK

■ **RIGHT**
In the early stages of training, the rider should not concern herself with the position of the horse's head and neck—only with learning to follow their movement so that a soft but constant contact is maintained.

The horse must respond the same way at all gaits. Here, at the trot, we can see the result of the rider failing to keep a contact with the horse's mouth, and the horse blatantly ignoring the rider's leg aids. The rider is working hard with her legs while the horse is being extremely lazy with his!

Free Forward Movement

The horse also has to learn to respect the rider's legs, i.e. when you use your legs against the horse's sides, he must respond by going forward if both legs are used together or by moving away from the leg if used as a lateral (sideways) aid. The vast majority of problems experienced both on the flat and over jumps are caused by the horse ignoring, or being slow to react to, the rider's leg aids. The horse's first reaction should always be to move forward. Once the horse respects the leg and is willing to maintain free forward movement without you continually having to reapply the leg aids, he is said to be in front of the leg and on the aids—he is attentive and ready to react to his rider's commands instantly.

In the early stages of training, you should use your voice combined with a squeeze from both legs to ask the horse to move forward. If the horse does not respond, use your voice again, backed up with a sharp nudge with both heels against the horse's sides. If this is still ignored, squeeze your legs against the horse, use your voice to ask him to walk on and give him a tap with the schooling whip or stick behind your leg at the same time as the leg aid is applied. You must be ready to allow forward movement with the hands, particularly if the horse jumps forward when the schooling whip is used. As soon as he moves forward, reward him by praising him verbally. You should then relax your legs against the horse's sides. As soon as he slows down again, repeat the process. Gradually the horse will learn to respond to the first light aid.

KEEPING A SOFT CONTACT

1 Here the rider has shortened her reins sufficiently to keep a contact with the horse's mouth. She has applied the leg again and backed it up with a tap from the schooling whip. Already the picture is one of greater alertness and activity.

2 The rider maintains the contact and uses the leg once more to ask the horse to walk on a little more energetically.

3 This time the horse responds instantly; the rider's leg can relax and the horse maintains the forward movement without further nagging. Note how the horse's outline is now much rounder and shorter as he begins to lighten his forehand.

4 At the trot, the rider takes up contact with the horse's mouth and backs up her leg aids with a tap from the schooling whip.

5 Immediately the horse offers much more in the way of forward impulsion. Now that he is thinking forward, see how he lengthens his steps and voluntarily raises his head and neck into a rounder, shorter outline.

6 The rider can relax her legs and enjoy the free forward movement that the horse is offering her. But as soon as he drops back from this pace, the rider starts the process over again.

Maintaining a Rhythm

Now that the horse accepts the contact and moves forward willingly from your leg, both you and he need to learn to maintain an even rhythm in all your work. This rhythm must not be too slow or the work will lack impulsion and power; also, it must not be too fast or the horse will tend to become unbalanced and will be pushed onto his forehand. Aim for a rhythm at each gait that gives you the feeling of free forward movement without feeling rushed. The ultimate aim is to use a light squeeze from the legs to ride the horse up into this rhythm; then to relax and enjoy the experience while the horse willingly maintains the rhythm, without continual nagging from either hand or leg.

Once the horse is responding quickly to the leg you are halfway there. Some horses have naturally rhythmic gaits and will automatically maintain the rhythm. Others will need a reminder from leg, voice and/or schooling whip to keep up to the rhythm, or they may need to be slowed down. Once the horse is thinking forward, be careful not to dampen his goodwill by restricting him with the reins if he goes too fast. The use of a neck strap to slow the horse is a better method to use; it prevents the horse from learning how to lean on the bit or to fight you by shortening and tensing his neck.

By pulling on the neck strap instead of blocking with the reins, you can slow the horse down. Practice in the arena, first using the strap to bring the horse from walk to halt, and then from trot to walk etc. Once the horse understands its use, this method can be used to steady him within any pace. But remember that you must still use your legs and voice, if necessary, in the same way you would if you were going to use the rein contact to slow down.

USING THE NECK STRAP

1 Here the rider is introducing the neck strap by using it to bring the horse back from trot to walk. She has put the reins in one hand and holds the neck strap in the other.

2 The rider then uses her legs with a light squeeze against the horse's sides, while using her voice and a firm pull on the neck strap to slow the horse down. Although the rider wants to slow down, the leg is still applied because it encourages the horse to bring his hindlegs further underneath him so that he can keep his forehand light. If the leg is not used, the horse will simply shift his weight on to the forehand and will become heavy and unbalanced in the rider's hand.

3 The horse comes back quite happily to the walk without the need to block with the rein. He is rewarded with a pat and praise from his rider.

4 When working at the trot, if the horse has a tendency to speed up out of the desired rhythm, the rider can just loop a finger through the neck strap and pull on it until the horse slows the rhythm down again.

5 When the horse responds, the neck strap is released and he is praised by his rider.

Bend and Flexion

∎ BELOW
The horse is bringing his hocks well underneath himself, the hindquarters are lowered slightly and the poll and jaw are relaxed so that the front of the face is on the vertical.

In all the horse's work, the rider is striving to ensure that the horse's hindlegs follow in the same tracks as his front legs, i.e. his quarters are not allowed to swing out or his shoulder to fall in. This is referred to as straightness in the horse, which is a term that causes some confusion. For the horse to be straight, i.e. for his hindlegs to follow in the same tracks as his front legs, when working on a turn or a circle he has to bend through his body; his whole body must form a slight, continual curve around the rider's inside leg. So in order to be straight the horse has to bend!

The degree of bend that the horse shows through his body is dependent on the size of circle or turn you are riding. For example, to ride a 65½ foot (20 m) circle the horse shows only a slight bend through his body, but to maneuver himself around a 33 foot (10 m) circle there will be a greater degree of bend.

ACHIEVING BEND

1 The rider should concentrate on making sure that the outside hand is really following the horse's movement in a soft, forgiving way, while still maintaining a light contact. This ensures that the horse's forward momentum is not stifled by a restricting outside hand. The rider then opens the inside hand, setting it in the open position by simply tensing the muscles of the arm, not by pulling back on the rein. The inside leg is used on the girth to keep the horse pushed out onto the circle, and a firmer contact is only taken up on the outside rein if the horse falls in on the circle, i.e. allows the circle to get smaller and smaller. If he does this, the rider must keep pushing the horse out with the inside leg and draw him back out onto the original circle by using the outside rein.

2 The rider should now feel the horse bending through the body and neck; if the horse resists and does not respond by offering some bend through his body, the rider simply opens the inside rein out further and sets it there—still without pulling back on it. The inside leg is kept on, and should be backed up with a tap from the schooling whip if the horse continues to fall in on the circle rather than bend through the body.

3 As soon as the horse offers the bend, i.e. when you can see a glimpse of his inside eye and nostril, use both legs against his sides to encourage him to bring his hocks further underneath him and to flex through his topline. When you feel the horse relax his poll and jaw so that the nose is lowered and his face is on the vertical, soften the inside rein and allow it to follow the movement in the same way as the outside rein. Praise the horse verbally— this is his reward for yielding to your leg and hand. The horse is now beginning to work in self-carriage, i.e. he is carrying more weight on his hindquarters and is lightening his forehand. Note that his head and neck are higher and more arched than in picture one; this is a result of the hocks being brought further under him.

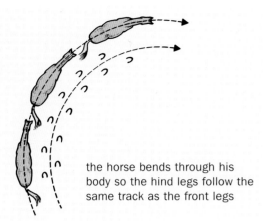

the horse bends through his body so the hind legs follow the same track as the front legs

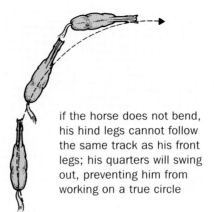

if the horse does not bend, his hind legs cannot follow the same track as his front legs; his quarters will swing out, preventing him from working on a true circle

■ LEFT
How a horse goes around a corner.

The more the horse has to bend his body, the more he has to use his hocks, and the inside hind leg in particular has to step much further across and under the horse's body in order to follow in the track of the inside foreleg. Having ridden simple turns and circles, you will know that the inside leg is used at the girth with an open inside hand to encourage the horse to bend around the inside leg, while the outside leg is used back behind the girth to prevent the quarters from swinging out. The outside hand is used to prevent the horse from bending his head and neck too much to the inside. On an unschooled horse the aids have to be exaggerated until he realizes what it is you are asking him to do. Once the horse is willing to offer you the bend through his whole body, you can ask him to flex right through his topline so that his whole outline becomes soft and round and he offers you no resistance whatsoever. The horse's topline describes the area from the top of the tail, over the hindquarters, back, withers and neck, and on up to the poll. When the horse flexes through his topline, his hindquarters are lowered as his hocks come further underneath him, he stays soft through his back, arches his neck and relaxes his poll and jaw so that the head is carried in a relaxed manner; the horse will lower his nose so that a vertical line could be drawn down the front of his face.

The horse should be introduced to this work at the trot—it is very easy to stifle his forward momentum if it is first asked for at the walk. Ride forward into the trot, bearing in mind the principles of having a horse who will respond happily to your leg and settle into a rhythm without being nagged by your leg or hand.

With time and practice, you will find that the horse will become more and more responsive to the request to bend and flex. After a while, you will not need to open the inside hand in such an exaggerated fashion; simply moving the hand over

OBTAINING THE CORRECT DEGREE OF BEND

The rider should only ask for a slight bend through the horse's body and neck, so that the outside of the horse makes a continual curve around the rider's inside leg. The rider only needs to see a glimpse of the horse's inside eye and nostril to know that the bend is correct.

A common fault is for the horse to bend only through the neck from the withers, so that his body is still straight. In this position the horse can avoid having to step under himself more with his hind legs, so his quarters will swing out as he goes around a corner. If his hocks are not underneath him, he can neither turn correctly nor flex through his topline when asked. The rider must use the outside rein to reduce the degree of bend in the neck, the outside leg to keep the hind-quarters from swinging out, and should reinforce the inside leg by tapping the horse with the schooling whip behind his or her lower leg.

Another fault is for the horse to tilt his head toward the inside. He is allowing the rider's inside hand to draw his nose to the inside but is ignoring the outside hand, so instead of bending through the neck and poll, the horse simply tilts his head to one side. More contact should be taken up with the outside rein to correct this.

BEND AND FLEXION—THE OVERALL PICTURE

1 The horse is ridden forward at the trot; the rider opens her inside hand and closes her inside leg on the girth to ask the horse to bend around her leg. The outside hand stays soft and allows the horse to move freely forward, unless it has to be used to prevent him bending too much through the neck.

2 Here the horse has responded by curving his whole body around the rider's inside leg; see how the neck looks more relaxed and softer than in the first picture. This is because the horse is working willingly, without resistance.

3 Now that the rider has obtained the correct amount of bend, she closes both legs against the horse's sides to encourage him to be more active and step further under himself with his hind legs. The horse is now flexing through his topline, i.e. his quarters are lowered and his back and neck are round and soft, which in turn raises and lightens his forehand.

4 The result is a picture of power with softness, and roundness with activity. See how the horse is bent around the rider's legs; he is also using his hind-quarters actively, which allows his forehand to be light and elevated. The increased power shows in the way the horse is stretching his front legs forward, and matching this up behind by stepping under himself further with the hind-legs. His neck is carried higher and is more arched than in the first picture but he remains soft and light in the rider's hand. This is the start of self-carriage.

about an inch will be sufficient. Much further down the line in the horse's training, it will also only be necessary to take up a feel on the inside rein and to close the legs against the horse's sides to achieve bend and flexion.

Once the bend and flexion are established at the trot, you can strive for the same result at both the walk and the canter. The vital thing to remember with this training method is always to reward the horse by softening the inside hand the instant that he offers you even the tiniest degree of flexion and relaxation. To begin with it will be a case of working quite hard to ask the horse to bend and then to flex, followed by the reward of softening the inside hand as soon as he does so. He may only offer you the bend and flexion for a few strides before you have to repeat the process and ask again, but as he begins to understand what is wanted and his topline muscles up as a result of the work, he will offer it to you for longer periods.

Gradually you will be doing less asking and more rewarding; you will find yourself riding for longer with both hands soft so that the horse is working on a light contact. But you will need to be persistent and consistent in your training.

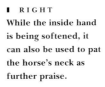

■ RIGHT
As soon as the horse
responds to the
rider's aids by
bending through his
body and then flexing
through his topline,
the rider must soften
the inside hand and
praise the horse
verbally as a reward.
This is the only way
that the horse can
know that he has
responded to the aids
in the right way.

■ RIGHT
While the inside hand
is being softened, it
can also be used to pat
the horse's neck as
further praise.

This horse has offered the rider the required degree of bend and flexion—note the arch of his neck and how his forehand appears lighter and higher than his hindquarters. You can see how he is really flexing his hock as he goes to step forward with his hind leg and, most importantly, note how the rider has softened the inside rein so that the horse is holding this outline himself.

CORRECT USE OF THE INSIDE HAND

It is vital to ask the horse to bend his whole body around your inside leg by opening the inside hand and using the inside leg to keep the horse out on the circle. By using your hand and leg in this way, when the horse does respond he will produce a continuous bend through his body, neck and head. You may have to open your inside hand very wide, you may have to back up the inside-leg aid with a tap from the schooling whip, and your outside hand may have to take up more of a contact to keep the horse from bending his neck too far to the inside, but, when the horse drops his resistance, relaxes and responds to these aids, he will be working correctly.

If the horse is slow to respond and refuses to offer the requested bend, it is very tempting to cheat! If you cross your inside hand over the horse's withers instead of opening the hand out and backing it up with the inside leg, the horse will instantly bend, but this bend will only be from the withers. It will not be right through the body. The crossing over of the rider's hand cuts off the horse's forward impulsion and cuts off the bend at the withers. So while you will be able to see the required glimpse of the inside eye and nostril, it will not be backed up by the correct use or position of the horse's hindquarters.

Crossing the inside hand over in this way is something that many riders, even at high levels

of competition, are tempted to do. Some do not realize that it is a false measure and are satisfied with the false bend that the horse offers them, but their future is limited and their potential will not be fully realized. The temptation to cross the hand over is simply a sign that the horse is not respecting the rider's inside leg and/or the outside hand. So instead of giving in to the temptation, use it as a reminder to yourself to use your inside leg and outside hand correctly,

even if this means not continuing with the exercise until the horse is prepared to move away from the inside leg (see Free Forward Movement). Always go back and correct the underlying fault if any training exercise is not progressing well. Never think that a short cut such as crossing the hand over or losing your temper will pay long-term dividends. Get the basics right and then you will have something permanent to build on. Be consistent, and be quick to praise your horse.

When asking the horse to bend, you must open your inside hand and use your inside leg.

If you cross your inside hand over, the horse will bend only from the wither.

Working Within Each Gait

Once both horse and rider have begun to understand
the basics of a correct and acceptable way of working
at each gait, the rider can take the horse's
performance a step further.

Having mastered the principles of free forward
movement and obtained a degree of bend and flexion,
you can further influence the horse by seeking to
improve his gaits. Plenty of horses have a pleasant
enough way of going—they are able to maintain a round
outline and a good rhythm at each gait—but this can be
nurtured to produce a horse who puts real power and
flair into his work. The use of half-halts and the introduction
of lateral work help the horse to become more balanced and
bring him nearer to working in self-carriage.

▌ OPPOSITE
The use of lateral work
—asking the horse to
travel sideways as well
as forward—can
greatly improve the
general performance
and gaits of the horse.

▌ LEFT
The ultimate aim in
the training of the
horse is for him to be
able to work in "self-
carriage" with his front
end remaining light
and elevated so that he
is a pleasure to ride.

The Half-halt

The half-halt describes what happens when the rider closes his or her legs and hands momentarily against the horse. This serves to rebalance the horse at whatever gait he is working; the rider's legs push the horse's hind legs underneath him further while the hand blocks any acceleration in pace that the horse might offer. The power that the legs have created is trapped by the rider's hand so that instead of accelerating, the horse lowers his hindquarters and elevates his forehand slightly, becoming better balanced and lighter in the rider's hand. The half-halt can be used to (1) rebalance

HALF-HALT AT TROT

1 This horse is producing an active trot, and is maintaining a good outline; considering that he is young the overall picture is soft and round. The rider is sitting quietly with the leg aid on, but only needs to maintain a light contact with the reins to the horse's mouth.

2 Now the horse is becoming unbalanced. He has probably overpowered himself with the push from his hind legs and is poking his nose forward and starting to lean on the bit in an attempt to balance himself. The soft, round outline is disappearing.

3 To rebalance the horse, the rider uses a half-halt. She closes her legs on the horse's sides and pushes him up into her hand which, just for a second, is blocked against the horse's forward movement. In effect, the horse's body is squashed up together; his outline becomes shorter because his hind legs are pushed further under his body so he is able to carry more weight on them, which in turn lightens and elevates his forehand.

4 The horse is rewarded by the rider relaxing the leg and softening the hand again. The softening, or giving of the rein, has been exaggerated in this picture to show that once the horse is using his hindquarters and hocks more actively he is able to carry himself and remain light in the rider's hand (self-carriage). So although the rein is completely loose, the horse is maintaining his own balance and a correct outline.

HALF-HALT AT CANTER

1 Here you can see how this horse is falling on to his forehand at the canter. The impression in the picture is that the horse's weight is falling forward and that he is leaning on the bit and, therefore, on the rider's hands for support.

2 The rider uses a half-halt to rebalance—she closes her legs against the horse's sides and blocks any forward acceleration with her hands.

3 Now the horse is balanced and light in the rider's hands. In picture one the hindquarters appear higher than the shoulders (on the forehand). Now the shoulders are higher than the hindquarters (the forehand is elevated and lightened).

the horse at any gait, (2) warn the horse that the rider is about to ask him to do something such as change direction and (3) build impulsion within each gait that can be stored to produce collected work, or released to produce extended work.

■ ACHIEVING THE HALF-HALT

Every horse will respond to a combination of hand and leg. You have to find out what combination is needed for your horse to obtain the desired result. Too much hand and the horse will either resist by throwing his head up, or he will simply slow down. Too much leg and the horse will try to accelerate and be pushed onto his forehand, which will unbalance him.

First, practice the half-halt at the walk. At a given point, close your legs against the horse's sides and reduce the degree to which you allow your hands to follow the contact, as if you were about to halt. Just as you sense the horse is about to halt, soften

THE RIDER'S SEAT AS AN AID

The rider's body weight can be used, through the seat, to influence the horse—it can create or block the amount of impulsion that the horse is working with. If you think about using your seat as an aid too soon, there is a risk that you will simply become stiff in your body and will no longer be able to move with the horse. The use of the seat will develop naturally once you have achieved that all-important independent seat. If you think back to the use of the hands and arms, and how these stay soft and relaxed so that they follow the movement of the horse's head and neck, that is how you should think of your own body weight. Just as you can change

the degree to which your hands follow the head and neck movement, when asking the horse to slow down or halt, for example, your body weight can be used either to encourage the horse to use himself more actively, or to slow him down. Letting the seat move freely with the horse encourages active movement; reducing the degree to which the seat moves with the horse slows him down. The use of the body weight or seat should always be subtle and sympathetic. The feel for its correct use will come naturally once an independent seat has been achieved, and once you understand how and why you need to influence the horse.

your hands forward again, keeping your legs on the horse's sides so that he continues at the walk. Once you get the feel of how much leg and hand is needed to produce this effect of almost but not quite halting the horse, you will have achieved a half-halt. Then practice it at the trot and

at the canter. Each time, act as if to bring the horse back to the slower pace and, at the last second, allow him to continue at the original pace. Once you have mastered the half-halt, you can use it more subtly to forewarn the horse that he is about to be asked to do something different.

TOO MUCH HAND

If the rider makes the mistake of using too much hand and not enough leg, the horse will soon let her know by not offering the desired response. Here the rider has tried to rebalance the canter by raising and pulling back with the hands, with no back-up from the leg. The horse responds by simply falling back into the trot.

Developing Lateral Work

The shoulder-in and half-pass are the most useful lateral-work exercises in terms of encouraging the horse to use his hocks more actively and effectively underneath him. The mistake that many people make is to think of them simply as requirements of a dressage test. This is not how they should be viewed—lateral work is used to improve the horse's overall way of going. These exercises teach the horse to respond to different uses of the hand and leg, to be supple through his body, and to place his hocks further underneath him in an effort to carry more of his body weight on the hindquarters rather than on the forehand.

SHOULDER-IN

COMMON FAULT

A common mistake is for the rider to ask for too much angle so that the horse works on four tracks instead of three, i.e. each leg is put down in a separate track. The rider has crossed her inside hand over the horse's withers so that the horse is only bending from in front of the withers, through the neck, instead of through the body and neck. The whole point of the exercise has been lost; the horse is not supple through the body, only through the neck, and the hind legs are not being encouraged to take any extra weight at all. To correct this mistake the rider needs to take up more contact in the outside hand to reduce the bend in the neck, use the outside leg to keep the quarters from swinging around any further, and the inside leg to push the shoulders back toward the track, which will reduce the angle of the horse's body until he is working correctly on three tracks.

■ SHOULDER-IN

The shoulder-in is similar to haunches-in, in that the horse moves on three tracks, but here it is the shoulders that are brought in, not the quarters, as the horse continues to move forward. The footfalls are as follows: the inside track is made by the inside foreleg, the middle track by the outside foreleg and inside hind leg together, and the outside track is made by the outside hind leg.

It is quite difficult in a shoulder-in for the rider to keep the horse moving forward in a straight line. The horse may try to swing his quarters out one way, or may drift sideways instead of holding the position and moving forward in a straight line. If you are working in an arena it helps to do the following: As you bring the

1 It is easiest to practice lateral movement in an arena so that you have a straight edge to work along; here the rider is about to ride a shoulder-in at the trot down the long side of the arena. She has already ridden a 33 foot (10 m) circle at the trot in the corner that she is just coming from. This circle gives the rider an idea of the correct amount of bend that the horse should hold throughout the shoulder-in. To start the shoulder-in she goes to ride another 33 foot (10 m) circle, but, as soon as the horse's front legs have left the track to start the circle, she uses the outside hand to prevent him from continuing on the circle, and the inside leg to keep him moving forward along the side of the arena.

2 As the horse progresses down the long side of the arena in a shoulder-in, you can clearly see how he is working on three tracks (inside fore, outside fore/inside hind, outside hind). This exercise encourages the horse to be supple as he has to maintain a bend through his body and neck; it also introduces the horse to the idea of carrying more weight on the inside hind leg. As the inside hind leg touches the ground, you can see that it is placed directly under the horse's belly and beneath the rider. So at this point the horse is carrying much of his body weight, as well as the weight of the rider, on that inside hind leg.

3 To help keep the horse moving forward in a straight line while in a shoulder-in, the rider should look straight ahead and think of her outside hip as pointing the way forward.

HALF-PASS

1 To ride the half-pass, shown here at a walk, the rider would turn down the long side of the arena and ask the horse for a shoulder-in. Instead of continuing in a shoulder-in, he would then use the outside leg back behind the girth to push the horse's hindquarters across until they are almost directly in line with the shoulders. The outside leg stays in place telling the horse to move sideways, while the inside leg also keeps him moving forward. The outside hand controls the degree of bend through the horse's body and neck while the inside hand remains open, inviting the horse to step forward and sideways.

2 In a half-pass the horse must remain bent around the rider's inside leg so that he is bent in the direction in which he is moving. In this picture, the rider's outside leg can clearly be seen in use behind the girth to push the horse sideways. Half-pass can be ridden at the walk, trot and canter.

3 This picture shows how, in a half-pass, it is the outside hind leg that has to come across and under the horse, thereby having to take the weight of both his own body and the rider's. The exercise also encourages the horse to be supple through his body and, in particular, through his shoulders.

horse's shoulders in off the track, make sure you are looking ahead yourself and think of your outside hip as a pointer; if you imagine keeping your hip moving forward in a straight line, the horse's outside shoulder will move forward on the same line. The correct position for the rider in a shoulder-in is for the hips to stay parallel with the horse's shoulders, but for the shoulders to be held straight as if you are riding forward in a straight line as usual. You should look straight ahead.

■ **HALF-PASS**

In half-pass the horse moves diagonally across the arena, taking good-sized steps forward and sideways, and keeping his body bent in the direction in which he is moving. His shoulders are allowed to be just fractionally ahead of his hindquarters as he makes this movement. His outside hind and foreleg cross over in front of his inside hind and foreleg.

COMMON FAULT

A common mistake is for the horse to try to make life easier for himself by not maintaining the correct bend. See how the horse is now bent to the outside which, in effect, means he is now simply leg yielding. The rider needs to ride the horse forward in a straight line so that he knows right away that his response was not acceptable. Shoulder-in should be re-established, and the rider should use the outside leg to bring the quarters over and to keep the horse stepping sideways. As soon as the horse offers the wrong bend again, he must be ridden forward in a straight line and the process repeated. The rider may need to tap the horse with the schooling whip just behind the inside leg to make sure he is listening to this leg and remains bent around it.

Variations Within Each Gait

The horse is capable of a number of variations in each gait, e.g. at the trot or canter the horse can work at a collected, working, medium or extended gait, and he can work at a collected, medium or free walk. As the horse's responsiveness to his rider increases and his training progresses, he should be able to offer all of these variations smoothly and without resistance. When asking the horse for variations within each gait, think in terms of asking for more power and impulsion rather than more speed.

MEDIUM WALK

The medium walk is the pace the horse naturally offers his rider—the sort of gait that would be produced out on a hack. The horse takes long, relaxed steps and he overtracks, which means his hind feet step further forward than the hoofprints left by the front feet.

▌ RIGHT
The medium gaits require the horse to work with increased impulsion so that he takes longer, rounder steps than he would do at the working gaits. He lengthens his whole frame slightly while still keeping a round outline.

WORKING TROT

The working trot is the gait the horse naturally offers his rider. It is an active gait with the horse maintaining a round outline while working in a forward-thinking rhythm. It is the sort of trot the horse would produce out hacking—relaxed but active. The same is true of the working canter.

COLLECTED TROT

At the collected gaits, which can be either walk, trot or canter, the horse shortens his whole outline by lowering his hindquarters and bringing his hocks further under him, and by elevating his forehand so that his neck is raised and arched. The horse takes shorter, rounder steps, with greater elevation.

MEDIUM TROT

EXTENDED TROT

At the extended gaits the horse stretches his whole frame and takes steps of maximum length with maximum impulsion. As with all the variations in pace, the horse must still remain in balance and in a rhythm. This horse could still afford to lengthen and stretch his neck a little more forward so that the overall picture is of a longer frame.

FREE WALK

LEFT
The free walk is often asked for in a dressage test—the rider offers the horse a long length of rein and the horse stretches his head and neck down and takes long, relaxed steps forward, with his hind feet overtracking his front feet. Because the horse has been taught always to expect a contact between his mouth and the rider's hand, when the rider offers him a long length of rein, he stretches his head and neck down to seek out the contact he is used to feeling. To allow the horse to stretch his head and neck fully, the rider allows her arms and hands to go forward and down so that there is still a straight line from her elbow, through the arm, down the rein to the bit.

EXTENDED CANTER

At the extended canter the horse lengthens his whole frame and fully extends his legs to take the longest possible steps while still remaining in balance. The horse in these pictures needs to lengthen his neck a little more and to take his nose forward a fraction so that he is not behind the vertical.

Achieving Collection and Extension of the Gaits

Producing these variations within each gait involves bringing together the techniques and principles with which you should, by now, be familiar. Whether the horse is working at the collected, medium or extended paces, he has to maintain the same rhythm in his work. In other words, you do not slow the horse down in order to achieve collection, nor should you go faster in order to extend the horse. To achieve collection, the rider uses the half-halt so that the horse's hocks are pushed further underneath him while the hand prevents him from accelerating. The trapping by the rider's hand of the power produced by the use of the leg causes the horse to shorten his frame and put that power into taking shorter, higher steps. Medium or extended work is achieved by first using half-halts to collect the horse and then releasing that power and energy in varying degrees by softening the hand forward, which enables the horse to lengthen his frame and his stride. Whether the resulting gait is medium or extended depends on the degree to which the rider softens with the hand while continuing to ask for more power and drive from the hindquarters. To be able to produce these variations in pace, you have to develop a feel for creating and storing energy for collected work, and for directing that energy forward into either medium or extended work.

COLLECTING AND EXTENDING THE HORSE

1 When practicing collecting and extending the horse, it is easier to work within the confines of an arena. The short side of the arena which provides two corners in close proximity to each other is a good place to ask for collection, while the long side, or even across the diagonal, provides room for extending the gaits. This rider is using half-halts to collect the horse as he progresses through the corner of the arena and begins to turn across the diagonal. A corner is a good place to start to ask for collection, as the horse has to bring his inside hind leg further underneath him in order to negotiate the turn anyway. Note the raised, arched neck and the way the hock is being raised and flexed.

2 As the horse starts to cross the diagonal, the rider continues to collect the energy that was built up as they came through the turn. The horse's outline remains relatively high and short.

4 The outline is now lower and longer as the horse extends his limbs forward to cover as much ground as possible with each stride.

3 Once the horse is completely straight, the rider asks the horse to extend. He continues to ask for impulsion and drive from the hindquarters by keeping his legs actively on the horse's sides, but now he releases that stored power by softening the hands forward so that the horse can lengthen his frame and strides. Note how the horse's hindquarters are still lowered, and how the first surge of released energy has really elevated his front end as the horse begins to extend his steps.

Introducing The Counter Canter

Counter canter is a movement required in many dressage tests, and it demonstrates the horse's suppleness, balance and obedience. Counter canter involves the horse cantering with the left leg leading while being worked on the right rein, and vice versa. The horse must keep his head and neck bent over his leading foreleg, so that he is in fact bent in the opposite direction to that in which he is moving.

Counter canter is introduced by cantering on the left rein across the diagonal to the opposite track. As the horse reaches the other side and turns onto the right

COMMON FAULTS

In this picture, the horse is still cantering with the right leg leading but, instead of maintaining the bend of his head and neck to the right, he has bent to the left, i.e. he is now bent in the direction in which he is traveling. The rider must correct this by opening the right hand and closing the right leg on the girth to ask the horse to maintain the bend to the right.

Another common mistake is for the horse to bend his neck too much to the right. This causes him to lose his balance and his whole body drifts back to the track instead of following the path of the 16½ foot (5 m) loop. When this happens the horse's hind legs are not following in the same tracks as the front legs—the horse is simply falling sideways or falling out through the shoulder. If the rider now took up more contact on the outside (left) rein to straighten out the bend of the head and neck, used the left leg behind the girth to stop the quarters swinging out to the left, and opened the right hand while keeping the right leg on the girth to encourage the horse to bend his neck to the right, the correct counter canter would be restored.

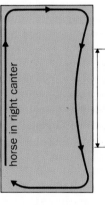

shallow loop where horse is ridden at a counter canter— still on the right lead but traveling toward the left

horse in right canter

rein, he should be asked to maintain the canter with the left leg leading for a few strides, before being brought back to trot.

Once horse and rider are comfortable with this, shallow loops can be ridden at the canter down the long side of the arena;

while the horse is on the track he is cantering as usual, whereas while he is negotiating the shallow loop he is in fact in a counter canter, provided he maintains the original bend of his head and neck over the leading foreleg.

RIDING A 16½ FOOT (5 M) LOOP IN COUNTER CANTER

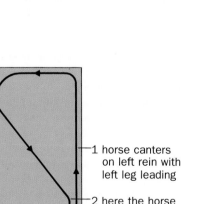

1 horse canters on left rein with left leg leading

2 here the horse is asked to continue in canter left although he is about to turn to the right

3 horse is brought back to trot

1 The horse canters around the arena on the right rein with the right leg leading as usual. Instead of continuing down the long side of the arena, the rider turns the horse off the track and rides a smooth 16½ foot (5 m) loop along the long side. As the horse negotiates the first curve of the loop he must continue to canter on the right lead.

2 With his head and neck slightly bent to the right, he starts to follow the loop around to the left. He is therefore bent away from the direction in which he is moving. The horse's body must remain straight—his hind legs must follow in the same tracks as his forelegs, with only his head and neck showing a bend to the right.

3 As the horse follows the loop around to the left and back toward the track, he must still maintain the canter on the right lead, with his neck bent to the right.

Riding a Flying Change

The flying change is when the horse changes directly from cantering with the left leg leading to cantering with the right leg leading, and vice versa. It is called for in some dressage tests and can be built upon in more advanced dressage so that the horse can literally change from one leg to the other on every stride, almost as if he were skipping! For the average rider, the flying change is most useful when jumping a course that requires changes of direction at the canter. For example, instead of landing over a jump with the left leg leading, then having to come back to a trot before picking up a canter on the right lead in order to turn right to the next fence, the rider can simply land, take

a few strides forward at the canter and then ask for a flying change as he turns toward the next jump.

Before the horse can be asked to perform a flying change, he must be responsive and obedient to the leg, and his canter must be balanced and show a degree of collection. He should willingly perform walk-to-canter transitions, be able to produce 33 foot (10 m) circles at the canter, and work at a counter canter before progressing to a flying change.

Some horses tend to become excitable or nervous when they are introduced to this movement, so be sure to teach it carefully and patiently.

CHANGING THE LEAD

1 This movement is best taught by asking the horse to change from counter canter back to normal canter. This horse has been down the long side of the arena on the right rein, and has then cantered a half-circle so that he is now cantering across the diagonal with the right leg leading.

2 As the horse nears the track and the ensuing left-hand corner, the rider must indicate to the horse that he must change from right canter lead to left canter lead. The rider momentarily blocks the horse's forward momentum by closing and setting the left hand, while at the same time changing her leg aids from asking for the right lead to asking for a left lead, i.e. the rider's left leg is now applied at the girth, and the right leg used behind the girth to tell the horse to put his right hind leg down on the ground first. Remember that if the right hind starts the stride off, it is the left foreleg that appears to be leading. In this picture, you can see how the rider's left hand has blocked the horse's forward momentum so his forehand is elevated as a result.

3 In this picture, the horse is in the period of suspension that follows each canter stride, and it is only at this point that he is able to perform the flying change. So the blocking of the forward movement makes the period of suspension just a fraction longer, giving the horse time to rearrange his legs so that he lands on the opposite lead, i.e. he changes from the right lead to the left lead. This young horse has overreacted to the rider changing the position of her leg aids (bringing her left leg back to the girth and using her right leg behind the girth). He has flicked up his back end higher than his forehand which unbalances him. As he strengthens up and becomes more relaxed about the exercise he will make a smoother flying change.

4 As a result of the rider changing her aids from asking for canter right to asking for canter left, the horse has landed on the left lead as required and can now continue to canter around the arena on the left rein.

Riding a Dressage Test

Once you have practiced everything that has been discussed in this book so far, it will be good for both you and your horse to go out and put it all to the test by riding in some dressage competitions. These can be anything from small, local affairs to affiliated competitions.

Always make the effort to learn your dressage test by heart, but do not practice it continually on your own horse because he will learn it himself and will start to anticipate the next movement instead of waiting for your instructions. At some competitions you are allowed to have your test read aloud, but if you are having to concentrate on instructions being read aloud, you cannot possibly concentrate 100 percent on getting the best out of your horse.

Your horse should be well groomed and have his mane braided for a dressage competition. You should wear a pair of white or beige jodhpurs or breeches, long or short riding boots, a riding jacket and a shirt and tie or stock.

All dressage tests begin with the horse and rider coming down the center line of the arena, and all but preliminary tests require the rider to halt the horse and salute the judge. This first movement is the first impression that the judge will have of you—the only thing the judge can see from that angle is how straight your horse is as he comes down the center line. So concentrate on riding the horse forward in a good active pace, as it is easier to ride a straight line if the horse is moving forward with impulsion. (Think of how a bicycle wobbles if you pedal too slowly—the same happens to a horse if he lacks impulsion.) A good straight halt will earn you good marks and put the judge in a good frame of mind for the rest of your test. Be ready with both hands and legs to correct any attempt the horse may make to drift one way or the other as you squeeze him forward from your legs into a blocking hand and into the halt.

▮ RIGHT
Notice how this young rider is looking across the arena to the marker where she has to make her next move. Keeping your head up and looking ahead to where you have to go next helps improve the accuracy and timing of the different movements you have to perform.

Once the horse halts, keep a feel against his sides with your legs and down the rein with your hand. This will keep him on the aids and attentive to your next instruction. A female rider bows to the judge by putting both reins in her left hand, and bowing her head as she drops her right hand to her side. Male riders are usually required to remove their hats unless fitted with a safety harness. The reins are put in the left hand and the hat is removed with the right hand and lowered to one side as the rider bows his head. Do practice this at home, otherwise your horse is likely to shy away as you lower your hat to his side. When you are

Every single dressage test includes at least one— and usually two—halts and salutes. A nice straight halt and a confident, unhurried salute create a good impression, and are aspects of the test that can be practiced at home.

ready to ride on again, concentrate first and foremost on straightness and maintaining a constant rhythm.

The various movements in a dressage test have to be carried out at the markers which are set around the arena. The correct point at which to carry out the next movement is as your shoulder is level with the marker. Always look up and think ahead to the next marker. Insist that the horse stays out on the track and uses the whole arena; do not be tempted to cut corners. If you ride the horse correctly around each corner, you will automatically be rebalancing him and asking him to use his hind legs more actively. Remember to balance the horse during and before each new movement, with a half-halt if necessary. All tests end with another turn down the center line and a halt and salute for the judge. No matter how well or badly the test may have gone, always perform this movement with good grace and manners. Remember that each movement in the test is marked separately, so that if you make a mistake in one movement all is not lost. If you keep your cool and improve upon the mistake in the remaining movements, you will pick up marks again. Never give up—there are always more good marks to be earned. On top of all that, do make a conscious effort to smile. It will immediately fill you, and the judge, with confidence and, more importantly, it will help you to relax and to stay that way.

Preparing for Take-off

One of the best things about riding is to experience the exhilaration of riding a horse over fences. A lot of new riders are put off by jumping due to a lack of confidence but, if you have developed any sort of feel for riding, jumping should simply be a natural and enjoyable progression.

All too often, when faced with a fence to jump, horse and rider seem to forget the basics they have been practicing up until then. Balance and rhythm are abandoned as they careen toward the obstacle! The secret of safe, enjoyable and successful jumping is to carry into the jumping arena the principles learned and mastered while riding on the flat.

▮ OPPOSITE
A relaxed and confident horse and rider will be able to enjoy their jumping.

▮ LEFT
Successful jumping comes down to horse and rider learning to remain relaxed, in balance and in a rhythm.

Rhythm and Balance

The two most important things for the would-be show jumper to keep in mind are rhythm and balance. If you can concentrate on keeping the horse balanced and in an even rhythm all the way to the fence, you have very little else to worry about.

You have already discovered how to encourage the horse to work in an even rhythm and to be responsive to your leg. Just because a jump appears in your path does not mean that anything changes—the horse must still be obedient enough to stay in the rhythm that you have dictated and, provided that you learn how to stay in balance with the horse throughout, clearing the fence comfortably and confidently will come naturally to both of you.

Horse and rider can practice working in a balanced rhythm by simply trotting and cantering over poles on the ground. This kind of work can be mixed in with your usual flatwork training so that the horse learns to remain calm and to apply

WORKING OVER TROT POLES

1 The horse is ridden in an active working trot through the corner and down to a line of trot poles set approximately 4 feet (1.25 m) apart, which gives the horse room to put his feet down between each pole as he takes each stride.

2 The horse must stay balanced and in the same rhythm as he approaches the line of trot poles.

3 The rider softens his hands forward so that the horse is able to stretch his head and neck forward as he negotiates the poles.

4 The horse should maintain exactly the same rhythm throughout the whole exercise—do not allow him to slow down at the end of the poles. Ride him through the next corner correctly, insisting he bends around your inside leg and maintains his balance and rhythm, and repeat the exercise.

WORKING THROUGH CANTER POLES

1 Exactly the same exercise should be practiced at a canter, except now the poles are spaced approximately 10 feet (3 m) apart to give the horse room to canter over them.

2 The rider must keep the horse balanced and in the same rhythm through the corner and all the way up to the poles.

3 As the horse negotiates the poles, the rider simply softens the hands forward so that the horse's head and neck are not restricted.

4 As when working over trot poles, the horse should maintain the same rhythm throughout the whole exercise.

5 As the horse completes the poles and canters on to the next corner, exactly the same rhythm and balance must be maintained throughout.

the same rules learned on the flat to his jumping work. Far too many horses are allowed, and often encouraged, to become overexcited and go too fast when they are asked to jump. The horse should be taught to use power to clear fences, not speed.

USING POLES AND LINES OF FENCES

Trot and canter poles are often used to help introduce horse and rider to jumping. They should be spaced out in such a way that the horse can easily negotiate them, without having to stretch himself or shorten himself up. Trot poles are usually set about 4 feet (1.25 m) apart and canter poles 10 feet (3 m) apart. But if these distances do not suit your horse, then, at this stage in his training, alter them to suit him. Adding lines of fences to the poles forms what is called a jumping grid. Gridwork is used to introduce the horse to the idea of jumping. Later in his training, it is used to increase his athleticism and to improve the way in which he jumps. It trains him to jump more carefully so he is less likely to injure himself or to knock fences down.

■ INSIST ON CONSISTENCY

It is only with practice and patience that you will teach the horse to carry out this exercise. Most horses thoroughly enjoy the idea of jumping but it is important to teach the horse to contain his enthusiasm so that he still remains obedient, balanced and in a rhythm.

A young horse who is being introduced to this work for the first time should have no reason to rush or get excited, provided he has been taught the basic principles throughout his flatwork training.

An older horse who already knows about jumping may get excited if he has been allowed to do so by previous riders, but practice and perseverance will teach him to keep an even rhythm.

If the horse really is inclined to rush, you should keep circling around the outside of the poles until he settles into a steady rhythm. If he still rushes as soon as he is allowed to go to the poles, simply circle him away from them again and keep repeating this exercise until he maintains the same rhythm. Alternatively, you can bring the horse back to a walk and insist

that he walks over the poles until he is prepared to keep the same rhythm at both a trot and a canter.

The opposite problem may occur with an inexperienced or nervous horse who may want to slow down on the approach to the poles until he is confident about what they are. The first few times the horse is introduced to the exercise, he should be allowed to slow down to give him time to take everything in. After that, insist that he maintains the same rhythm. It may be worth choosing a slow rhythm at the trot so that the horse does not feel he is being hassled, but do insist that the horse sticks to this rhythm throughout. Once he is confident, the pace can be picked up a little and a slightly faster rhythm maintained throughout. The horse should never be rushed through these exercises—his pace should be active and yet balanced.

In jumping it is the power of the horse that is critical, not his speed. As a rider you are trying to create and store power and energy on the way to the fence so that all that power can be used by the horse to clear the fence.

Jumping Fences

It is your job to bring the horse to the fence in a balanced rhythm, to remain in balance with him over it, and to land in balance so that you can continue to the next fence.

Most riders attempt to do far too much on the approach and over a fence, which only unbalances and distracts the horse. When jumping, keep a light seat on the approach to the fence. About 22–33 yards (20–30 m) away, while still retaining exactly the same rhythm, lower your seat deeper into the saddle and actively close your legs against the horse's sides. Keep your shoulders slightly forward. Having closed the legs more against the horse's sides, you may have to take a slightly stronger contact in the hand to prevent the horse accelerating. As the horse takes off over the fence, remain in the same position but close your knees and lower legs tighter against the horse's sides to help you stay over the saddle, and stretch your hands and arms forward to allow the horse to stretch his head and neck forward over the fence.

BASIC TECHNIQUE

1 Here the rider is in the forward seat. Note how her seat bones are raised just off the saddle so there is less weight directly on the horse's back. This encourages the horse to remain soft through his back and to move along actively beneath her. The rider keeps her shoulders slightly more forward than they would be when cantering on the flat, but it is this position that allows the weight to be taken off the saddle while still allowing the rider to keep her balance. The lower leg is closed on the horse's sides, and the rider's weight is now taken by the stirrup iron. The horse is producing a light, active canter with his forehand nicely elevated.

2 As the rider approaches a fence, she lowers her seat into the saddle but keeps her shoulders in the forward position. The lower legs are closed more firmly against the horse's sides so that his hocks are pushed under him, but the rider's hands prevent him from accelerating. The aim is to collect the horse so that he has plenty of energy to power himself over the fence.

3 Just before the horse takes off, the rider softens her hands forward so he can lower his head and neck to produce a supple, clean jump. The rider's seat is still deep in the saddle, her lower legs are closed against the horse's sides, her heels are pushed down and, at this point, she also allows her knees to close against the saddle to keep her body balanced as the horse jumps.

4 As the horse takes off, all the rider does is to allow her hands and arms to stretch forward to follow the movement of the horse's head and neck. The rider remains perfectly still and balanced over the horse and, in this way, leaves the horse free to jump athletically and comfortably over the fence.

5 By adopting this technique over a fence, the rider is able to remain in balance with the horse; this means that, as they land, the two of them are still balanced and ready to face whatever comes next. If another fence were to follow immediately, they would both be in the correct position to tackle it.

6 Horse and rider look equally balanced on the approach and on landing over the fence. If horse and rider can maintain this same rhythm and balance around a whole course, they have every chance of producing a clear round, be it cross-country or in a show-jumping arena.

COMMON JUMPING FAULTS

GETTING IN FRONT OF THE MOVEMENT

These two pictures show one of the most common faults of which any number of riders, of all levels, are guilty. Faced with a fence, many riders seem to be overwhelmed by an irresistible desire to anticipate when the horse is going to take off and to "jump" with him! Instead of sitting quietly and maintaining their position, the rhythm and the balance, they fire their seat out of the saddle, hurl their upper body up the horse's neck and generally do about ten times more than they need to. The effect on the horse is both unbalancing and distracting. This can result in the horse hitting the fence with his front legs because the rider has loaded too much weight onto his forehand or, worse still, the horse may be tempted to put his feet back down again in front of the fence. The horse is then unable to jump at all.

You can see how easy it would be for the horse to put his front feet back down on the ground and, because the rider has come right out of the saddle and thrown all her weight forward, she would have very little chance of staying on. In the second picture, the rider is still in a relatively weak position; her weight is balanced on her knees instead of being pushed down into the stirrups and her heels, with the result that her lower leg has slid backward.

The rider is going to be out of balance with the horse as he lands and will not be in a very strong position to regain the balance and rhythm that they started with. If the horse stumbles as he lands, because the rider is not supporting her weight in her lower legs and heels, she will probably be thrown forward. Again she could fall off or, at the very least, she would not be able to help the horse recover as well as if she had maintained her balance.

IN TIMES OF TROUBLE!

While the horse must not be allowed to rush toward his fences, it is just as important that he is not allowed to slow down to the point that he runs out of impulsion and stops. If you sense that the horse is reluctant to keep progressing forward to a fence, you must adopt a more aggressive style of riding to encourage the horse to keep going. In this situation it is more important than ever that you keep your seat in the saddle the whole time. If you are tempted to anticipate the take-off and get in front of the movement, the reluctant jumper is presented with the ideal opportunity to stop dead!

In these pictures, the rider has pressed both legs very firmly against the horse's sides. If necessary, both heels should be used to kick the horse forward. The seat remains deep in the saddle and the rider arches her back slightly to allow her seat as well as the legs to drive the horse forward. The rider must not throw her hands forward at the horse as often happens—she is trying to ride the horse up into the contact so that while contact is maintained it does not actually restrict the horse's forward movement.

CHASING THE HORSE INTO THE FENCE

Another fault commonly adopted by any number of riders is to chase or rush the horse into the fence. The rider is meant to maintain the same rhythm and balance as he or she rides from fence to fence, but many people feel unable to wait for the fence. As soon as they are a few strides from it, they drive the horse forward, immediately unbalancing the horse and pushing him onto his forehand.

This approach usually results in the horse taking off much too far away from the fence and really having to stretch to clear it. In these pictures, even the horse looks angry at this unwanted interference from his rider. If the horse is made to jump like this, he is likely to knock fences down. He is being made to use speed to clear the fences rather than power and the athleticism of his body. If he is ridden like this cross-country, particularly to a very upright fence, he will find it difficult to get his front legs up in the air quickly enough and risks hitting the fence; if it is a solid cross-country fence, this would be enough to unseat his rider or, at worst, would cause the horse to fall as well.

▌ RIGHT, TOP TO BOTTOM
In the first picture the horse's canter stride is already plenty long enough, but in the second you can see that the rider has continued to drive the horse, stretching out his frame and stride even further. Compare the look of this canter to the approach made in the first pictures in this chapter. In those pictures the canter looked light and active, and the forehand was elevated. In these pictures you can see how flat and stretched out the canter is and how all the weight is falling on the forehand.

Maintaining Balance and Position

The easiest way to learn to maintain the correct position while jumping is to learn how to stay in balance with the horse—and the easiest way to learn that is to remember always to maintain the same rhythm when jumping. Having already practiced maintaining the rhythm, balance and your position over trot and canter poles, this exercise can be extended to include your first jump about 14 feet (4.25 m) away from the last pole. You should simply concentrate on keeping the horse trotting in a balanced, even rhythm through the trot poles and on to the fence. The horse will fit in three trot strides after the last pole and will be perfectly placed to jump the fence.

If you find that you cannot resist the temptation to "jump" as the horse jumps, or if you feel yourself tensing up as the fence gets nearer, try the same exercise without looking at the fence at all. It's quite simple, and the horse will cope perfectly well without your eyes looking out for him, provided you do still maintain the same even rhythm.

POSITION AT TAKE-OFF

1 Think about maintaining the correct position, keeping your seat in the saddle as you approach the trot poles but allowing the shoulders to be carried forward a little.

2 Close the knees and lower legs against the horse's sides just in front of the fence, and soften the hands forward.

3 As the horse takes off, allow the hands and arms to go forward in order to follow the movement of his head and neck.

LOOKING AWAY FROM THE FENCE

1 Once you have lined the horse up in front of the row of ground poles, look to one side so that you cannot anticipate the fence itself. As you feel him take off, just allow your hands and arms to follow forward.

2 Keep the rhythm throughout, sit deep in the saddle, allow your shoulders to move forward a little, and close your legs and knees against the horse as he trots over the last pole (you will feel him do this).

3 As you feel him take off, just allow your hands and arms to follow forward.

Trotting and Cantering to a Fence

Having experienced your first jump, it is now just a matter of getting the feel of cantering to a fence while maintaining the same principles as described already. This is most easily done by extending your existing line of trot poles and small fence to include a second fence, which the horse will jump from a canter. This should be placed approximately 18–20 feet (5.5–6 m) from the first fence; this allows the horse to trot to the first fence, land and take one canter stride before taking off over the second fence.

Many riders at this stage feel tempted to interfere in an effort to help the horse, but the grid is set up to allow the horse to find his own way through. The biggest help you can be to your horse is to maintain the even rhythm and balance.

JUMPING TWO FENCES

1 The horse trots over the ground poles and up to the first fence, just as he did in the previous exercise. The rider retains the same position and rhythm throughout.

2 Having allowed forward movement with the hands and arms over the fence, the rider now makes sure his legs are closed against the horse's sides to encourage him to canter forward in the same rhythm. As the horse lands, the rider's hands return to the normal position.

3 Here the horse takes the one canter stride that brings him up to the second fence; the rider continues to concentrate solely on keeping his position and the same rhythm.

4 The horse clears the fence, but the rider has anticipated the jump and has allowed his lower leg to slide back a fraction and brought his seat out of the saddle. The next time he comes to this fence it would be good practice for the rider to look away so that he cannot anticipate what is going to happen!

MAINTAINING BALANCE

■ RIGHT
This is another horse and rider completing the same exercise. In the second picture you can see why it is so important for the rider always to soften the hands forward on the last stride in front of the fence—see how this horse has really stretched his head and neck forward toward the jump before taking off. This is to be encouraged as it helps the horse to produce a powerful, athletic and round jump.

In the last two pictures you can see how this rider has kept her seat in the saddle, which has allowed her to land in balance with the horse and ready for the next challenge.

The Circle Exercise— Balance, Rhythm and Trust

Trotting poles and grids make it easier for the horse and rider to keep their rhythm and balance—the real test is whether or not they can maintain the same principles when cantering to a single fence. One of the best ways to ensure this is to practice this very simple exercise. Build a small jump somewhere that allows you room to canter in a large circle to it, say on a 33 yard (30 m) circle. Pick up a canter and just practice maintaining a good, even rhythm as you canter around the circle, bypassing the jump to begin with. When you feel settled enough to jump, make sure that you stick to the same rhythm— don't speed up or slow down just because you are thinking of jumping. As you come onto the last quarter of the circle before the jump, sit deep into the saddle, close your legs against the horse's sides and contain him in the same rhythm with your hand, and then look away from the jump. Maintain the rhythm and allow the horse to look after the jump. As you feel him take off, allow your hands and arms to go forward to follow the contact. Have a friend standing in the middle of the circle to remind you not to look at the jump.

Practice jumping at different speeds on the circle—the faster you go the further away from the fence the horse will take off, the slower you go the closer he will

FINDING THE RIGHT RHYTHM

1 On the last quarter of the circle the rider sits deep in the saddle, closes the legs and hands to collect the horse while still maintaining the same rhythm, and then looks away from the fence.

2 The rider continues to look away from the fence, concentrating only on keeping the same rhythm and balance. Note how the horse, left undistracted by his rider, is totally focused on the fence.

3 The horse has the fence measured up and is about to take off.

4 The rider allows his arms and hands to follow forward while the horse clears the fence.

get before take-off, provided you maintain the same rhythm. This exercise will help you find the rhythm from which your horse jumps best. Once you get the idea of

trusting the horse and waiting for the fence, you can go back to looking where you are going, but return to this exercise whenever you get the urge to interfere.

LEARNING TO TRUST THE HORSE

1 Nine times out of ten, if the rider looks at the fence at this stage he or she feels obliged to interfere by either checking or chasing the horse. This simply distracts and unbalances the horse.

2 The rider is trusting her horse to do the job; note how the horse is fully concentrating on the task in hand and is about to clear the fence.

3 A horse can jump as big a fence as you wish in this way. Provided you keep the rhythm and balance, he will do the jumping.

Improving Horse and Rider's Jumping Ability

In the same way that, when learning to ride, the rider is more concerned about his or her own position and balance than about how well the horse is going, when learning to jump you must first master the art of keeping a balanced, rhythmic approach before worrying about trying to improve the horse's actual jumping ability.

Gridwork can be used to help in both instances—jumping the grids allows you to concentrate on improving your own balance and position, and can also be used to improve the horse's agility and ability over a fence.

Some horses are naturally more careful jumpers than others; some horses tend to throw long, flat jumps, while others may have a tendency to jump very high but with little scope to clear spreads. In either case, gridwork exercises can enhance the horse's performance.

■ GRIDWORK AND JUMPING DISTANCES

When gridwork is first introduced, the distances should be set to suit the horse. Once the horse is confident with the exercise, the distances can be altered—either lengthened or shortened—to improve the horse's technique. So with a horse who tends to throw a long, flat jump

the distance should gradually be reduced so that he has to collect himself up and use himself more athletically, while a horse who is very short strided should be encouraged to stretch out a little by using longer distances.

You may well wonder why it is necessary to alter what the horse does naturally. The reason is that, in the competition world, show jumps and cross-country fences are built to set measurements and distances. The course designer has to build fences that can be jumped safely by different sizes and types of horse, so he has to find an average distance to use and build his fences around that. For example, an average measurement used in course designing is based on the assumption that the horse will cover 12 feet (3.65 m) with every canter stride. Extra room has to be allowed for the distance away from the fence that the horse will take off, and further distance must be allowed on the other side of the fence for the horse to land. A rule of thumb is 12 feet (3.65 m) for one canter stride, plus 6 feet (1.9 m) for take-off and 6 feet (1.9 m) for landing. If the course designer wants the horse to fit in one stride between two fences, he will place the fences 24 feet (7.35 m) apart. To fit in two

strides the fences would be placed 36 feet (11 m) apart—two canter strides equal two times 12 feet (3.65 m), plus 6 feet (1.9 m) for landing over the first fence and 6 feet (1.9 m) for taking off at the second fence.

If your particular horse is to fit in the same number of strides as the course designer intended, he needs to cover the ground that the designer has based his figures on. Higher up the competition ladder, the course designer may include an extra-long or an extra-short distance to test riders' ability to adjust the distance their horses cover. Some riders may choose to collect their horses and fit in three strides; others may push for two.

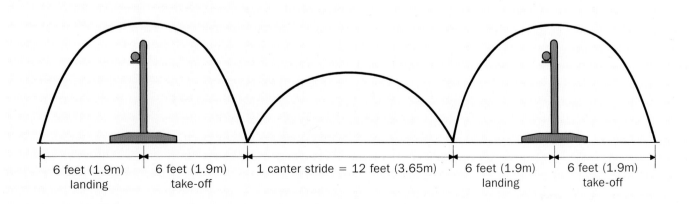

6 feet (1.9m) landing   6 feet (1.9m) take-off   1 canter stride = 12 feet (3.65m)   6 feet (1.9m) landing   6 feet (1.9m) take-off

BOUNCE GRID

Gridwork Exercises

Jumping grids can be adapted and altered as much as your imagination allows, the only confines being that you use distances that are acceptable and safe for the horse. But you should always have some aim in mind when designing a grid, otherwise you may dishearten the horse or simply end up undoing with one exercise any improvement you had created with another. So don't just go blindly on—feel the difference the grid is making to the horse and change it accordingly. And if the horse throws a truly fantastic jump early on in the session, it sometimes pays to stop at that point rather than risk undoing the good work you have just created.

It is very helpful to have someone knowledgeable watching you from the ground. Sometimes they can see, better than you can feel, exactly what the horse is doing as he progresses through the grid.

■ RIGHT, TOP TO BOTTOM

The fences in this bounce grid have been set at 10 foot (3 m) intervals. The horse is introduced to the exercise by first using one bounce, i.e. two fences. This horse has approached this exercise at a canter, but if the horse has never seen a bounce before you may prefer to shorten the distance and approach at a trot, so that the horse has more time to work out what to do. When he is confident about tackling this, an additional fence can be added to make it a double bounce.

As you can see, a bounce distance means that the horse lands over one fence and immediately takes off over the next without taking a stride in between. It is a good exercise for improving the horse's physical and mental agility. He has to think quickly in order to organize himself correctly. Another advantage of this exercise is that it helps to make the horse confident enough to tackle lines of fences in competition. If he is used to seeing—and picking his way through—lines of poles and fences in front of him at home, he will feel more confident when faced with a complicated combination of fences in a competition.

Practicing with a bounce grid also improves the rider's balance and ability to follow the movement of the horse.

■ THE COMBINATION GRID

This grid aims to improve the way the horse jumps. It starts with the horse trotting to a small cross-rail, set one canter stride away from a spread fence or oxer. This is set at a distance that suits the horse's natural stride. The distance to the oxer is increased gradually, by up to 2 feet (0.5 m), and the fence is altered to become an ascending oxer, i.e. the back pole is raised higher than the front pole. Once the horse is jumping well through this, it is altered again. This time the distance is shortened gradually, up to 2 feet (0.5 m) less than the original distance, and the fence is adjusted to make it a descending oxer, i.e. the back pole is now lower than the front pole. An ascending oxer encourages the horse to be neat and careful with his hind legs over a fence; the descending oxer teaches him to be neat and careful in front while still being able to stretch forward to clear the spread.

SQUARE PARALLEL

The horse is brought to the grid at a trot. The two trot poles are set 4 feet (1.25 m) apart and are, in turn, 8 feet (2.5 m) away from the small cross-rail (the first jump). These serve to bring the horse into the grid balanced and straight. He takes one canter stride before jumping the oxer.

ASCENDING OXER

The approach through the trot poles and the cross-rail remains exactly the same. But the one-stride distance to the oxer (now ascending) has been increased. To encourage the horse to take a longer stride to help him cover the distance to the oxer, the rider simply "clucks" to the horse and closes her legs against his sides to tell him to stretch forward. The horse responds by taking a longer stride than he did in the first grid sequence. In the last picture you can see how the horse is really using his hindquarters, and has snapped up his hind legs to make sure he clears the back pole.

RIDER'S WEIGHT

Here the horse tackles the same grid and, from this angle, the interesting point to note is shown in the last picture. The rider has, to some degree, thrown her body weight forward and up the horse's neck, rather than keeping her seat in the saddle. Note how she has thrown her weight to the left side and look at the effect this has had on the horse's left foreleg. Because the rider's weight is over the horse's left shoulder, it is harder for the horse to bring his left foreleg up as quickly and cleanly as the right foreleg. It would therefore be very easy for the horse to knock this fence down with the trailing foreleg. To avoid this, the rider's weight must stay balanced centrally in the saddle.

DESCENDING PARALLEL

The approach to this exercise is the same as before, but the one-stride distance is shortened to less than it was in the very first grid, and the oxer is now descending. The horse has to land over the cross-rail, collect and shorten his stride and then be quick and neat with his front legs to clear the front pole of the descending oxer. The previous exercise will have reminded him to be really tidy with his hind legs, so this exercise should produce his most impressive jump. Note in the last picture how very neat and correct this horse has been with his front legs—exactly the aim of the exercise.

■ THE DOUBLE OF OXER

This exercise is aimed at helping the horse who tends to jump high, but not necessarily very wide. Two square oxers are built one stride apart, with the distance set to suit the horse's stride, i.e. approximately 24 feet (7.35 m). The horse is cantered through this once or twice and then the distance between the two fences is shortened by simply making the two oxers wider—the back rail of the first fence and the front rail of the second fence are moved 1 foot (30 cm) or so toward each other. This encourages the horse to jump wider than usual over the first oxer; he must land and shorten himself up to fit in one stride before having to make another scopey jump over the second oxer.

INTRODUCING TWO OXERS

The exercise is introduced by cantering the horse to two square oxers, set one stride apart at a distance to suit the horse's stride. Note how soft and sympathetic the rider's hands are—allowing the horse to use himself without restriction.

ADJUSTING TO THE JUMP

Now the oxers have been made wider so that the distance between the two fences has become shorter—the two green standards have been moved in toward each other. In the first picture you will see that the rider has been caught by the huge jump that the horse has made—she really needed to allow her arms and hands to go forward more so as not to restrict the horse.

Having made such a big jump, the horse now has to shorten and balance himself quickly in order to clear the second fence. Note the improved position of the rider's hands.

Riding Related Distances

Over a whole course of fences, two of them will often be placed at what is called a related distance. This means the designer intends the competitors to ride a set number of strides between the two. Combination fences refer to jumps that are one or two strides apart, whereas related distances refer to jumps that are anything from three to, say, six strides apart.

Gridwork exercises at home will have shown you whether or not your horse has a naturally short or long stride, and you should use this knowledge to your advantage when faced with combinations or related distances. If the horse has a naturally short stride, you will need to encourage the horse to open up his stride; you may need to ride with more pace than, say, the rider whose horse has a long, ground-covering stride. Whatever the case, when riding combinations or related distances the aim is to maintain an even stride length between the fences, not to land over the fence and then have either to check the horse or to chase him forward toward the next element.

Watch a number of horses tackling a related distance and you will start to see how it rides best. Some riders may approach in a short, collected canter and fit in an extra stride, while others may let their horses jump, canter and jump out of a longer stride and fit in one stride less. If you practice the options at home you will learn which approach suits your horse, but whatever the number of strides you opt for they should be of an even length. So, to fit in the maximum number of strides, approach in a more collected canter, with a little less pace. To fit in the minimum number of strides, approach on a longer stride with more pace.

TAKING FIVE EVEN STRIDES

These two fences are set 60 feet (18.25 m) apart, and in this first exercise the rider intends to fit five strides between them. She approaches in a reasonably collected canter which encourages the horse to jump in quietly over the first fence. As she lands, the rider successfully maintains the same rhythm that she had on the approach, and this allows the horse to fit in the five even strides as required between the two fences.

TAKING FOUR EVEN STRIDES

Now the rider needs to open the horse up a little to fit in only four strides, so she approaches with a longer stride and in a stronger rhythm than previously. The horse jumps in more aggressively, which helps him to make up some of the distance required. The rider again thinks about keeping the horse going forward and in the rhythm that she had on the approach. This allows the horse to take four strides of even length between the fences.

TOO MUCH PACE

This rider, attempting the same exercise, shows how not to do it! Her plan was to fit in five strides, but instead of coming at a quieter rhythm than normal she has ridden the horse strongly into the fence so that he throws an extravagant jump. She is now going to struggle to fit in the five strides and resorts to checking the horse back, i.e. using her hands to make the horse continually shorten his stride. In the third picture, you can see how the horse is objecting to this treatment by throwing his head up and resisting the rider's hand. The horse has kindly cleared the fence for her but could easily have knocked it down, or even refused. Once the horse throws his head up, his eye is taken off the fence and he is unable to judge what he needs to do. It also makes him tense and hollow so that he cannot be as athletic. As you can see from these pictures, instead of taking five strides of even length, this horse's strides were being gradually shortened. Having made the initial mistake of coming in with too much pace, the rider may have been wiser to allow the horse to continue in the stronger rhythm and to fit in only four strides. Practicing these exercises at home will give you a feel for how to get the distance right on the day and for how best to react when things go wrong.

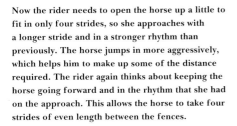

Riding a Course of Fences

Successfully riding a course of show jumps is simply an extension of the principles practiced at home—except that you need to concentrate for longer. Instead of having to keep the rhythm and balance over just one or two fences, you have to maintain them around the twists and turns of a course. But the principle is exactly the same—choose your rhythm and stick to it. Keep the horse balanced, especially on the turns, and maintain that balance and rhythm every inch of the way around the show-jumping course.

■ RIDING YOUR ROUND

As soon as you have entered the arena, pick up the canter you will be jumping from and give the horse a good canter around and in between the fences. Always be aware of being in the right position to keep cantering around to the first fence once you start your course. You will be eliminated if you blatantly show your horse the fences before you

However large or small the course you are about to jump, always take the opportunity to walk it so that you can measure the distances between fences and decide the exact line that you intend to ride.

start, but if there is a particularly spooky fence in the arena it is a good idea to happen to canter past it on your way to the first fence!

Once you begin, stay relaxed and just concentrate on holding the rhythm and balance all the way around the route you have planned to ride.

Fences can come up on you very quickly once you are jumping in a show-ring, so look up and ahead the whole time. Look for the next fence before you have even landed over the previous one. If you have to land over a fence and then turn, say, right to the next fence, open your right hand slightly once you are in the air over the first fence, and just bring your left leg back behind the girth at the same time, to encourage the horse to land and canter away with the right leg leading. If you fail to get to the turn with the correct leg leading, either ask the horse for a flying change or bring him back to a

Make good use of the practice jump. Keep it very low to begin with so that you both get a confident and happy start to your warm-up. Then gradually raise it to the height of the fences in the ring. If you have a fall of any sort, put it back down and jump it a few times until you are both confident again.

WATCH THE COMPETITION

If there is time, try to watch several other horses and riders negotiate the course. In a jumper course, listen for the judges' signal to start. Remember that you must start within sixty seconds of hearing it.

Watch to see whether or not each of the distances between the fences is riding as you envisioned. Are the horses finding the distances long or short?

Note the turns that the other riders make to the fences and see which route appears to give the horse the best chance of clearing the jump.

▌ R I G H T
The aim is to have a happy partnership, as is illustrated here.

WALKING THE COURSE

At some show-jumping competitions the rider is given the opportunity to walk around the course before the class starts. Make the most of this time to note the following relevant points:

■ Find the start markers. In a jumper course, you must pass through these once you get the signal to start, or you will be eliminated.

■ Walk the route you intend to ride. Do not simply take the shortest line from fence to fence in order to learn the order of the course. Walk exactly where you intend to ride and memorize it.

■ As you walk, note the conditions of the ground—are there any slippery areas to try to avoid? Pace out the distances between any combination or related-distance fences. Remember that 24 feet (7.35 m) equals landing, one stride and take-off. Every stride after that takes 12 feet (3.65 m). So a one-stride distance between the fences is 24 feet (7.35 m), a two-stride distance is 36 feet (11 m) etc.

■ As you walk any turns, ensure that you really are allowing enough room to get the horse straight and lined up for the next fence. Do not be tempted to cut corners at this stage.

■ Relate the distance that you measure out to the knowledge you have of your own horse's stride length. You will know from practicing at home whether your horse covers the ground easily or whether you need to open him up in order to fit in the designated number of strides.

■ Note where the finish markers are. In a jumper course, you have to pass through these once you have jumped the last fence.

trot and then pick up the correct canter lead. If you simply let the horse canter on around the corner on the wrong lead he will be less balanced. There is also a risk that he will attempt to change onto the right lead but may only change his front legs, rather than the hind legs as well. This is called cantering disunited and is very unbalancing for horse and rider.

If you have to pass the in-gate during your round, just be aware that your horse may be tempted to try to join his friends outside the ring. Keep your leg on and back it up with a tap from your stick if the horse drops back from the rhythm you asked for.

If you do have a refusal or a runout, make sure you go far enough away to give your horse a good approach on your second attempt. It is very easy to panic and just swing the horse around and fire him at the fence again, which will only invite a second refusal. Turn him away, pick up the canter and make a good, balanced turn back to the fence. Do not be tempted to go faster and chase the horse into the fence—that will only push him onto his forehand and make it easier for him to stop again. Think of collecting him and riding him from a strong, determined leg up into your hand. Contain the power you are creating and channel it toward the fence. Keep the rhythm consistent and do not get in front of the movement.

Make use of the turns to collect and balance the horse. Remember that to go around a corner properly he has to bring his inside hind leg further underneath himself, which in turn helps to lighten and elevate his forehand.

After jumping the last fence, bring your horse down to a trot and then a walk, reward him with a pat on the neck, and leave the arena at a walk.

If disaster strikes and you have a really bad round, remember that losing your temper is not going to improve things. Never punish the horse after his round—the time for a smack is the instant that the horse misbehaves. And never ever punish your horse with a yank at his mouth, or a jab with the spurs. If things have gone wrong, the place to put them right is back at home. Learn from what happened—analyze the mistakes and use exercises at home to correct them. Then come out another day and do it right!

Once you start jumping a course of fences, you will find that everything comes up on you very quickly. You must keep looking ahead to the next fence so that you can plan your turns accordingly.

Cross-Country Riding

Riding cross-country is a true test of a horse-and-rider partnership—whether it be the genuine article, when you are quite literally crossing the open countryside and jumping whatever natural hazards block your path, or the more organized version of riding a course of cross-country fences. Cross-country riding requires bravery and fitness from both horse and rider, as well as obedience and trust from the horse. Cross-country fences do not fall down. Very often the horse cannot even see where he is going to land, and he cannot judge the depth of any water which he might be required to jump into. Far from being a sport for the reckless, cross-country riding requires trust, obedience and technique.

▌ OPPOSITE
This sort of fence requires a brave horse who trusts his rider.

▌ LEFT
Horse and rider must remain balanced and in a rhythm as they negotiate varying terrain and obstacles.

Cross-country Jumping

▌ BELOW
When galloping cross-country your weight should be kept out of the saddle, unless riding downhill or directly on the approach to a fence. This allows the horse to stretch out underneath you unhindered by your weight in the saddle.

Jumping cross-country fences involves exactly the same principles of rhythm and balance that have already been discussed. The two main differences are:

■ You are generally required to ride cross-country at a faster pace than you would ride a course of show jumps. It is harder to balance a horse when he is traveling fast, so the rider has to work harder to achieve the same balance as when show jumping while traveling in a faster rhythm.

■ The terrain and the types of fence that you have to jump are far more varied than when show jumping. The cross-country course designer will use the natural terrain of the countryside to add to the questions he is asking of horse and rider. He might place a fence right at the top of a hill, or on a hillside. He may set the course so that the rider has to cross some rougher, more uneven ground on the approach to a fence, making the job of balancing the horse harder still. If you are riding cross-country while out hunting, for example, you will have no idea of what kind of terrain or fences may come up next. Whatever the countryside throws at you, you have to find a way of crossing it.

SPEED CROSS-COUNTRY

When riding in a cross-country competition there is nearly always what is called an optimum time to aim for, laid down either by the appropriate rule book or by the event organizer. Anyone exceeding the optimum time will incur time penalties. This often results in riders trying to finish the course faster than they are capable of doing. It may be good to be competitive but it is always better for the horse, and for the rider's long-term success, for horse and rider to finish the course safely rather than first. You should never ride faster than you can ride safely.

Remember that you will have a better round, and probably a faster time, if you settle in a rhythm and jump from that rhythm, than if you set off too fast and then have to fight for control in front of every fence. So think long term—ride your horse safely so that he learns how to deal with things properly and, just as importantly, so that his enjoyment and confidence grow. Gradually you will find you are recording good times cross-country without realizing you are even trying. That is how you produce a good cross-country horse.

DOWNHILL APPROACH

As you approach an uphill fence you should elevate your shoulders so that you lighten the horse's forehand; this makes it easier for him to get his front end up in the air and clear of the fence.

On the downhill approach to this fence, the rider keeps his seat well back in the saddle, and uses his legs and hands to keep the horse together so that he does not fall on the forehand. Just in front of the fence the rider elevates his shoulders slightly to lighten the horse's forehand further and to make it easier for the horse to get his front end up and over the fence. The rider must land in balance with the horse, ready to restore the balance and rhythm immediately.

Coping with the Terrain

LEFT
Just as when working on the flat or show jumping, the cross-country rider must keep the horse balanced between her legs and hands, over all kinds of terrain.

Keeping the horse balanced and in a rhythm across all kinds of terrain is the secret of good cross-country riding. When galloping on the flat in between fences you should adopt a forward seat, i.e. raise your seat off the saddle so that your weight is carried down through your lower legs into your heels and the stirrup irons.

In the same way that you use a combination of leg and hand when riding on the flat to keep the horse balanced and in a rhythm, do the same cross-country. You must be physically fit and strong to do this, as you not only have to support your own weight by keeping your seat out of the saddle, but you must also continue to use your lower legs effectively to keep the horse pushed up into your hand so that he is balanced. In front of a jump, do the same as you would when show jumping— lower your seat into the saddle, close your leg and hand sufficiently to keep the horse together and to keep him in the same rhythm, and then let your hands follow the horse's movement over the fence.

When galloping uphill, shift your weight further forward so that the horse's hindquarters are free to propel him up the hill. Still adopt the forward seat, but bring your shoulders further forward to keep your weight forward. Although uphill fences can look imposing, the horse will generally jump them very well as he is already actively using his hocks. On the approach to an uphill fence, slightly elevate your own shoulders, and drop your seat down into the saddle. This has the effect of driving the horse's hocks up underneath him and lightening his forehand so that he is able to raise his front end easily to clear the fence.

Downhill fences are harder to negotiate. When running downhill the horse is more likely to fall onto his forehand, which unbalances him and usually results in him leaning on the rider's hands for support. With all his weight falling onto his forehand he may not be able to raise his shoulders and forelegs quickly and cleanly enough to clear the jump. A good number of cross-country falls occur at downhill fences simply because the rider has failed to follow the golden rule of maintaining balance and rhythm. So when riding downhill, keep your seat in the saddle, your weight well down in your heels and your lower legs pushed slightly forward. There should be no need to lean back unless it is an exceptionally steep slope. Do not let the horse pull his head and neck down because in so doing he will pull you forward out of the saddle and then all your weight, as well as the horse's, will be on the forehand. Keep your shoulders up, use your legs and seat to drive the horse's hocks under him and use a stronger contact to balance the front end. Elevate your shoulders more in front of the fence to help the horse lighten and raise his front end, and give his head and neck plenty of freedom over the fence. As you land, keep your own weight back so that you don't get pushed onto the horse's shoulders. Take up contact, close the lower legs and work on rebalancing the horse and restoring the rhythm again.

Preparing for the Unexpected

When competing at a cross-country event, the rider walks the course and is therefore familiar with the terrain and the questions that the fences ask. The horse, however, has no idea what is coming next, and it is your task to use your knowledge of the course to prepare the horse.

Having left the start box, settle the horse into a good strong canter. Any straightforward single fences are jumped out of this canter; you simply have to maintain the same rhythm and balance and allow the horse to jump out of his stride. But when you know a more complicated jump is coming up, you must prepare the horse for it. So if you know that after the next rail there is a ditch to be jumped just one stride from it, prepare the horse for this unexpected obstacle. On

the approach to the rail, slow the horse and collect him so that his stride is shorter but he is still in an active rhythm. Hold this strong, more collected canter all the way to the rail. An experienced horse will take this as a signal that there is more to this fence than meets the eye. It gives him time to realize that a ditch follows the rail. On an inexperienced horse, this same action will help focus the horse's attention on the fence, and will give him time to see the ditch on the other side. However, you must be prepared for the horse to be wary of the ditch, and you may need to ride more aggressively so that he keeps going and tackles both the rail and the ditch that follows.

Similarly if the next fence is followed by a step down, or involves a combination

of various obstacles, always re-collect and balance the horse on the approach. If, having walked the course, you know that the distance between two fences is very tight, shorten the horse's stride on the approach and keep this new rhythm all the way to the fence so that the horse jumps it tidily and has room to take the designated number of strides. If there is a long distance between the fences, open the horse's stride up well before he gets to the jump and hold the new rhythm all the way to the fence. On landing you may need to send the horse forward actively in order to encourage him to continue the opened-up stride on the approach to the second fence.

Landing over a drop or into water also requires some warning for the horse, and

JUMPING INTO WATER

On the approach to this log into water, the rider has shortened the horse's stride and really pushed him together. This has elevated the horse's forehand and has helped to focus him on what is coming up. Just in front of the log, the rider is ready with a strong leg to insist that the horse keeps going now that he has spotted the water on the landing side of the fence. The rider keeps her upper-body weight back as the horse drops down into the water, and she slips the reins through her fingers to allow the horse the full use of his head and neck. Once in the water there is not enough time for the rider to shorten the reins again; she therefore draws her elbows back behind her, which in effect takes up the slack in the reins and allows her to regain the contact and control.

you should rebalance and collect him on the approach. As the horse lands, use your own body weight to help balance him. Make sure you don't get tipped forward; keep your body weight back by keeping your own shoulders elevated. Although the reins will have slipped through your fingers so that the horse's head and neck are not restricted over the jump, you still need to keep a contact with his mouth so that you can help balance him again as

you land. If the horse trips or stumbles as he lands, or if he is taken by surprise at the size of a drop, or by landing in water, you can use the contact through the reins to support the horse and to keep his head up slightly, and you may well be able to save him from falling. In contrast, if you have leaned forward and let the reins go loose, if anything untoward should happen on landing both you and the horse are likely to fall.

▌ **ABOVE LEFT**
When jumping into water, you must keep your weight well back. However, at the same time it is vital that you let the reins slip through your hands so that you do not restrict the horse's use of his head and neck. Note how this rider maintains a contact so that he can help to balance the horse as soon as they have landed in the water.

▌ **ABOVE RIGHT**
When cantering through water the rider must keep a contact with the horse's mouth so that the horse can remain balanced and light on his forehand.

It is quite difficult to stay in balance with a horse when he jumps up onto a step or bank. The idea is to keep your seat close to the saddle, but with your weight just raised out of it so that the horse feels he can really use himself. Your upper body needs to fold forward and your hands must also move forward so that, once again, the horse has enough freedom of the rein to stretch and use himself as he jumps.

PATIENCE AND DETERMINATION

You can spend a lifetime mastering the art of horsemanship because, like any artist or craftsman, it is perfection that you are seeking. You may not wish to take your riding to the highest levels but you should never close your mind to the opportunity to improve. You may have no ambition to compete seriously but you should always have pride in the care and well-being of your horse. Enjoy him to whatever degree you wish but always repay him by making sure you know how to care for him. Every horse and pony, whatever his job in life, deserves to be looked after properly.

Those who do wish to strive for perfection will need patience and determination in equal measure. Patience is vital because all horses are individuals, and some will react and learn more quickly and easily than others. You must be prepared to take time to teach the horse the basics so that you have a strong foundation to build on later. A horseman should always be working for the long-term good of the horse, not for short-term gain.

Determination is needed because somehow horses always seem to create as much

heartbreak as happiness. Things do go wrong—some horses simply aren't cut out for the sport for which they were bought. In the same way that not all human beings can cope with the same pressures or stresses in life, horses vary in their degree of tolerance and aptitude. Many a failed competition horse has become someone else's adored hack or hunter. So always be realistic about what you are asking of the horse. If he really isn't up to the job, it is kinder to sell him to someone who will appreciate his other talents, rather than for both of you to endure a life of frustration and misery.

Horses do go lame or become ill, often just before your main target of the season, and riders have accidents with a similar degree of bad timing! Years of work and preparation can appear to be wasted when such things go wrong, but if you have trained and prepared your horse thoroughly and carefully your chance will come.

You will never stop learning about how to get the best from your horse. Even the top riders continue to go to people more experienced than themselves for help and advice—and remember that they never stop practicing their art either.

COPING WITH AN EARLY TAKE-OFF

This rider has taken quite a risk at this widespread fence by asking her horse to take off very early. On a less scopey horse there is every chance that this sort of riding will result in a fall, as the horse may be physically unable to clear the spread of the fence and will land on it. In the first picture the rider has kept the horse balanced and in an even rhythm, but in the second picture she has suddenly opened the horse up and asked him to take off. Had she maintained the rhythm and balance all the way to the fence, the horse would have been able to fit in another stride and would have taken off a little closer to the fence. As it is, having taken off early, the rider has reacted in the correct way over the fence. She has kept her body weight balanced over the middle of the horse and has let the reins slip so that he can really stretch himself out and clear the fence.

TACKLING TWO CORNERS—1

This horse and rider are tackling a combination of two corners set three strides apart. See how the rider lands over the first corner and, using his knowledge of his horse's stride length, he sits quietly and lets the horse take three even strides to the second corner.

TACKLING TWO CORNERS—2

Another horse and rider tackling the same combination. Note how this rider, having landed over the first corner, knows that she has got to open up her horse's stride in order to make up the three strides to the next fence. She has sat down in the saddle and is really riding the horse forward. Knowing her horse very well, she has even dropped the rein contact with his mouth, and thus lessened her control, to encourage him to stretch everything forward in order to reach the fence. In this instance, it has paid off for her because she knows her horse well enough to trust him. Usually at a fence like this, which demands accuracy, you cannot afford to drop the rein contact in this way as the horse is then free to run out if he so wishes.

■ WHEN THINGS GO WRONG

Successful cross-country riding requires an ability to cope with the unexpected—even though you may have walked the course and know exactly how you intend to ride everything, sometimes the horse has other ideas. Despite your best intentions he may jump or react differently from how you imagined. Then you need to know what to do to make the best of the situation. For example, if your horse is normally long strided you might expect him to make up the distance in a combination easily, but if there is something in that combination that makes the horse back down, such as a ditch under the jump, suddenly you may not take off at the distance you imagined. Experience will teach you whether it is best to shorten your horse's stride and let him fit in an extra one, or whether you are better off riding even more aggressively, forcing him to open up his stride again and to take the fence. Some horses jump very big over ditches, or off drops, and this may alter the distance to the next fence.

Most importantly, if and when the unexpected happens, you are of most help if you can stay in balance with the horse and give him the necessary freedom of his head and neck. This all comes down to having an independent seat. If you can stay balanced without needing to hang on to the reins, and can at the same time keep thinking ahead and judging what you need to do to help the horse, you are the best asset he can have. A horse can jump out of some seemingly impossible situations, and can correct seemingly disastrous misjudgements, if his rider is not hindering him. The golden rule is to maintain rhythm and balance.

World of
the Horse

The Competition World

Competing with your horse can be as low-key or as serious as you wish to make it. Some riders make a living out of riding and competing with horses, others simply enjoy giving the family horse a quick wash and brush-up once a year for a local show. Whatever you opt for within that scale, there are certain things to be aware of. Before attempting any form of horse sport you must be sure that your horse is fit and mature enough, both mentally and physically, to take part. He should be sufficiently well schooled to be obedient to your commands, and should have seen enough in his daily hacks and general training regime not to be overawed by the competition scene.

Most horses should be versatile enough to take part in any number of sports at the lower levels. But if you decide to take up a particular sport seriously, check out the requirements and skills needed to ensure that you are both suited to that sport.

▮ OPPOSITE
A day at a show can be just so exhausting! All the best riders take time out to relax and contemplate what lies ahead of them.

▮ LEFT
The sport horse must be both mentally and physically mature enough to cope with the sometimes rigorous demands of the competition world.

Types of Competition

The wide range of horse sports that is now available means there is something to suit all types of horse and rider. From the more genteel, such as showing and dressage, to the rough and tumble of team sports such as polo and horseball, all manner of skills, both mental and physical, are tested. Some sports are judged very subjectively. Dressage and showing, for example, are reliant on the opinion of the particular judge on the day. Others are out-and-out contests of stamina and tactics, such as horse racing and endurance riding. In show-jumping and cross-country riding competitions, the skills of each horse and rider are not only pitted against their fellow competitors, but also against the questions set by the course designer. However great or small your competitive streak, there is something to suit all tastes.

■ LEFT
The main aim of competing at any level is that it should be fun. It is not so much the winning that is important—although everybody likes to win sometimes!

HEALTH REQUIREMENTS

■ Some affiliated competitions may state the age at which horses or ponies are allowed to compete in that particular discipline. For example, event horses are not allowed to compete in some events until they are five years old. You will need to be aware of such restrictions before planning a competition season with your horse.

■ Competition horses must have an up-to-date vaccination certificate that proves that they have received their annual vaccination booster.

■ As a rider and competitor you have a responsibility to your horse and to other competitors to ensure that, if you suspect your horse is suffering from something contagious, he is kept isolated from other horses. Obviously if your horse is clinically ill you would not consider taking him to a competition but some diseases, such as ringworm or mild viruses, do not greatly affect the horse's general well-being. When this is the case you should not be tempted to hope for the best and still go—you must keep your horse at home, away from other horses, until he is fully recovered.

■ BELOW
...to the sheer elegance of dressage...

■ RIGHT
...and the test of all-around horsemanship, eventing.

■ AFFILIATED AND UNAFFILIATED COMPETITIONS

Most countries have a good selection of organized horse sports, and these are usually split between what are regarded as affiliated and unaffiliated competitions. The **affiliated competitions** are generally stricter and require horse and rider to be registered as members of that particular sport's governing body.

At the top end of the scale, the International Equestrian Federation (FEI) governs all international competitions involving the sports under its jurisdiction—dressage, show jumping, carriage driving, eventing, vaulting and

endurance riding. The FEI controls their rules, and approves the program of events at the regional, championship and Olympic level.

Each country's own national federation is, in turn, answerable to the FEI. They organize competitions for all levels of experience within their own country.

Unaffiliated competitions, usually run along the same lines as the affiliated competitions, are put on by individuals who are happy about taking on the organizational responsibility. To enter these you do not need to be a registered member of any governing body, but you

will need to be familiar with the affiliated rules as these are often used. Many of the riders who compete in the affiliated competitions will take advantage of the more relaxed atmosphere at unaffiliated shows to introduce a young horse to the sport. The unaffiliated competitions also act as an introduction to the sport for novice riders.

■ RESTRICTIONS

Many sports split their competitions into classes for either different age groups of riders, or different standards or sizes of horse or pony. Pony classes are restricted either to recognized pony breeds or to any equine standing under 15hh. Showing classes are classified by size and type of horse or pony—working hunter, show hack, cob, etc.

The affiliated organizations run competitions for horses of the various grades recognized by their governing body, e.g. event horses are graded from novice through to advanced, dressage horses from preliminary through to grand prix, and so on.

Local unaffiliated classes are divided up into rider age groups, size of horse or pony, or prize money or placings previously won. The novice class may be

restricted to horses or ponies who have never been placed in any competitions, the next class may be limited to horses who haven't previously won a competition. The open class, as its name suggests, is open to any grade of horse or pony and is usually the most competitive of all.

To avoid disappointment and embarrassment or, worse still, elimination, do make sure you have read the rules and regulations of any competition you intend on entering and comply with them.

The happy winner of a show class in England salutes his appreciative audience.

Choosing a Sport

It is a good idea to find out if you enjoy and have an aptitude for a particular sport by entering unaffiliated competitions before going to the expense of registering with an affiliated body.

If, for example, you decide that dressage appeals to you, start out by competing quietly against friends and neighbors at local unaffiliated shows. Having decided that this sport really is for you, register with your national federation and start to work your way up through the grades of affiliated competition. If you have the talent, dedication and time to commit to the sport, there is nothing to stop you from reaching the top. If your sights really are set on the giddy heights of world championships or the Olympics, do remember that competitors at this level not only have to qualify to take part but also have to be selected by their national federation to enter as individuals or team members.

If you are lucky enough to be able to take your sport that seriously, you should investigate the opportunities that your national federation offers. Most countries that have an affiliation to the FEI also offer training to their members, as well as competitions culminating in international championships for riders of different age groups. The sports of dressage, show

▪ LEFT
When choosing a sport to take part in, it is important to consider the suitability of both your own and your horse's temperament. For some riders the excitement becomes too much—can you cope with this? Will it add to your fun or will it worry you?

▪ ABOVE AND BELOW
If you wish to compete regularly then some form of transportation is going to be necessary. This can be a vehicle and trailer or a horse box, either of which can be purchased, hired or shared. Not only will the trailer or truck provide a safe haven for your horse in between classes, it will also tend to become the social center of the event.

EQUIPMENT NEEDED FOR ALL EQUESTRIAN SPORTS

▪ You should wear a certified safety helmet complete with safety harness for all horse-riding activities. If you intend to ride and jump cross-country, you should also wear a body protector.

▪ Each sport has its own recognized and accepted style of dress. Dressage, show jumping and showing classes require the rider to be wearing a riding jacket, jodhpurs or breeches, short or tall riding boots and a hard hat. For cross-country riding, you can wear a sweat shirt instead of a riding jacket.

Polo, horseball and polocrosse require breeches and tall leather boots to be worn, along with a shirt instead of a riding jacket, plus protective padding such as knee pads.

Endurance riders wear either standard jodhpurs or breeches, or more lightweight ones for hot conditions, as well as rain gear for wet weather. They are not expected to wear riding jackets but dress according to the weather conditions.

▪ Your horse or pony will need a well-fitting saddle and bridle, and it is also advisable to protect his legs against strains or scrapes by using boots or bandages.

▪ You will need water, buckets, sponges, sweat scrapers and towels so that the horse can be washed and dried off if he is hot and sweaty after competing.

■ RIGHT
■ RIGHT
This competitor rewards her horse with a pat and a swim at the World Equestrian Games Endurance competition. Endurance competitors are allowed to dress according to the weather conditions.

jumping and eventing have championships specifically for pony riders, juniors and young riders. When you reach the age of twenty-one, you have to join the senior ranks.

Within the other equestrian sports there is usually a very good choice of competition designed to cover all levels of ability and ambition. In the showing world this ranges from local shows to regional competitions, right through to national championships. For some of these classes, your horse or pony may have to be registered with a breed society or showing association; these, in turn, help to govern and organize the various competitions, local and national.

Team sports such as polo, polocrosse and horseball require greater organization and facilities, as does learning the skills of vaulting. To take part usually entails joining a local club.

■ BELOW
Whether you have a good or a bad day, you must always put your horse's or pony's needs first. Make sure he has time to relax and enjoy the experience as well.

■ BELOW
Equestrian sports involving jumping offer variety and fun. Show jumping, for example, has classes available for anyone from lead-line contenders, through junior classes as shown here, to international senior competitions.

TRAVELING EQUIPMENT

Once you decide to compete regularly, unless you are very lucky in having regular competitions held within hacking distance, you will need to transport your horse in either a horse box or trailer. The horse must be kept safe and comfortable when traveling.

■ There should be bedding on the floor to cushion his legs and to help soak up any urine or manure he produces.

■ He should be secured with a halter and rope that is tied through a piece of string attached to the fixed tie ring. This is so that, should the horse fall or struggle, he will be able to free his head and neck—otherwise he may injure himself very badly.

■ He will need a selection of blankets, chosen according to the weather conditions on the day, so that he becomes neither too hot nor too cold on the journey.

■ He should wear protective boots or bandages on his legs, a tailguard or bandage (or both) to protect his tail from rubbing, and a poll guard to protect the top of his head.

■ You should offer your horse water to drink during the journey, and a haynet, although this should be taken away at least an hour before he is due to be ridden. Take food and hay for him to eat during the day and on the journey home, and keep a check on how warm or cold he is while traveling.

Non-Jumping Sports

Horse sports are so varied that they are difficult to categorize. For the purposes of this book, they are split into a selection of non-jumping and jumping sports. To make it to the top of any one, you need to specialize. But most riders enjoy taking part in a number of different activities, so first look at the different things you can try. Unless you have your heart set on one particular sport, it is worth experimenting to find out what really suits you and your horse. The discipline and perfectionist nature of dressage may suit your personality, or perhaps you would prefer the more light-hearted approach of mounted games. Once you have outgrown those, there are team games such as horseball, polo and polocrosse to enjoy, or perhaps Western riding appeals to you. Whoever you are, whatever your ability, there is bound to be something to which you can aspire.

▌ OPPOSITE
Whatever sport you choose to take part in, make sure your horse or pony is fit enough to enjoy it. His exercise routine must be a mixture of fitness and schooling work.

▌ LEFT
Endurance riding is rapidly growing in popularity around the world. It tests the horse's fitness and stamina, and the rider's ability to judge pace and ensure their horse has enough energy to complete the whole ride in good health.

Mounted Games

If you can envision a cross between party games and a race on horseback, you will have some idea of what mounted games involve. Although adults do compete, it is primarily a sport for children—the energy, enthusiasm and agility that this sport requires ideally suit youngsters and their ponies. The beauty of these games is that there is one to suit every type and ability of pony and rider.

Mounted games can be organized for fun between a group of friends or as a serious form of competition, with regional, national and international championships provoking great rivalry between the various clubs and associations taking part. But at whatever level they are played, mounted games will help to develop your riding skills, your confidence in handling yourself and your pony and, most importantly, the realization that riding is fun.

■ HOW MOUNTED GAMES BEGAN

Surprisingly for a sport that is now dominated by children, mounted games were first played by adults. It was in India that the games we are familiar with today developed. They were then known as gymkhanas, which translated as gymnastic or athletic displays on horseback. The word *gymkhana* is still used in many countries today to describe the sport. The British Army, which was based in India in the late nineteenth century, adopted the games, although their mounts included donkeys, mules and camels. The games, such as "Kiss the Girl," "Tent Pegging" and "Grab the Hat," were a popular and light-hearted way not only of helping to keep horse and rider fit and supple, but also of fostering strong regimental loyalty.

When the soldiers returned to Britain, they introduced the games to their home country where they proved most popular with children, their small, nimble ponies being ideal mounts for the games. The Pony Club, which was formed in 1929 and quickly grew to become a world-wide organization with over 100,000 members, developed and spread the benefits of the games. Pony Club Mounted Games are now played in over twenty-five different countries at interbranch, interstate and international level.

BELOW
Some games rely on your pony's skills; others are down to the rider. In "Apple Bobbing" you have to retrieve an apple from a bucket of water without using your hands!

For those who do not wish to lose out on the enjoyment of mounted games once they are over Pony Club age, there is the International Mounted Games Association. They hold an annual World Mounted Games Championship in a different host country each year, and membership of the Association goes up to the age of twenty-one.

Other opportunities to play mounted games are offered at local shows and gymkhanas, where there are classes for lead-line competitors as well as for older children.

A flying start is a big advantage, whatever race you are in. Practice at home by gradually asking your pony to go straight into a canter from the walk, and then from a halt.

■ SKILLS REQUIRED

To enjoy mounted games for the fun and entertainment they offer requires no great skill on the part of horse or rider. But if you want to be the winner of many ribbons, or to make it onto a team and compete more seriously, certain skills are necessary.

Your pony will need to be fit, obedient, agile and unflappable—he will encounter

▍ LEFT
Another great asset is the ability to vault onto a moving pony. It is a bit easier than it looks—if you time it properly the pony's forward motion helps propel you through the air and up onto his back.

the ability to dismount at speed without losing your balance and falling.

You must be able to control your pony with only one hand on the reins, as the other hand is often needed to do whatever the game entails. If the pony can be taught to neck rein, i.e. to respond to pressure on the neck from the rein rather than to a feel on the bit, controlling him with both reins in one hand will be easy.

■ TRAINING THE MOUNTED-GAMES PONY

Obedience in the form of quick responses is what is required of the mounted-games pony. He must be able to start and stop quickly, turn tightly and, amidst all the excitement of the race, remain stock still while his rider carries out whatever task the game requires.

You cannot begin to improve your pony's responsiveness until he is working obediently to the basic leg and hand aids. Unless he is already at the stage where you can quietly ask him to go forward at the walk, trot and canter, to halt, to turn left or right and to move to the side, i.e. leg yield, he is not ready to be asked to do

THE RANGE OF GAMES

Each year more and more ingenious games are developed to test the pony's and rider's speed, agility, coordination, fitness and sense of humor!

The easiest games are designed for young riders whose ponies are being led—musical mats, musical chairs and musical statues. The children are led around on their ponies until the music stops, when they must leap off and pounce on a chair or mat. One chair or mat is taken away each time so that the rider who finds him- or herself without a chair or mat is out. In musical statues the pony, rider and leader must remain absolutely still when the music stops. The first to move is out—more often than not it is the pony who doesn't have the patience or desire to remain still.

For those who want to test their speed and agility there are the races. These can be as simple as a bending race, where horse and rider thread their way between a line of poles, or as complex and extravagant as such team races as the "Dragon Race." There are even games that include the fun of jumping. In "Chase Me Charlie," the competitors follow each other over a jump. If they clear it they stay in the game, if they knock it down they are out. The jump is raised each time until only the winner remains. "Barrel Elimination" involves jumping over a line of barrels. After each round, one barrel is removed so that the jump becomes narrower and narrower until there is only one barrel remaining to be jumped over. If the pony stops or runs out to either side, he is out of the game.

all kinds of strange objects in the varied races offered. Most riders opt for a pony who for most other sports would be considered a touch too small for them, but a smaller pony makes it easier to reach down to deposit or retrieve objects and to mount and dismount on the move.

As a mounted-games competitor, you too will need to be fit and agile. Good coordination and balance are called for, as well as good speed as, in many games, the rider may be dismounted and leading the pony for much of the race. Similarly, the ability to vault onto your pony while he is cantering along is a great asset, as is

▍ LEFT
It takes a tolerant pony and two agile riders to manage this feat!

■ LEFT
It helps to be fit and supple and to have good coordination. Here the rider has to retrieve a tennis ball from the top of the cone.

NECK REINING

In countries where horses have always been used for herding livestock, such as America, Australia, New Zealand, parts of Africa and the Far East, neck reining is commonly used. This allows the rider to carry both reins in one hand. To turn the horse to the right, the rider simply brings his left hand, which is holding the reins, over to the right-hand side of the pony's neck. The reins press against the left-hand side of the pony's neck, the pony moves away from the pressure and so turns to the right. Do the opposite to turn left.

In most European countries, ponies need to be taught to respond to neck reining. If you apply the correct leg aids before you bring the rein across the pony's neck, and at the same time incline your body weight slightly in the direction you want to go, the pony will quickly get the idea of responding to neck reining.

anything beyond this. As in all things, establish the basics first and it will be easy to teach your pony any number of new skills.

THE QUICK START

To have any chance of winning you need to get a good start—your pony should be able to leap forward from a halt to full speed ahead. He will already know how to go up through the gaits to canter; now he needs to speed up the process. You should first practice going forward into a trot from a halt, and then try halt to canter. The correct aids should still be applied and they should be backed up by the voice, and, if necessary, a tap behind the leg with the schooling whip, rather than resorting to giving the pony a kick with your heels. If you teach the pony to go forward by kicking his sides with your heels, he will gradually become less responsive and will certainly be spoiled for any other activity. Treat this training in the same way as your flatwork—you are still looking for a quick response to a light aid.

THE QUICK STOP

Similarly, the pony must be able to come back rapidly from flat out to a halt whenever required. This is not achieved by simply hauling hard on the reins. As in your flatwork training, ask the pony to halt by using your legs to drive him up into your hands which, on this occasion, do not soften or yield to him, so he is brought back to a halt. Using your voice to ask him to "Whoa" will also help him to understand and respond more quickly to the request to stop. Shift your weight slightly further back in the saddle as you ask your pony to halt. This will help push his hindquarters further under him and allow him to sit down on his hocks so that, when he halts, his forehand is still light and elevated, ready for the all-important quick getaway.

In the stepping-stones race the rider has to tackle the stepping stones before vaulting onto the pony and racing for the finishing line.

▌ LEFT
Mounted games aren't just for children and small ponies—here an American Quarter Horse shows how good he is at bending.

that there is pressure on the right-hand side of the pony's neck. It is sometimes helpful to use the reins slightly higher up the pony's neck when you would like him to turn particularly sharply.

GETTING USED TO THE EQUIPMENT

In a serious mounted-games competition your pony will face any number of strange objects. He must be prepared to go up to whatever the target of the game is, he may have to go under a clothes-line strung with laundry, or a post hung with signs—all kinds of items have to be acceptable to him. He must allow his rider to carry flags, buckets, swords and balloons without being worried by them. He must be accustomed to noise and the general hustle and bustle, including a very noisily appreciative audience, which is all part of a mounted-games competition.

All these strange and startling things should be introduced to the pony at home. As long as you give him time to realize that none of these peculiar objects is going to

TURNING

Your pony will need to be able to turn quickly and sharply, and this can be practiced at home by using a barrel as a turning point. Practice first at a trot, riding up to and around the barrel, keeping your pony as close to the barrel as you can. Remember that it is your outside hand and leg that will prevent the pony from drifting away from the barrel. Once you have mastered a tight turn at a trot using both hands on the rein, try it at a canter. When the pony is familiar with what is required, try it with the reins in one hand. To turn tightly to the left around the barrel, your right leg will be back behind the girth to keep the pony's quarters close to the barrel, your inside leg will be used at the girth to make the pony bend through his body and you will bring your rein hand across to the left, so

The "Dragon Race" is one of the most spectacular—the riders have to kill the dragon by bursting the balloons attached to him. Then they can rescue the damsel in distress.

■ LEFT
Mounted games are as much to do with team work
as with individual ability and success.

harm him, he will soon accept them. There is no point in using force—his trust has to be won and this takes time and patience. When you show your pony something new, allow him time to make up his own mind that it is harmless. Do not force him to approach a strange object too quickly. Reward and reassure him all the time that he is prepared to face it, even if he is still not very close to it. Only become stronger in your riding if he actually turns away from the object. Then you must be positive and use your legs and hands to turn him back. Once he is facing it again, reward him. Let him know you are displeased each time he tries to turn away, and gradually he will realize that you are determined that he will meet this new thing. Usually curiosity takes over and he will dare to get closer and closer. Take things slowly—go one step at a time—and this will ensure that your pony's confidence and enjoyment increase.

THE CHANGEOVER

Many races require a fast changeover of equipment—usually a baton—between two riders. This has to be practiced, first to accustom the pony to the idea of another pony and rider bearing down on him at great speed—the last thing you want is your pony shying away. Second, both riders involved need to know how to hand over the item without dropping it. It should be held at arm's length so that the receiving rider has a good view of the

target to be grabbed. The riders should be positioned so that the receiver can grab the baton with his or her best hand (the right hand if he or she is right-handed) and the first rider should not release the grip on the baton until he or she is positive that the second rider has taken hold of it. It is quicker to turn around and hand it over again than for the baton to be dropped and the rider to have to dismount.

■ PRACTICE FOR THE RIDER

Once you are familiar with even a small number of mounted games, you will realize that a wide range of skills is called for. All demand dexterity and agility, but some demand more specialized skills. If you are a good shot you will excel at games such as the "Hi Lo Race," where a tennis ball has to land in a high net, or the "Sharpshooters' Race," where a soft ball is thrown at a line of comic models until it succeeds in knocking their heads off. In the "Sack Race" you will need to be able to race along, leading your pony, while your feet and legs are trapped in a sack!

All these strange skills can be practiced on foot at home, with simple homemade equipment. Practicing the races on foot will also help to promote your overall fitness and agility, which will be all to the good when you try them out on horseback again.

VAULTING ON AND OFF

To be a truly successful mounted-games player you will need to master the art of

mounting and dismounting at speed. A small pony coupled with a rider with long legs has the advantage here, although there is an art to vaulting on that makes it easier than it looks. The trick is to use the momentum created by the pony's movement to help lift you into the saddle. To begin with, practice mounting a moving pony with someone leading the pony so that he can be kept straight and at a steady speed. You should run beside the pony, who will be trotting or cantering, keeping level with the pony's shoulder. Stretch your right hand over the pony's back and take hold of the front of the saddle flap on the far side. Your left hand is holding the reins and can be rested on the pony's withers. As the pony's near-side foreleg touches the ground, spring upward and swing your right leg over his back. If your timing is good, the pony's forward momentum will help to lift you up into the air.

To dismount from a moving pony, organize yourself so that you land facing forward and are immediately able to run forward so that you do not lose your balance. If you have ever stepped off a moving bus or carousel platform, you will know that unless you start running as soon as your feet touch the ground you will fall flat on your face.

Take both feet out of the stirrups, put your right hand on the pommel of the saddle and your left hand on the pony's neck. Lean forward over the pony's neck and swing your right leg up and over his back. Use your hands to push your body clear of the pony's side and to help balance yourself as you land. Make sure you land running.

For those competing seriously, team-training sessions will be necessary, possibly even with a coach; here it is possible to see which riders and ponies are best suited to which games, and also to discuss team tactics—an important weapon on the road to victory.

The Games

As you will have gathered, any number of mounted games can be dreamed up. The Pony Club probably has the most comprehensive list, which is used for their national and international competitions. It has a good rule book, including—to avoid any breakdown in international relations—an Official International Exchange Visits rule book. Despite the fact that mounted games are meant to be fun, they can become very competitive, so it is always safest to be sure everyone is agreed on the same rules. The following is a selection of team games. Most can be adapted to suit team or individual competitions, but do not feel you have to be limited to these. Let your imagination run riot!

SACK RACE

Gallop your pony to the end of the arena where there is an empty sack. Jump off the pony, get inside the sack, and make your way back to the start, hopping, shuffling or tripping along, while still leading your pony. One trick is to rest an arm across the pony's withers as this will help support your weight and keep you upright. The other hand holds the sack up around you. Jump forward, allowing the pony to take your weight and to carry you forward a little way before landing again.

An even more amusing adaptation of this game is the "Big Sack Race." Four team members gallop to the end of the arena where a fifth team member is holding a huge sack. She takes her teammates' ponies while all four of them climb into the sack and, *en masse*, wriggle their way back to the start.

GROOM'S RACE

This calls for an additional skill—the ability to control two ponies at once. You have to ride your own pony, and lead one of your teammates' ponies, up through a line of bending poles. At the changeover point, your teammate mounts her own pony, and leads the third rider's pony back

through the line of poles. And so it goes on until all the riders and ponies have had their turn and are back at the start.

LAUNDRY STAKES

One pair of riders gallops to a clothes-line, carrying a basket of laundry between them. They hang up the clothes and gallop back, handing the empty basket to the second two members of the team. They have to gallop to the clothes-line, remove the clothes, and bring them back safely to the start in the laundry basket.

ROPE RACE

Set off at a gallop through a line of bending poles carrying a piece of rope about 3 feet (1 m) long. At the end of the arena, one of your teammates grabs the end of the rope and you both gallop back through the bending poles together. At the other end you drop your end of the rope and a third rider picks it up; the second and third rider hold the rope and gallop through the bending poles, and so on. Be careful not to allow your pony to step on the heels of the one in front.

■ BELOW AND OPPOSITE
The greatest opportunities to play mounted games
are provided by the Pony Club, which is an
international youth organization. These groups of
riders from many different countries are taking
part in the annual Euro Camp.

BALLOON RACE

A bunch of balloons is tied to a post.
Gallop to the post, collect a balloon,
gallop back and pass it to your
teammate. He or she gallops with it
to the post, collects a second balloon
and hands both balloons to the third rider.
This goes on until the last team member
crosses the line with all the balloons
in his or her hand.

FISHING RACE

You are given a fishing rod, which is
actually a piece of wood with a hook on
the end. Gallop to a bin full of wooden
fish with rings in their noses, hook a fish,
gallop back to the start and hang it on a
peg. Your teammate then sets off, catches
a fish, brings it back, and so on until all
the fish are caught.

BALL-AND-RACKET RACE

You have to balance a tennis ball on a
tennis racket while riding your pony as fast
as you can through a line of bending
poles. You then hand the racket and ball
to your teammate who races through the
bending poles, and so on.

STEPPING STONES

Race to a line of stepping stones—usually
a line of upside-down buckets—dismount
and negotiate the stepping stones while
leading your pony alongside. Then
remount your pony before crossing the
finishing line.

SHARPSHOOTERS' RACE

This race calls for another asset—a pony
willing to carry two riders on his back! At
the start of the race sit bareback on your
pony. When the whistle sounds your
teammate has to jump up behind you, and
you race to the far end. Your passenger
jumps off and has to throw soft balls at a
row of comic figures until their heads are
broken. Your passenger has to remount,
and you both race for the line where the
next pair of riders is ready to set off.

FIVE-FLAG RACE

Gallop with a flag in your hand to a pot
at the end of the arena. Put the flag in
the pot. On your way back, grab another
flag from a line of pots and hand it to

your teammate. He or she gallops to the far end and puts it in the furthest pot along with the first flag. On the way back, he or she grabs another flag from the line of pots to hand to the next rider, and so on.

DRAGON RACE

This is one of the most spectacular races to watch. It requires some quite elaborate equipment in the form of the dragon, and so it usually tends to be reserved for major championships.

The centerpiece is a model dragon with balloons attached to him. For added effect he is often made to puff great clouds of smoke. One team member plays the part of the damsel in distress, captured by the fearsome dragon. Her teammates are the knights attempting to rescue her. As a gallant knight, you race to the damsel and collect a token from her, which you tie to your lance. You then attack the

IMPORTANT RULES

Most competitions are run under Pony Club rules. Points to note:
■ Ponies must be at least four years old, and not more than 14.2hh.
■ If you weigh more than 117 lb (53 kg) when dressed for riding, your pony must be over 12.2hh.
■ Your pony must wear a snaffle bridle and a conventional saddle; racing saddles are not allowed. Whips or spurs are not allowed, nor may you use the baton or your hand to encourage your pony to go faster.
■ Riders must wear recognized safety helmets with a proper safety harness.
■ The winner of the race is the pony who manages to get his head across the finish line first.
■ If the race involves leading the pony, the winner is the first rider across the line provided he or she still has hold of the pony. In a race involving pairs of ponies, the placing is judged from the moment that the second pony's head crosses the line.

dragon by bursting a balloon. When the last knight succeeds in bursting the final balloon, the damsel is rescued and led to the finish on her pony.

BENDING RACE

In contrast to the "Dragon Race," this requires a minimum of equipment—just a line of flexible poles pushed into the ground at intervals. You have to ride your pony in and out of the poles, turn tightly at the end and either race for the finish or thread your way back through the poles. Barrels can be used instead of poles.

EGG-AND-SPOON RACE

Holding a spoon with a hard-cooked egg resting in it, you have to race through a line of bending poles, out and back, without dropping the egg.

These are just a sample of what is offered if you take up mounted games. More important than the games themselves is the opportunity they provide to ignite a spark of interest in children, so that their enthusiasm for horses and riding, for fun or for sport, may continue long after they have outgrown the fun of mounted games.

Dressage

The simple aim of dressage is to produce a horse who can carry his rider easily, and is supple, balanced, correctly muscled, active, eager and responsive to his rider's most subtle command—yet far too many people look down on dressage as an option for those who are too scared to jump!

If you wish to succeed in any horse sport, you have a much greater chance of doing so if your horse is a well-schooled and responsive ride. Whatever sport or sports you decide to take part in with your horse, you should discipline yourself to practice the art of dressage, even if you never set foot or hoof in a competitive dressage arena.

Your horse cannot perform to the best of his ability, nor be a true pleasure for you to ride, unless he has had some help and training to improve his balance and responsiveness. A horse is a far greater joy to hunt, to jump, to hack out or to compete with in any form, if he is able to balance himself so that he carries more of his weight, and that of his rider, on his hindquarters, which in turn will lighten his forehand.

■ LEFT
Dressage is as much about power as it is about obedience—the horse must look as though he is moving with purpose.

■ BELOW LEFT
As soon as your horse is able to keep a steady rhythm in all paces, and has enough balance to trot and canter 20 meter circles, he is ready to try some of the easier dressage tests.

■ THE HISTORY OF DRESSAGE

As far back as the fourth century BC, Xenophon, a Greek, wrote a book on training the riding horse. Prior to that, most interest in training lay in driving horses for chariots, rather than in riding.

From the sixteenth century on, a succession of excellent European horsemen laid down the foundations of classical riding and training as we know it today. The aim of these early trainers was to improve the lightness and balance of the horse. Much of the work involved training from the ground using long reins, so that the horse learned the movements without the hindrance of a rider. Only after that was the rider taught how not to hinder the horse!

Interest in dressage fluctuated over the following centuries. In Great Britain there was far more interest in hunting and cross-country riding which, in those days, was performed very much on a wing and a prayer. The horses jumped what they were asked to jump either because they were naturally bold or because their riders were able to use enough brute force to get what they wanted. School riding or dressage was laughed at. Typically, instead of the good influencing the bad, in this particular instance the British attitude drifted across to France after the Napoleonic Wars, and

the interest in dressage faltered there for a while. The nineteenth century saw a revival of interest in Europe. The principles laid down centuries before were refined and adapted, but the basic requirements of free forward movement, suppleness, obedience and lightness of the forehand remained and are still the aim of dressage riders today. In many other parts of the world, such as America, Argentina, Africa, New Zealand and Australia, the horse was still primarily used either as a beast of burden or as a stock animal for the herding and control of large herds of livestock. But the influence of the great riding masters, particularly those of the Spanish Riding School in Vienna and the Cadre Noir in France, spread throughout the world until dressage became a truly international sport and a passion for many riders.

■ DRESSAGE AS A COMPETITIVE SPORT

Dressage is an Olympic sport, and its governing body is the FEI. It is therefore affiliated, and there are various levels of competition for affiliated members. However, dressage is a popular and easy sport to organize, which means that many unaffiliated competitions are run by various show organizers.

Dressage tests are split into the internationally recognized FEI tests and national tests, devised by each individual country. The national tests generally start with the lowest level, preliminary or novice, progressing through elementary to medium and advanced tests. Unaffiliated shows normally only offer classes up to elementary level, and may also make use of the simpler dressage tests taken from the sport of eventing. Most countries hold national and regional championships as well as participating in the international

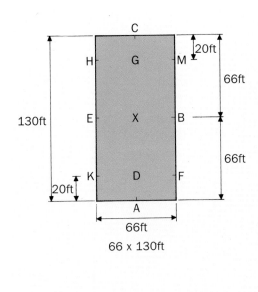

66 x 130ft

66 x 200ft

■ LEFT
As the horse progresses through the levels he is expected to show more expression in his gaits. His outline should be shorter and higher, and his gaits more powerful and elevated.

■ BELOW
Something to aim for—this combination won the gold medal at the 1988 Olympic Games. Nicole Uphoff on Rembrandt at Aachen.

FEI competitions. All tests are ridden in a dressage arena, which is a rectangle marked out by boards and letters. The letters signify where various movements should be carried out. The lower-level tests are performed in the minimum-sized arena of 22 x 43¾ yards (20 x 40 m), whereas more advanced tests are carried out in an international-sized arena of 22 x 65½ yards (20 x 60 m). The marker letters are always the same. At the Olympic Games and other FEI championships, the arena must have an all-weather surface of sand, but at other competitions it may be of grass, or may be indoors.

Lower-level tests are judged by just one person, who awards marks for each set

FEI TESTS

- Prix St. George
- Intermediare 1
- Intermediare 2
- Grand Prix
- Grand Prix Special
- Free Style Test—this is the same standard as the Grand Prix but is performed to music.

movement in the test, plus an overall mark for the horse's way of going and the rider's performance. The judge stands behind the C marker, directly in line with the center line of the arena. Higher-level competitions are judged by three or even five judges. Each judge sits to one side or the other of the center-line judge and awards his or her own scores. These scores may well vary, as each judge will see the test ridden from a different angle. The final score is taken as the average of all the judges' scores.

In all dressage competitions, you are given a precise time at which your test will start. You must figure out how much loosening up and schooling work your horse needs so that he is well prepared for his test at the allotted time. Once you are sent over to the appropriate arena, you must not enter it until the judge signals you to start, usually with a bell or horn. You can ride around outside the arena, continuing to work on keeping your horse balanced, calm and attentive, until the judge's signal. Enter the arena at A, proceed down the center line to X, the halfway point, halt and salute the judge. A female rider is required to put both

reins in the left hand, bow the head, and drop the right hand to the side. A male rider is expected to remove his hat and bow likewise. After this, you can proceed down the center line and into the first movement of the appropriate test. The test always ends with another trip down the center line to halt and salute once more. Then proceed at a free walk, giving the horse a long rein, and leave the arena at A. After that it is a case of waiting for your scores to be posted.

■ WHO CAN DO DRESSAGE?

Any rider can, and should, practice dressage, even if you choose not to compete. Once your horse is basically obedient, can maintain a rounded outline and can work in a reasonable rhythm at the walk, trot and canter, he is equipped to perform the simpler dressage tests. The lower-level tests only require the horse to work at a medium walk, working trot and canter, and may require some lengthening of the horse's stride. The horse must be able to produce a good halt, as all tests end with a halt and salute to the judge, and the vast majority of tests also start with one. A few of the very basic tests allow the

The aim of dressage is simply to produce a fit, supple, obedient horse who is so responsive that his rider appears to be doing nothing.

horse to enter the arena and begin the test immediately. You will need to be able to ride basic schooling movements such as 20 or 15 meter circles, and serpentines or half-circles, but none of these is outside the scope of a reasonably well-schooled horse.

International tests have to be ridden from memory, as does the dressage test in horse trials. In lower level tests you are allowed to have the test read out loud to you. But it is worth making the effort to memorize the test, both out of respect for the judge who has given up a day to come and mark you, and because to ride a really good test you need to concentrate fully on getting the best out of your horse, not wondering what command is going to be called out to you next. The movements of the test should become second nature to you if you are to ride your horse to the best of your ability.

■ SKILLS REQUIRED

To be successful in any equestrian sport you need to develop a secure independent seat but, in dressage, it is equally important to develop "feel." You should be able to feel exactly what the horse is doing underneath you. Is he straight, is he giving you the correct bend, are his hocks really coming underneath him, is he relaxed enough

through his neck and jaw? This feel can be developed with experience, but some riders are simply never able to accomplish it. Be patient and dedicated. The correct training of a dressage horse is a very long, careful process—there are no shortcuts.

Any horse who has been correctly schooled is already doing dressage, and can therefore compete, but some horses find this discipline easier than others. A calm temperament helps, along with a willingness and quickness to learn. If the horse has good conformation and naturally good gaits, he is going to find his work easier than a horse who has an awkward build and therefore struggles to move as freely. The horse should be forward thinking, and ideally he should have naturally active hocks—some horses have naturally "lazy" hocks and will find it harder to use their hindquarters. Finally the ideal dressage horse should have presence—he should make people want to stop and watch him. But don't be deterred if your horse lacks some of these qualities. Careful and consistent training can do wonders for the most unpromising candidate—it just takes more time and determination.

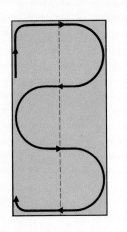

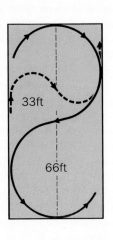

33ft

66ft

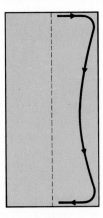

17ft

The World of Showing

The showing scene probably offers a wider range of opportunities for all types and abilities than any other equestrian sport. If you are the sort of person who takes pride in appearance, manners and performance—both yours and your horse's—you will enjoy exploring the showing world.

There are no Olympics or world championships for showing, but there is ample opportunity to compete. In most countries there are regional and national championships for the different categories of show horses and ponies.

If you wish to compete at the higher-level shows, you will need to register your horse with the appropriate society. Which you register with depends on the type of horse you own and which classes you wish to compete in. It usually means registering with a breed society, a show-pony society, or a hunter or hack society or association. Small, local shows do not usually require their entrants to be registered with anyone.

▌ LEFT
Mountain and moorland ponies are shown off in a more natural state than their show-pony colleagues. Their manes and tails are left full and unbraided or braided; their legs are not trimmed either. It is probably harder to produce a well-turned-out native pony than it is to produce his show-pony counterpart who may be braided, clipped and trimmed. NOTE: This would be only in the British Isles.

Different countries vary in the interest and opportunities that are afforded to showing. In terms of expense and facilities required, it is a relatively easy sport to accommodate. A grass enclosure and some respected judges are all that most classes require. Generally speaking, there are classes available to suit all ages and types of horse and rider.

■ IN-HAND SHOWING

Mares and foals, yearlings, and two-, three- and four-year-old horses and ponies can all be shown "in-hand," i.e. they are led by their handlers and are judged on how well they are turned out, their conformation, their manners and paces, and their potential suitability for adult life. As the handler, you are expected to be very

neatly dressed yourself, and your horse should be sensible and obedient enough to stand in line with the rest of the class, and to walk and trot in-hand when he is required to do so by the judge.

Your horse should appear in the ring without a saddle, and with no boots or bandages of any sort. He can be led with either a halter or a bridle.

You can practice all the requirements at home, teaching your horse to halt squarely and to remain still, and to walk and trot calmly beside you when asked.

EQUIPMENT NEEDED

For nearly all showing classes, apart from side-saddle, you can use your normal saddle and bridle. If given the choice, a saddle that is not too forward cut is usually more appropriate. It shows off your horse's shoulders and front end rather than covering them up, and gives you more chance of impressing the judges. At higher levels of competition it may be more appropriate to wear either a top hat or a bowler hat instead of a traditional hard hat. The showing world in general strives to uphold tradition and standards, and it is worth bearing this in mind when you are buying any clothing or equipment. Keep everything clean, tidy and workmanlike and you won't go wrong.

Pony and rider showing off their paces in the Working Hunter Pony class.

In many classes you have to be able to show off your horse at the gallop despite the confines of the arena. A safe, all-weather surface is provided for this show cob.

■ RIGHT
You may find yourself competing against "professional" showmen who will arrive with a whole string of horses or ponies to enter. This is Great Britain's Robert Oliver.

■ BELOW
In some horse-show classes all the competitors ride around together while the judge assesses them. They are then asked to line up, after which they may be given individual tests.
NOTE: In the U.S. the individual tests are usually only given in certain equitation classes such as Medal or MacClay, and could involve jumping.

SUCCESS IN THE SHOW RING

To maximize your chances of success in the show ring it is worth making use of your "ring smarts." All this involves is using your common sense to ensure that the judge gets the best chance to view your horse. When you are all going around the ring together, make sure you keep some open space around your horse. If everyone is bunching up, circle away to make some more room for yourself. Do not hold your horse back and make him tense, as this will restrict his pace. Let him stay in his natural rhythm and circle away to.make room.

If you are asked to give an individual test, remember that the aim is simply to demonstrate your horse's gaits, obedience and general way of going. Have something planned before you go in; do not do too much at the walk as this takes up so much time, and the judge will have had plenty of opportunity to view your horse at the walk already. Make sure you demonstrate the trot and canter on each rein. Keep your movements simple and smooth so that your horse is able to stay in a rhythm and in balance, and to show himself off to the best of his ability. Think of it as a short but sweet dressage test, using the same degree of accuracy and concentration in the show ring as you would in the dressage arena.

■ BREED CLASSES

Some classes are restricted to particular breeds so that the entrants can be judged on their trueness to type. Each breed of horse or pony should have certain characteristics that identify him as being true to type. These characteristics are listed by the appropriate breed society. Breed classes can be judged either as in-hand or under saddle classes and, once again, turnout, manners and conformation are the key criteria.

Some breeds have very specific traits that they are judged on; for example, the Tennessee Walking Horse on his walk.

If the class is ridden, you are expected to wear jodhpurs or breeches with the appropriate short or tall boots, a shirt and tie or stock, and a hunting, show or

■ ABOVE
Many of the bigger shows are held indoors, with classes going on late into the evening. Your horse will have to become accustomed to spotlights and a far more claustrophobic atmosphere than he will have experienced at an outdoor show.

■ LEFT
Many classes are judged in-hand, which means that the horse is led rather than ridden.

▮ LEFT
When showing in-hand your horse must be trained to trot quietly alongside you when required.

fences, a water ditch or a bank.

It is usual for each competitor to enter a "division" consisting of three or four classes, some of the classes will be over fences, while some will be "under saddle" or "on the flat."

Your horse may be judged on his overall performance, manners, soundness, suitability to purpose, turnout, and the quality and evenness of his gaits.

■ **EQUITATION CLASSES**

In other horse-show classes, called equitation classes, the rider's form and ability are judged. Equitation classes are usually divided by the age and the level of experience of the rider. There are equitation divisions for beginners of all ages right up to the highest levels for the most advanced competitors. In equitation classes, the judge may test the riders without stirrups and at the higher levels may ask riders for further individual tests that can range from verbal testing to changing horses with another rider.

hacking jacket. A helmet with a cover or a traditional velvet hat should be worn.

■ **TYPE CLASSES**

These classes are not restricted to breeds but to types of horse and pony. Within each type, the classes are often split by height or weight. The type of horse or pony might be regular hunter, pleasure, show hack, cob, three or five-gaited horse, ladies' horse, etc. The regular hunter

classes will probably be further divided into lightweight, middleweight and heavyweight, gaited horse classes may be divided by sex, while other classes are usually split according to height or age of rider.

The classes designated "working," such as the working hunter pony, involve the competitors completing a course of fences. These are usually rustic show jumps as opposed to solid cross-country fences, but may include a coop, brush

Breed classes are popular with many competitors. These Arab horses will be judged on their breed characteristics as well as their gaits, manners and general condition.

The judge may study your performance from a variety of angles.

Sometimes you will find yourself eligible for several different types of class. This young rider on her Welsh mountain pony can enter the lead-line class as well as the Welsh mountain-breed class.

▌ LEFT
Everybody loves to dress up—showing classes often offer the chance to compete in costumes.

▌ BELOW
Side-saddle riding is growing in popularity. Here Jennie Loriston-Clarke gives a superb side-saddle dressage display.

▌ BELOW
It takes a competent side-saddle rider to be able to jump well—note how this rider is giving her horse a good length of rein so that he is not restricted.

■ SIDE-SADDLE CLASSES

Riding side-saddle, as opposed to astride, used to be the only acceptable way for a lady to be seen on a horse, but, as competitive sports became more popular with both sexes, riding astride became the norm. However, the elegance and splendor of side-saddle riding have made a comeback in many countries, and shows are held specifically for side-saddle riders. Additionally, some lady riders of show hunters have enhanced their appearance and their prospects in the show ring by competing side-saddle against the majority of astride riders. Many riders take up side-saddle having ridden astride for years; others are taught to ride side-saddle in the first place—both approaches seem to be equally successful.

It is, however, an expensive sport in terms of the equipment needed—a side-saddle and riding habit will cost more than a conventional saddle and riding outfit. Second-hand equipment may prove even more expensive, as the more authentic saddles and habits are in great demand. But if you enjoy creating a real spectacle, there is nothing to beat the elegance of a well-turned-out side-saddle rider.

It takes a good horsewoman to jump successfully—too many seem unable to give their horses sufficient freedom of head and neck, but this is also true of a good many astride riders, male and female! Many ladies still hunt side-saddle, although, presumably for safety reasons, riders are not allowed to compete side-saddle in horse trials.

Although much to do with side-saddle riding is judged on turnout and overall appearance, some classes are judged on equitation, i.e. on how well you ride your horse. This is a popular class with those who have taken the trouble to learn to ride well, and who have schooled their horses carefully and skillfully.

▌ LEFT
Equitation classes are popular, as riders are judged on how well their horses perform for them rather than on how expensive or well bred they look.

Endurance or Long-distance Riding

▌ BELOW
The horse's weight is checked at the beginning and end of the ride so that the amount of condition he has lost can be judged.

There are two types of long-distance riding—endurance riding (which has FEI status) and trail riding. Trail riding does not involve racing—the idea is to complete the ride with your horse still in good condition. Trail rides vary from about 25 miles (40.25 km) to over 100 miles (160 km). Endurance riding does involve racing—it is a competition against the clock that tests the speed and stamina of the horse. It also tests the rider's horsemanship and judgment of pace, and of his or her horse's well-being. Each competition is split into a number of phases, each one being usually just under 25 miles (40 km) long. At the end of each phase the horse is checked by a veterinary surgeon for sores on his back or in his mouth, overreaches, and general well-being; his heart rate is monitored.

Competitions vary in length, but an international event that takes more than one day is usually over a minimum distance of 50–62 miles (80–100 km). A championship one-day competition usually covers nearly 100 miles (160 km)

The horse's pulse rate is monitored at intervals throughout a long-distance ride; the horse has to finish in good condition.

with a winning riding time of somewhere between ten and twelve hours.

■ DEVELOPMENT OF THE SPORT

For many centuries the horse has been used to transport man and his possessions over great distances. Most countries can boast feats of great endurance riding— there has always been someone who has wanted to go further than those before him on the back of a horse—but endurance riding as an organized competitive sport did not start in earnest until the 1950s.

Endurance riding today puts the horse's welfare first and foremost with strict veterinary checks. The organizers have the authority to eliminate any competitor whose horse shows signs of having had enough. Before this, some of the earliest long-distance races tested the horse's endurance to the limit, with equine contestants literally being ridden until they dropped. The care and attention lavished on today's endurance horses is some recompense for the suffering endured by the horses who gave their all in previous centuries.

Interest in competitive endurance riding spread most quickly in Europe and America. The first endurance rides were actually organized to demonstrate the suitability of different types of horses as cavalry mounts. It was in California in 1955 that competitive endurance riding started.

The endurance horse must learn to remain balanced, settled and in a rhythm, even on the lightest rein contact.

▮ RIGHT
All kinds of natural hazards have to be tackled.

TACTICS

To succeed as an endurance rider you will
need to be happy with your own company,
have a good rapport with your horse and
your back-up team, and an awareness of
winning tactics. Who is ahead of you, who
is behind you, are you keeping up with the
pace, how can you avoid overtiring your
horse, how can you help him if he does tire?
What is your strategy at the checkpoints and
the meeting points *en route* where your
horse is allowed to rest? Whose horse can
still put in a sprint for the finish, and how far
ahead of them do you need to be to make
sure you sprint over the line first?

▮ BELOW
**Endurance or long-
distance riding is
suitable for many
different types
of horses.**

Interest was sparked by the ride
undertaken by Wendall T. Robie and a
group of friends. They followed the old
mining and emigrant trails over 100 miles
(160 km) from Squaw Valley, through the
Sierra Nevada range and on to Auburn.
This trail became the world's first official
endurance ride, and was named the
Western States Trail Ride.

Today the popular sport of endurance
riding, which has been approved as an
international discipline since 1982, is
governed by the FEI.

■ THE ENDURANCE HORSE

The main requirements of any endurance
horse are that he has strong, dense bone,
strong, healthy hooves, and a willingness
and confidence to tackle whatever he is
faced with because he will encounter all
kinds of natural hazards on a long-
distance ride. He should have a light,
ground-covering action, and be balanced
and sure-footed over all manner of
terrain. He should be trained to settle into
a steady trot or canter when required, and
should accept a loose rein with minimal
contact. A calm temperament means he
will take less out of himself.

EQUIPMENT AND
BACK-UP TEAM

A special gel pad is essential under the
saddle to reduce the risk of any rubbing or
bruising, and purpose-designed endurance
saddles can be purchased. Stock or
Western-type saddles are popular as far as
rider comfort is concerned. Many horses are
ridden in hackamores (bitless bridles) to
reduce the risk of sores or bruising, but
these take practice and skill to use.

A good back-up team of between one and
three helpers is essential during an endurance
competition. They, as well as you, must be
able to map read so that you all follow the
same route and arrive at the same meeting
points. They carry and provide everything that
horse and rider may need along the way—
food, water, clothing, spare tack (especially
pads and girths, as these may need changing
several times during a ride), spare horseshoes,
a first-aid kit, a tack-repair kit, a flashlight,
and a grooming kit and towels.

Western Riding

Western riding is predominant in countries where the horse is still used to work cattle, such as America, Argentina, Australia, New Zealand and parts of Africa. It also has a growing following in other countries where riders are keen to enjoy the experience of riding a light, balanced, responsive horse, along with the novelty of trying many of the Western riding skills.

■ **WHAT IS WESTERN RIDING?**

America is the home of Western riding, which developed directly from the needs of the early pioneers. They depended on horses for their survival—for transport, for hunting food, and later for herding and

managing vast herds of cattle. They had to be able to sit comfortably, for very long hours, in the saddle. They also needed horses who were both fast and responsive and yet also calm and easy to handle. The

skills that horse and rider had to learn in order to earn a living in those times form the basis of the Western-riding competitions held today.

In Western riding you adopt a longer leg position than is usual for general riding. The reins are held in one hand, leaving the other free to rope cattle, fire a gun etc, and the horse is controlled mainly by the seat and weight, rather than by hand and leg. A Western horse is not ridden in an outline. He carries himself in a relaxed, but light and balanced manner, with his rider keeping the reins virtually slack. The weight of the reins is used as an aid, rather than the contact with the horse's mouth.

Western-riding competitions test everything from how the horse feels to

■ ABOVE
In Western riding it is the seat and weight distribution of the rider that are used to control the horse, rather than the hand and leg as is usual in English riding.

■ LEFT
Western tack is designed to offer comfort, practicality and security to riders spending many hours in the saddle.

EQUIPMENT NEEDED

Many riders simply enjoy riding in the Western style—hacking or long-distance riding—without going as far as competing.

A Western or stock-type saddle adds authenticity and comfort to the proceedings but is not essential during the training of horse and rider. Similarly, a standard bridle and bit can be used, rather than the simpler Western-style bridle which may or may not be bitless. But once Western tack is used, no doubt you will want to be properly decked out too. Cowboy boots, which have a raised, supported instep and a higher heel than a standard riding boot, along with a pair of long, leather chaps are the two essentials.

■ RIGHT
In cattle-cutting competitions the horse has first to "cut" a selected calf out from the rest of the herd, and then to prevent the selected animal from rejoining the herd. This Quarter Horse is using his own "cattle sense" rather than his rider's instructions to keep the calf he is facing from joining the herd behind him.

ride, his ability to perform complex reining exercises and his skill at cutting out and controlling cattle, to his ability to race around barrel, or bend poles. There are World and European Championship titles to be won, as well as numerous regional and national events to compete in.

Many Western riders get caught up in the whole Western phenomenon. As well as learning the ridden style they may also practice other "Wild West" skills, such as trick roping, whip cracking, knife and axe throwing, as well as the fast draw and gun spinning. It is amazing what sitting in a Western saddle can do to the imagination of even the most retiring rider!

■ THE WESTERN RIDING HORSE

Any horse can be converted to Western riding, but not all horses will have the temperament or inherent traits for all the Western-style competitions. The American Quarter Horse is a popular and successful choice—he has the speed, stamina, agility, intelligence and in-bred "cattle sense" to succeed. Other American types, such as the Appaloosa, the Paint horse and the Pinto also feature strongly. But any horse with natural balance and agility, who can be taught to respond to weight and seat aids rather than being held between hand and leg as is usual in English-style riding, can be taught Western skills.

■ SKILLS REQUIRED

As a rider you must have good balance, the patience to build a rapport with your horse, which allows your commands to appear invisible to the onlooker and, if you are to become involved in cattle-handling skills, the overall fitness and

In Western riding the horse is expected to be versatile and cooperative. At the Cowboy Ski Challenge in Jackson Hole, Wyoming, the horse demonstrates his ability to carry out any number of duties, from providing the power for the skiers...

■ RIGHT
...to showing how essential they were to the survival of the early pioneers.

■ BELOW AND BELOW RIGHT
The sliding stop is one of the most dramatic Western-riding skills. The horse wears special skid boots to protect his fetlocks and to aid the slide.

toughness that these require. For most Western showing classes, the horse has to be taught the jog and the lope—these are basically a slow, smooth trot and canter. These gaits were developed for rider comfort and to reduce wear and tear on the horse's legs and joints. For most equestrian disciplines, the horse is trained to put spring and elevation into his paces, but for Western riding the paces are smooth and flat, with less knee and hock action than normal. Other classes require the horse to be taught various Western moves—the rollback, which is a fast 180° turn, the spin or pirouette, which is a 360° turn, the side pass (lateral work), the rein

▌ LEFT
The spin is one of the many Western skills that the horse has to learn.

back, the sliding stop, and the flying change.

■ SHOWING CLASSES

These are the easiest Western classes to train for and take part in.

▌ The **Western Pleasure** class is the simplest. The horse is judged on how much of a pleasure he is to ride. He must work at all gaits on both reins, with the rider keeping the reins in one hand and a minimal contact. He is judged on how smooth his gaits and transitions are, and on how calm and responsive he is to his rider's commands.

▌ The **Trail** class tests the horse's ability to cope calmly with the sorts of hazards he might encounter when riding the trail. There are a number of tasks you and he will have to perform in the ring, such as opening and closing a gate, backing through or around an obstacle, and jumping some logs. You may have to carry an object, and your horse may have to allow himself to be hobbled (tied up) on his own.

▌ The **Western Riding** class imitates some of the tasks a ranch horse might have to carry out. The horse must demonstrate a good walk, jog and lope, and may have to tackle various tasks or obstacles similar to those also found in the trail class.

▌ The **Reining** class tests some of the most advanced Western-riding techniques. The horse demonstrates at speed a pattern of various Western movements—turns, circles, spins, flying changes, rollbacks and sliding stops. All of these movements are performed from the lope—the slow, smooth canter.

■ CATTLE-HANDLING CLASSES

These require more extensive practice, training and facilities than the Western showing classes.

▌ In the **Cutting Horse** class, the rider indicates to a judge which calf he is going to separate from the herd. The calf has to be "cut out" from the herd and driven out into the arena. The rider must then adopt

a loose rein and leave the job of preventing the calf from rejoining the herd to the horse. The cutting horse must be fast, athletic, brave and clever. The ability to outwit and outperform the calf is called "cow sense" and is thought by many to be an inherited trait, rather than an acquired skill.

▌ The **Working Cow Horse** class is judged in two sections: first the horse performs a reining pattern which demonstrates the various Western movements, and then he has to hold, maneuver and control a cow within the arena, turning it several times as well as driving it along a fence line.

▌ **Barrel Racing** is a fast, furious, grown-up version of that most popular of mounted games, the bending race! Horse and rider race around a course of barrels—they are allowed to touch the barrels but not to knock them over.

▌ Other competitions, such as **Steer Wrestling** and **Calf Roping**, demonstrate and test the skills still required by the working cow pony and rider.

Vaulting

■ BELOW
Vaulting teams are often called upon to give displays at various shows.

The sport of vaulting is probably most simply described as gymnastics on horseback. Although it is now recognized as an international sport, governed by the FEI since 1982, it developed from an early teaching method that was used to accustom novice riders to the movement of the horse, and to instill a sense of balance and confidence.

Cavalry schools in particular used vaulting exercises to teach new recruits to develop their balance while the horse was in motion. Vaulting also served as a good fitness and strengthening exercise for riders, as well as giving them confidence when on horseback.

■ **SKILLS REQUIRED**

If you wish to be a vaulter you will need to have good natural balance, be naturally athletic and have an air of grace and elegance. The sport also requires confidence—it takes a brave person to carry out many of the exercises with poise.

The horse needs to be quiet-natured, strong, unflappable and able to hold a steady, rhythmic, balanced canter on the lunge throughout the exercise.

The main disadvantage of the sport is that the vaulter always requires help—someone has to be on hand to lunge the horse and, unless you are to compete only as an individual, you will need a partner or even a full team of eight to work with. Riders interested in vaulting therefore really need to join a club, although much of the actual gymnastic work can be practiced on a wooden horse.

■ **THE COMPETITIONS**

International vaulting competitions are made up of team, individual and pair

■ FAR LEFT
Vaulting competitors need time to warm up in the same way as other gymnasts.

■ LEFT
The wooden horse is used for warming-up exercises as well as for practicing set movements.

classes. The upper age limit for team vaulters is eighteen, but there is no upper age limit for individuals. A team comprises eight vaulters, one horse and one lunger, and a reserve vaulter. Both the individual and the team competitions include a compulsory and a free-style test.

The horse always works on the left rein, at a canter, and must complete a circle of no less than 42½ feet (13 m) in diameter.

There are two classes of international competition—CVI one star, and CVI two star. The World Championship is held every two years, and there are also intercontinental championships, including classes for all-male, all-female and mixed teams.

DISPLAY TEAMS

As well as taking part in competitions, vaulting teams are now often called upon to provide displays at shows and exhibitions. Such demonstrations are certainly an exciting, elegant and colorful way in which to entertain a crowd of spectators.

▌ ABOVE
It takes a good athlete to maintain the grace, poise and balance of a gymnast while on a moving horse.

▌ LEFT
The team horse must maintain a consistent rhythm throughout all the exercises.

Polo

Of all the team ball games played on horseback, polo is the most widely played and recognized. The sport of polo carries an unashamedly glamorous image. It has always been expensive to take part in, mainly because of the string of ponies that is needed if you are to be a professional player. Despite the growing number of polo clubs, and the opportunities for children to learn to play provided by the Pony Club, polo remains an expensive sport, the greatest opportunities being open to the wealthy or the very talented.

Polo is thought to have originated in Persia about two-and-a-half thousand years ago. Its popularity spread to China, Japan, Tibet and Manipur, where British soldiers learned the game and wrote home about it. Soldiers in England started playing their own version based on the description they had been given, and British settlers took the game to Argentina. The late 1800s and early 1900s saw the foundation of many polo clubs, including London's Hurlingham, which was the first in the Western world. Hurlingham's rules later became universal. Polo is now played all over the world.

■ LEFT
Polo is only too happy to flaunt its reputation for wealth and glamour. Spectators gather at the Palm Beach Polo Club.

■ THE GAME

Polo is played on a grass—or snow—field that is 901 feet (274 m) long by 600 feet (183 m) wide. Most of the field is framed with low boards to help keep the ball in play, and there is a goal at either end, 24½ feet (7.5 m) wide. Indoor polo is also growing in popularity.

There are four players on each team, each of whom has a specific role. The Number One is the front player; his job is to play well up the field to take forward passes and to shoot at the goal. When he is not in a position to score, he tries to keep the opposing team's back player (their Number Four) away from the goal so that one of his teammates may have a chance to score.

The Number Two is another front player; he is usually the most influential attacking player. He works closely with his Number One to keep moving the ball up the field to maximize their chances of taking a shot at the goal.

The Number Three player is the link between the two forward and the back. He is central in turning the play back from defense to attack and must be an extremely versatile player, able to defend, attack and score. He is usually the strongest and most experienced player in the team and is often the captain.

EQUIPMENT NEEDED

To play polo you must be properly dressed—breeches, long boots, helmet with optional face guard, and knee protectors. You will also need your own polo mallets.

You must have at least two ponies—there is no longer a height restriction but polo mounts are still referred to as ponies. The rules insist that ponies wear standing martingales and that they have their tails tied up so that there is no risk of them becoming caught up in anything. The polo pony needs to be brave, responsive, quick-thinking, agile, fast and tough.

■ LEFT
Practice makes perfect. Even the most complex shots can be practiced without getting on a horse—at least not a real one.

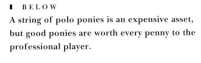

▐ LEFT
Polo ponies need to be as alert and enthusiastic as their riders—and often quicker thinking.

▐ BELOW
A string of polo ponies is an expensive asset, but good ponies are worth every penny to the professional player.

▐ BELOW
Polo originated in far hotter climates than these, but continues as a winter sport in St. Moritz.

▐ BOTTOM
Polo ponies have their legs protected by thick bandages during play.

The Number Four is the back player; his main task is to defend the goal but he must also be a good hitter, able to send the ball long and hard up the field to give his forward a chance of attacking the goal.

A full polo match is divided into six seven-minute periods called chukkas. One pony should only ever be used for two chukkas per game, and should never have to play two consecutive chukkas.

Each player uses a mallet (a bamboo stick with a wooden head) to drive the ball down the field to the opposition's goal. The opposing team is obviously doing its utmost to prevent any progress down the field and to turn the ball back so they can drive for a goal of their own.

All polo players are given a handicap—this varies between -2 goals and +10 goals. The handicap indicates the player's value to the team, not the actual number of goals he has or is expected to score. Teams are given overall handicaps that dictate at which level they play—high goal, medium, intermediate or low goal.

■ SKILLS REQUIRED

To succeed as a polo player you should be quick-thinking, fit, have very good co-ordination and balance, be physically and mentally tough and have good anticipation of how the game is going to proceed.

There are four main playing strokes to be mastered, as well as another eight subsidiary strokes. The four main strokes are the off-side forehander, off-side backhander, near-side forehander and near-side backhander. These strokes can be practiced on a wooden horse as well as on your pony. Would-be players spend many hours simply "stick and balling," i.e. cantering up and down a field, hitting a shot, chasing the ball and trying another stroke—up and down, again and again gradually getting a better result every time.

The rules of polo are quite complex and the game itself is fast moving, with the direction of play changing all the time. As a player you need to have an intimate understanding of the rules, as well as a continual awareness of where everyone is in relation to the direction of play.

Horseball

Horseball is for those who enjoy a real contact sport—it resembles a cross between rugby football and basketball played on horseback. There are two teams of four players. The ball is about the size of a football and has leather loops sewn to it to use as handholds. The ball is thrown between the players and can be pulled from your opponents' hands, but if it drops to the ground it must be picked up without dismounting: riders have to bend down and scoop the ball up off the ground by grabbing hold of the leather loops. Whenever a rider is retrieving the ball off the ground, the other riders have to keep a distance as a safety precaution; otherwise they are offsides. The stirrups are tied together under the horse's belly, making it easier for the rider to reach down.

A goal is scored by throwing the ball through a suspended loop that has a net attached to it. The game is started, and restarted after a goal, by a throw-in similar to that used in rugby. The ball is tossed in the air between two riders who each strive to grab it first. The game can be played

■ LEFT
Horseball has grown rapidly in popularity in recent years, as a game for both adults and children.

■ BELOW LEFT
The ball is moved rapidly down the arena toward the goal. In order to score, the ball has to be thrown through a high loop with a net attached.

EQUIPMENT NEEDED

The joy of playing horseball is that the equipment required for the sport is cheap and simple. The ball can be made by having leather loops sewn to a soccer ball and the goal can be made from a kind of post, using a hoop and a net. If you are going to play bareback, whoever sews the loops to your ball can also be asked to sew handholds to a surcingle, which will hold a saddle pad in place on the horse's back and give you some security.

indoors or outdoors, and is a sport enjoyed by both adults and children.

Because the ball can only travel as far and as fast as you can throw it, horseball does not require the same speed from its contestants as, say, polo. For this reason any horse or pony who is well behaved in company, i.e. can be trusted not to kick or nip an opposing pony or rider, and who is reasonably well schooled, can be introduced to the game.

The greatest advantage of horseball is that, because the equipment is relatively cheap and easy to make, it is ideal as a fun, impromptu game for a group of friends on horseback. At the other extreme it can be played fast, furious and mean by teams with their hearts set on regional and national championship glory.

PONY CLUB HORSEBALL

The Pony Club adopted the game with enthusiasm, as the organizers could see its potential as a fun way of improving riding skills and confidence. To make it additionally beneficial as a training exercise, at Pony Club level horseball is played bareback. You sit on a saddle pad held in place with a surcingle which has two handholds. When you have to reach down to scoop the ball off the ground, you can use the handholds to help keep your balance. To ensure that the ponies don't get pulled in the mouth, you have to drop the reins when you catch the ball.

Polocrosse

Polocrosse is based on the mounted game of polo and on lacrosse, a ball game that is played on foot. While polo originated in the Far East and lacrosse in North America, both were introduced to Europe by returning servicemen and travelers. Polocrosse was first played in 1932 in London. It was used as an exercise to encourage better riding skills and was originally played by teams of two, indoors. It quickly developed into a four-man team

EQUIPMENT AND SKILLS NEEDED

To play polocrosse you need one horse and a polocrosse racket. The only other necessary equipment is protective boots and bandages for your horse's legs. All kinds of horses and ponies play the game, from Shetland ponies to thoroughbreds, making it a good family game. You need to have a safe and secure seat in the saddle; beyond that, it is just a case of practicing your catching and throwing skills, which can be done on the ground as well as mounted.

each chukka so that only three of the six team members are on the field at one time. The game is played on a large area slightly bigger than a rugby field. The field is divided by penalty lines over which the ball must not be carried—the player must either bounce and retrieve it, or throw it to a teammate.

There is a goal at each end consisting of two poles 8 feet (2.5 m) apart. The ball must be thrown between these in order to score. Only the Number One player is allowed to shoot at goal. The defending Number Three player is allowed in the goal-scoring area to protect the goal and to tackle the attacking Number One. The Number Two players are only allowed in the midfield area.

▌ BELOW
Many younger riders are introduced to team ball games on horseback by the Pony Club. Polocrosse is a popular alternative to polo, although the Pony Club fields many high-quality polo teams as well.

outdoor game. In 1938, an Australian couple who watched the game in England took the idea back home with them to Australia, where it became the fast and exciting game that it is today. Polocrosse is played in many different countries around the world, and there are numerous inter-club championships as well as a World Championship.

■ THE GAME

Polocrosse is played between two teams of six, all of whom are equipped with a long-handled racket that has a net on the end of it. A soft rubber ball is the object of play; it is caught in the net of the racket and passed between players by throwing or bouncing it.

The game is split into six chukkas, each lasting for eight minutes. Each team is divided into two and they alternate for

Driving

Horses and ponies are well designed for the task of pulling a vehicle of some kind or other. Remember that a horse has to be taught how to rearrange his balance and posture in order to carry a rider, whereas pulling something comes more naturally.

Driving is a lot of fun—although many riders find it more nerve-racking than riding—and it can be undertaken in as simple or elaborate a way as desire and finances allow.

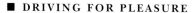

■ DRIVING FOR PLEASURE

Many a family pony has been converted from riding to driving once the children have outgrown him. Given a patient and common-sense approach, most horses and ponies of an equable nature will convert to driving; many even show a preference for it, though there are always exceptions.

The first stage in training a driving horse is to accustom him to wearing blinkers. He should be lunged and long reined in these, and finally hacked out in them. After that, introduce him to the rest of the harness. The next stage involves

▌ ABOVE
The second phase of driving trials is the marathon, in which competitors cover a set route following various roads and tracks. This phase incorporates a hazards section where cross-country-type obstacles have to be negotiated.

▌ LEFT
In show-ring driving the overall turnout and performance of the competitors is judged. This smart little Welsh mountain pony is creating a good all-around impression in the ring.

getting him to pull something safe, such as an old tire. It is not the weight of what he is pulling that is likely to bother him, but his awareness of something following behind him and the noise it makes. Once he is comfortable with this he is well on the way to being introduced to a simple cart of some sort. Straightforward as it all sounds, experienced help should always be sought in the training process.

Driving clubs will provide a social dimension to a leisure activity that can otherwise be quite a solitary one.

■ COMPETITION DRIVING

The world of competition driving revolves around the show ring and driving trials. Show-ring driving follows a similar format to ridden showing classes; driving trials resemble ridden horse trials and consist of three disciplines—a dressage test, a marathon and an obstacle competition.

In show-ring driving, the full turnout of horse or pony, his harness, the cart, the furnishings and the appearance of the driver and groom are all judged, as well as the behavior and way of going of the whole team. Competing in driving trials requires far more time, practice and equipment than show-ring driving.

Harness racing, which involves specially bred trotters or pacers pulling a lightweight racing cart, is another specialty sport that attracts a great spectator following. The horses can travel at a tremendous speed at the trot, and race each other around an oval track. The

▌ OPPOSITE
For competition
purposes a team
of four is about as
complicated as you
want to get, but horses
can be driven in larger
teams than this.

▌ BELOW
Driving horses and ponies, and the vehicles they
pull, come in all manner of shapes and sizes, and
can be driven in different ways. This pair of ponies
is being driven abreast.

▌ BELOW
This pair is being driven in tandem, i.e. one behind the
other.

necessary equipment is relatively
inexpensive, as the carts are lightweight
and basic in design, but it is a fiercely
competitive sport.

SHOW-RING DRIVING CLASSES
▌ In **Private Driving** classes the
competitors may be sent off for a drive
around the surrounding roads with the
judge following in a car to see how they
react and behave.

▌ **Light Trade** classes are for horse-drawn
vehicles that were, or still are, used for
trade purposes, such as deliveries of
goods. An additional requirement in these
classes is for the horses to stand still
unattended, which they would have to do
while their goods were being unloaded.

▌ The **Concour d'Elegance** class is judged
more on overall poise than on close detail.

▌ **Scurry Driving** is a popular class at many
British shows. Pairs of ponies, which must
be either 12hh and under, or between
12hh and 14.2hh, are harnessed to small,
four-wheeled vehicles carrying a driver
and groom. They race around an obstacle
course marked out by cones, which
involves tight turns and high speeds and a
lot of noise from the spectators. Any cones
knocked over are penalized by adding
extra seconds to the overall race time. The
groom has to play a very active role—

leaning out to either side to help maintain
the vehicle's balance as it swings around
the corners.

▌ Additional show-ring classes include the
likes of **Drive and Ride** competitions and
Heavy Horse classes. There may also be
the opportunity to put on a display to
entertain the public.

DRIVING TRIALS
▌ For the first phase, you have to perform
a simple dressage test within the confines
of a large arena; this is given a score based

Water is a popular hazard in driving trials. This pair
of ponies is negotiating a simple water crossing with
great enthusiasm.

on the performance and on the overall
presentation.

▌ The marathon, which comes next,
involves covering approximately 15½ miles
(25 km) in about two hours. There are five
different sections and two compulsory ten-
minute breaks.

– The first section can be completed at
any gait but trotting is usually sufficient to
make the time.

– The second section must be
performed at a walk and is followed by a
ten-minute rest.

– The third section usually involves
a stretch of more arduous terrain, and
a fast trot is required to make the time;
cantering is not allowed.

– The fourth section is another walk
section, followed by a ten-minute break.

– With the fifth section the excitement
really begins. This involves negotiating
various man-made or natural hazards at
speed, as this section is timed.

▌ The final phase is the obstacle or cone-
driving competition. This tests the horses'
obedience and the driver's ability to drive
accurately between sets of cones that mark
out the course. Once again, this section is
timed.

▌ The overall winner is the one with the
best combined score over the three
different phases.

Jumping Sports

Jumping requires confidence, rhythm and balance. Once you have a fair degree of these three skills you can start to discover the world of jumping sports. Show jumping offers competitions for fun as well as for fortune seekers, and provides an excellent and safe way to practice your jumping skills and gain experience. Once you feel confident about show jumps—which fall down if you hit them—you may want to try your hand at jumping solid obstacles. Hunting and hunter trials provide you with the opportunity to do this— and when you are feeling confident enough you can progress to team chasing or eventing. For the brave and robust there is race riding—the ultimate way to jump at speed.

▌ OPPOSITE
Hunter trials are an excellent way of introducing horse and rider to the more demanding sport of eventing. This pair is showing sufficient confidence and style to be ready to move onto greater things.

▌ LEFT
Point to pointing and race riding offer the ultimate thrill of jumping at speed. Despite the speed factor this horse has maintained a good shape and technique over the fence. All too often jumping technique is sacrificed in pursuit of sheer speed.

Hunting

There is little to beat the exhilaration of riding fast cross-country. You and your horse must tackle whatever is thrown in your way—balancing your horse over all kinds of terrain with the wind making your eyes stream, mud splattered in your face, encouraging him over every manner of obstacle, letting him jump out of his stride and land running, looking eagerly ahead for the next challenge.

The thrill of the chase as experienced when hunting on horseback usually succeeds in lifting the spirits and the courage of all horsemen and women. The hedge that you sailed over effortlessly when running behind hounds may look completely unjumpable when viewed in cold blood. Hunting, for many, provides an opportunity to tackle much greater challenges than they might otherwise contemplate. There is neither judge nor

▌ **A B O V E**
Hunting etiquette requires that you and your mount are smartly and tidily turned out. Your horse's or pony's mane should be braided, your tack should be gleaming, and you should be turned out in clean jodhpurs, boots and jacket.

▌ **B E L O W**
The hounds are controlled by a huntsman; he is usually assisted by a whipper-in who helps to keep the hounds together as a pack.

winner, except in the hearts and minds of those taking part. You can be sure that even the mildest-mannered horseman may suddenly feel the desire to ride his way to the head of the field when inspired by the sweet music of hounds.

■ DIFFERENT TYPES OF HUNTING
HUNTING QUARRY

Ever since man learned to ride a horse he has used the horse's speed and agility to his advantage, including in his hunt for food. Today, hunting on horseback is a country sport rather than a means of survival. It also has a valuable role to play in the conservation of the countryside and in the management of the wildlife it hunts.

A wide variety of animals is hunted from horseback around the world. The most common ones are the fox and stag in

▌ LEFT
You are never too young or too old to go hunting.
Many children are taken out, and an abundance of
youthful seniors still hunt regularly.

England and Ireland, the wild boar in other parts of Europe, and the coyote in North America and parts of Africa. The hunting of any of these animals relies on the cooperation and permission of the landowners whose property is crossed.

Packs of hounds are bred and trained to pick up the scent and track down the hunted animal. The hounds are controlled by a huntsman and whipper-in, who are the only people actively involved in the work of the hounds. The hunt followers, or "field," as they are often known, are sometimes helpful in observing the whereabouts of the hounds or the direction the hunted quarry has taken, but their main role is to help pay for the upkeep of the hunt's hounds, horses and hunting country. In return for an annual subscription and a "cap"—an additional donation to hunt funds made on the day of the hunt—the hunt follower enjoys seeing hounds at work and the thrill of the chase.

In fox hunting, after a convivial half an hour or so at the meet, the huntsman heads off with the hounds to the first cover. This is usually a piece of woodland or scrubland where a fox is likely to be found. The field follow, led by the field master whose instructions you must obey at all times—and whom you should avoid overtaking! The hounds are "cast" into the cover, i.e. sent in to hunt around until they find the scent of the fox. Some days are good scenting days and the hounds can easily follow the scent; other days are not so good.

Once the hounds are on the scent of their quarry, they will follow it across all manner of country. The mounted followers keep up as best they can, the bravest and most talented jumping everything in their path, the rest finding a way around the

edges of fields, through gates and along roads. A good knowledge of the local countryside helps in the task of keeping up with the hounds. If you are crossing country that has been planted with crops, only the hounds and huntsman are allowed to take the direct line after the prey. The field have to find a way around that minimizes any damage to the crops; an intimate knowledge of your surroundings makes this easier. Etiquette demands that you follow the lead of the field master, but after a good run behind hounds the field often gets split up and strung out, and it is up to you to find the hounds again.

The hounds will either succeed in catching their prey or they will lose track

▌ LEFT
Whether you are
hunting foxes, coyote,
rabbit, or with drag or
bloodhounds, nothing
very exciting happens
until the hounds pick
up the appropriate
scent and set off.

▮ LEFT

Out hunting there will always be those who want to jump obstacles and those who want to go around them. The choice is yours, but should be based on an appreciation of ability—yours and your mount's—rather than on pride.

of it, or may have to be called off if the fox crosses land that the hunt doesn't have permission to cross. In any case, the hounds are taken to another cover to see if they can pick up the scent of another fox, and so it goes on.

Most hunt meets are organized for mid-morning, and hunting continues until late in the afternoon. At about lunchtime "second horses" are arranged. This means that the huntsman, whipper-in and master will change to fresh horses who have been brought to a prearranged point. Their first horses are taken home, washed and dried off, blanketed, fed and stabled. Hunt followers may also change to second horses if they have another horse and have been able to organize someone to deliver it for them.

While hunting is a thrilling way of enjoying cross-country riding, it carries a lot of risks because there is no time to check out what you are about to jump. Many a horse and rider have fallen when, having taken off over what looks like an innocuous hedge, they see in mid-air that there is a wire or timber fence running alongside it on the far side. A quick-thinking, focused horse can usually get himself out of such a muddle, but only with experience, which can be painful in the making.

DRAG HUNTING

This involves a pack of hounds and mounted followers but, instead of hunting a live quarry, the hounds follow a trail that has been laid earlier in the day by someone dragging a bag laced with a strong scent that the hounds have been taught to pick up and follow.

Drag hunting gives you the chance to ride fast cross-country, behind hounds. It is safer and more predictable than hunting live quarry because you are following a pre-set course. The jumps will be either safe, natural features or man-made fences. A knowledge of the country is not necessary, as the course the hounds take is predetermined. Many hunts offer days specifically for the novice or nervous, when they will make sure the jumps encountered are smaller than usual.

Subscriptions from the field help to pay for the upkeep of the hounds and kennels.

BLOODHOUNDS

Hunting with bloodhounds is another form of drag hunting. This time the hounds are following the scent of a man

EQUIPMENT NEEDED

Your horse should be well turned out with his mane braided. He will need a good, strong set of tack, as a good-quality saddle and bridle will add to your own safety. Hunting entails long hours in the saddle, often in bad weather conditions. The last thing you want is for a rein or stirrup leather to snap when you are in the middle of nowhere, riding at a flat-out gallop and heading for a large and solid post-and-rail fence!

Put an especially good saddle pad under the saddle to make it more comfortable for the horse and to reduce the risk of him being rubbed.

Whether or not your horse wears boots to protect his legs is a matter of personal choice. Your horse's legs are at great risk of being knocked or scratched out hunting, but many boots, once they are wet and muddy and have been worn for several hours, start to rub anyway. You will need to decide which is the lesser of two evils.

As a rider you are expected to be smartly turned out. You should wear traditional-colored breeches or jodphurs, teamed with either tall riding boots or short jodhpur boots. You must wear either a hacking jacket (tweed jacket) or a plain blue or black jacket. A helmet with a black velvet cover should be worn and this should have a well-fitting safety harness. If you wear a hacking jacket it is correct to wear a shirt and colored stock tie (similar to a cravat or broad neck tie) held in place with a stock pin. A plain white stock tie should be worn with a blue or black jacket.

Gloves should be worn and a stick carried. You should carry in your pockets some good, thick string, such as baling twine, and a folding jackknife so that you can help make repairs to any gates or fences that get broken by the less able jumpers in the field. A day's hunting can end up being a very long day—find room in your pockets for a couple of

sandwiches or a bar of chocolate to keep you going.

If you are going to hunt a lot, a hunting whip and a pair of wire cutters are worth buying. A hunting whip is a shaped cane with a long leather lash on the end. The cane is useful for helping you to open and shut gates, and the lash, if let down so that it hangs by your horse's legs, can be used to prevent hounds from going right underneath your horse where they are more likely to get kicked or trampled. A leather carrying pouch can be fitted to your saddle in which to put a pair of wire cutters. No matter how diligent you are, when you are crossing unknown country it is possible to get caught up in one of the hazards of agriculture—wire netting or barbed wire. A pair of wire cutters is invaluable to cut your own horse free or to help anyone else unfortunate enough to be caught.

BOTTOM
At the end of a long, hard day's hunting the field is greatly diminished. It is one of the most satisfying feelings in the world to be among the few left at the end of the day.

BELOW
Ladies traditionally only rode side-saddle, and the elegant picture it creates is one reason for a growing number of people returning to the habit.

who sets off some time before the hunt starts. The runner will follow a previously agreed trail, making this form of hunting as safe as drag hunting. You might find the thought of a pack of bloodhounds bearing down on a fleeing man alarming, but they will not harm him when they catch him. He will most likely be smothered in wet, warm licks by his friendly canine pursuers.

SKILLS REQUIRED

Hunting suits all types of horse and pony—it seems to inspire the less cautious to be even braver, but it can also cause a great deal of overexcitement. It is important to have developed a reasonably strong and secure seat and to be able to balance your horse in order to help him tackle the varied terrain and obstacles that you will encounter. Whether you are riding around a cross-country course or are genuinely crossing the country out hunting, the approach to jumping is the same: Keep the horse balanced and in a rhythm. Keep in contact with the horse with your legs, seat and hands so that you can help balance him as he negotiates the unexpected.

Those brave and able enough to jump everything in their path will take the most direct line, following the lead of the field master. But there are plenty of others who will find their way around as best they can so as not to have to jump too much. Consider your own riding ability and the experience of your horse before deciding which party to join. When you do get the chance to jump, always give your horse room to see what it is you want him to do. Don't follow blindly behind the horse in front—your horse will not be able to judge the fence and, if the horse and rider in front fall or refuse, you will have a

problem. In a crowded gateway, or if there are several riders waiting to jump a narrow fence, slow your horse down well beforehand, so that you don't run into the back of everyone else. Wait your turn and give your horse room to make a good, balanced approach, and the chance to see what the fence involves.

Your horse needs to be fit, as he will be required to gallop and jump, often with little chance to rest. He should be well mannered; he must accept other horses all around him. If you have even the slightest suspicion that he may panic or kick out, keep him out of the crowd. It is your responsibility to prevent your horse from hurting anyone else. A young or inexperienced horse should be introduced quietly to the hunting field. It is often a good idea to avoid the first hour of the meet when all the horses are fresh and excited, and perhaps join the hunt later in the day. Keep the horse moving and thinking forward but do not allow him to get caught up in the crowd of the field until he is used to all the sights and sounds. It is considered an unforgivable sin to let your horse kick a hound, so be constantly aware of where the hounds are in relation to your horse. Keep his hindquarters turned away from the hounds if they approach or pass by you.

In the excitement of the chase do not overlook your horse's well-being. At all times, keep in mind how tired he might really be—horses get very caught up in the excitement of the chase and may not appear to be tired, as their excitement and adrenaline gives them additional stamina. But this should not be abused—think of how fit your horse really is, and how much galloping and jumping he has done. Do not keep him out for too long—there will always be another day. Think responsibly about what you ask him to jump. Never be tempted to jump wire—find a gate instead. Look out too for hazards such as rabbit holes and discarded farm machinery.

Hunter Trials and Team Chasing

For those who want to be judged on their cross-country riding skills, there is the option of competing in hunter trials and team chases. In a hunter trial you may ride the course as an individual or as one of a pair. In team chasing there are four team members to motivate each other.

In hunter trials you are expected to tackle a course of cross-country fences, the height of which varies depending on the class you enter. Some competitions cater to lead-line riders, others offer a range of classes with fences varying from about 2 feet 6 inches to 3 feet 9 inches. The organizers decide upon an optimum time, which is based on horse and rider tackling the course at what is commonly described as a fair hunting pace. Within the course there is usually an additional timed section that often includes a gate that has to be opened and shut—not jumped! The winners are the horse and rider who jump clear and complete the course nearest to the optimum time—which is not revealed to the riders until after the competition. If more than one rider finishes on the optimum time, the winner is the fastest one through the timed section.

■ ABOVE
Water is one of the most common problems encountered at a hunter trial. There is no reason why it should be feared provided it is introduced quietly and calmly. This pony looks a bit tentative and needs to gain more confidence before he is likely to tackle water with enthusiasm.

■ BELOW LEFT
Hunter trials offer a huge variety of challenges for all ages and abilities. Even lead-line riders can take part, provided their helpers are as agile as their ponies!

■ **SKILLS REQUIRED**
The main difference between hunting and competing in a hunter trial is that at a hunter trial you have to jump alone and in cold blood. You do not have the rush and excitement of hounds running and the rest of the field following to give you confidence. You and your horse have to be prepared to jump for the fun of it, although some classes are open to pairs,

■ LEFT
Cross-country riding is tiring for both horse and rider, but it is always a kind and correct gesture to dismount and lead your horse or pony once you have pulled up over the finish line.

■ BELOW
This horse and rider have both taken a good soaking at the water hazard, but the joy of team chasing is that, provided the rest of the team got through, there is still a chance of winning. It just means there is little consolation for the faller—his team will have galloped away into the distance!

■ LEFT
Competing as a pair is a good way of introducing an inexperienced or nervous horse or rider to the thrill of cross-country riding, as they can gain confidence from their partners.

Once you are up to speed it is a case of staying in that rhythm and keeping the horse balanced.

■ TEAM CHASING

Team chases are held over a variety of different-sized cross-country courses. Teams of four riders set off around the course, and progress is timed from the moment a team sets off to the moment the third rider crosses the line. So if one member of your team is left behind you still have a chance of winning.

The winning team is the one whose first three riders complete the course in the fastest time. Penalties are not given for falls or refusals—it is all judged on speed. For this reason the number of falls can be quite high. If the lead horse falls and the others are coming too fast and too close behind, at least one other member of the team is likely to fall also. But there is never any need to give up hope—even if one of the team stops or falls, provided the team can make up time somewhere else they still have a chance at placing. Regional and national championships are held.

in which case a less confident horse can take a lead from his bolder partner. Some horses make great hunters but will not jump an inch outside the hunting field. Remember to let your horse take his own line out hunting—do not just blindly follow the horse in front. If you have balanced him and helped him so that he regards hunting and cross-country jumping as fun, there is no reason why your hunter should not happily complete a hunter trial for you.

In the timed section you will have to open and shut a gate quickly without

dismounting. It should be easy if your horse has learned to listen and respond to your hand and leg aids. You just need to be sure that your horse will rein back, and move over to the right or left when you ask him, and you can practice all these skills at home.

To win the competition you will need to have a good sense of speed and timing. If you have hunted, try to think of the speed you travel at when hounds are running, and to go at that same speed on the hunter-trial course. You will know the terrain, having already walked the course.

EQUIPMENT NEEDED

To compete in a hunter trial you need to be turned out in your hunting attire, although most organizers allow you to wear a sweatshirt or polo shirt instead of a jacket. They will, however, insist that you wear a proper safety helmet and harness, as well as a body protector.

Your horse will need his usual saddle and bridle, as long as these are clean and in good condition, and his legs should be protected with either boots or bandages.

A normal riding stick or hunting whip may be carried; for hunter trials a proper hunting whip may help in opening and shutting the gate quickly in the timed section.

■ RIGHT
Team chasing involves a team of four riding fast and furiously cross-country. The competition is based on the time it takes for the first three team members to complete the course.

Show Jumping

The sport of show jumping involves tackling a course of artificial jumps, as opposed to natural cross-country jumps. It takes place in an arena that can be grass or have an all-weather surface, indoors or outdoors. An Olympic sport governed by the FEI, it is also a popular unaffiliated sport with any number of classes being held at local shows.

Show jumping requires accuracy and care. Almost every horse or pony can jump, but they do not all have the technique or the will to clear the fences.

Show jumping developed from the "leaping competitions" that were held at various shows in Europe and America during the late nineteenth century. There were high-jump and long-jump competitions for horse and rider, but the idea of jumping a course of fences was, at the time, mainly restricted to natural cross-country fences. Jumping was first included in the Olympic Games in Paris in 1900. It incorporated the high and wide competitions plus a timed competition over a course of artificial show jumps. In 1907, the first International Horse Show was held at Olympia in London, England, and the show jumping proved to be very popular. From then on competitions were organized throughout Europe and America for major trophies such as the

▌ LEFT
Teaching your horse to go well on the flat is as important to his success as teaching him how to jump correctly; look at the beautifully round and elevated canter that this show jumper is producing—with a canter like this, jumping the fence is almost a formality.

▌ BELOW LEFT AND RIGHT
If you can invest in a few jumps of your own, or team up with some friends to share them, there is much that can be practiced at home. A simple thing to practice is always looking toward the next fence. This helps you to judge your turns and your approach. Once you have taken off over a fence you should be looking toward your next target; as you ride around the course you should always be looking toward where you have to go next.

Nations Cup. This began as a military competition open to three officers of the same nationality who had to compete in uniform. Today it is open to four riders of the same nationality, male or female, military or civilian.

■ SHOW-JUMPING COMPETITIONS

The simplest form of unaffiliated competition is the Clear-round Class, held in the U.K. This is an excellent way of introducing an inexperienced horse and rider to the sport. Each rider pays a small fee to tackle a course of jumps. If you jump a clear round you win a ribbon, but the real usefulness of the competition is that if you jump a fence badly you can turn around and jump it again. Most organizers of these classes are extremely tolerant and will even lower a fence for you if your horse continually refuses. In a proper competition you would be eliminated after three refusals.

**It is important that the horse learns to jump
straight, unless his rider is asking him to turn in the
air. In this picture you can see that the horse is
looking in the opposite direction from his rider,
suggesting he has a tendency to jump crookedly.
Gridwork and the use of cross-rails help to teach
the horse to stay straight.**

The next stage is the two-round
competition. Each competitor tackles the
same course of fences and if you jump a
clear round you go through to the jump
off. This is ridden against the clock and
the fastest clear round wins.

Fences in unaffiliated classes start as
low as the organizer wishes. There may
even be beginner classes with jumps only
18 inches (45 cm) high. Fences usually go
up to about 3 feet 11 inches (1.2 m).
Affiliated competitions start with a novice
class with fences at about 3 feet 3 inches
(1 m) and continue through the levels to
courses with jumps which are well over 6
feet (1.8 m) high.

There are also other types of jumping
classes such as "Gambler's Choice." This
involves a course of fences that each have
a different value in terms of points to be
won. You jump as many fences as you can
in the time allowed, in any order you like,
with the aim of accumulating the
maximum number of points. The
Puissance involves jumping a short course
of fences; these include a wall, which is
always the highest jump. The fences are
gradually raised until nobody is able to
clear the wall.

Derby competitions have cross-country-
type obstacles in the arena, such as banks
and ditches. Some shows also hold relay

EQUIPMENT NEEDED

To develop your show-jumping skills you need to
have access to at least three or four sets of jump
standards and poles. Other than that, all that is
needed is a reasonably flat surface to practice
on, which can be a grass paddock when ground
conditions permit, or an outdoor or indoor arena
with an all-weather surface. Your horse needs
only his usual saddle and bridle and should wear
protective boots of some sort. Most show
jumpers use open-fronted boots on the front legs
so that the tendon area is protected but the
horse will feel the knock if he hits a pole, and
short fetlock boots behind. At smaller shows you

may wear riding boots and chaps, jodhpurs or
breeches. At higher level shows, proper show
attire is required.

While almost any horse or pony can be
persuaded to go around a show-jumping
course, once the fences get bigger you do need
a horse who is athletic and balanced. There are
plenty of horses who will make their way around a
course, gaily sending poles flying without
appearing to be the least bit bothered by the
experience. There is a great deal you can teach a
horse but, at the end of the day, he has to want
to clear the top pole.

competitions between teams of show
jumpers, or for added entertainment they
may build two identical courses side by
side over which competitors race. Time
faults are added for knock-downs.

One of the advantages of show jumping
is that jumping a course of fences does not
take as much out of a horse as, say, a day's
hunting or a hunter trial, so the show
jumper can compete far more frequently
than many other sports horses. You could
compete in a couple of different classes on
the same day and, provided your horse is
fit enough and enjoying his work, you
might compete nearly every weekend. In

■ RIGHT

Riders all develop
their own jumping
style as they gain
confidence and
experience, but one
of the things you must
always do, no matter
what your technique, is
to ensure that you give
your horse plenty of
freedom of his head
and neck. Your hands
must always move
forward when the
horse is jumping over
the fence.

theory this offers horse and rider the
chance to gain experience relatively
quickly.

■ **SKILLS REQUIRED**

Flatwork training is as important to the
show jumper as jump schooling. A
balanced, rhythmic and elevated canter
is essential if the horse is to jump
successfully. Whatever it is you are
jumping, your chances of clearing it safely
are mainly reliant on how good an
approach you give the horse to the fence.
The horse must be able to negotiate
corners and turns while still keeping his
rhythm and balance, so he needs to be
supple and responsive.

How much actual jump training you
do depends on what suits your horse.
Naturally careful horses are best not
jumped too often—just enough to keep
them in practice and their muscles toned
up. A horse whose technique needs
tidying up may be jumped up to three or
four times a week.

Jump training rarely involves jumping
huge fences. It concentrates on improving
the horse's technique and ability over

smaller fences—this reduces the risk of
injury or loss of confidence. Gridwork is
used to make the horse more supple, and
to influence his technique and the shape
he makes as he goes over over a fence to
maximize his chance of going clear.

The distances between fences in a grid
can be shortened to encourage the horse

to shorten up his stride and snap his front
legs up quickly and neatly as he takes off.
They can also be lengthened, which
encourages the horse to stretch and to
lengthen his stride and jump.

Poles can be rested on the fence or on
the ground in such a way as to encourage
the horse to stay straight as he jumps;
many horses have a tendency to veer off to
the left or right. Gridwork also gives you a
chance to concentrate on refining your
own position and improving your balance.

The ability to lengthen or shorten your
horse's stride and to react quickly when
he jumps into a combination or related
distance in a different way from the one
that was planned, is an essential skill for
the successful show jumper. Some riders
have a natural eye for distances, which
means that as soon as they land over one
fence they are able to gauge whether they
need to alter the horse's stride length in
order to meet the next fence at a good
distance. Those not born with this skill can
develop a good eye by practicing riding
different distances between fences at
home, and getting a feel for the pace at
which they need to approach the first

■ LEFT

This little pony is
showing superb
technique—see how
tightly he has snapped
up and folded his
front legs, which gives
him every chance to
clear the fence.

▌ LEFT
Show-jumping competitions usually just involve jumping over fences. However, in Derby classes cross-country type obstacles are introduced; this is the world-famous Hickstead Derby bank.

horse and rider to progress through the levels. They can go as far as their ability, time and/or finances allow them.

For those looking for greater rewards, show jumping also offers very good opportunities. Through the FEI there is a training and team-selection program for pony riders, juniors, young riders and seniors. There are also Pony Club and riding club competitions and championships. To be considered for team selection usually involves informing the appropriate selection committee of your interest and then entering a number of specified competitions where your performance will be noted by the selectors. If you are a likely candidate for a team place, you may be invited to attend various training courses—but remember that the ability to operate as part of a team is as important as being a good enough competitor to warrant selection.

▌ BELOW
In show jumping the horse has to be taught to jump *over* water, whereas in cross-country riding you are always trying to encourage your horse to jump *into* water.

fence in order to fit in the required number of strides to the next fence.

Among the most important attributes the rider needs are patience, a cool head and confidence—if you have all three of these you will no doubt succeed in whatever sport you choose.

■ OPPORTUNITIES

In all sports there are those who compete purely for their own enjoyment and entertainment, and those who compete with a view to being selected for team competitions and, who knows, maybe ultimately the Olympics. Show jumping caters extremely well to both types of competitor. For the less ambitious there are no end of unaffiliated and affiliated classes and competitions that still allow

Eventing

The sport of eventing, or combined training, is really a complete test of all-around horsemanship on the part of the rider, and of all-around performance on the part of the horse. Horse and rider are tested on their ability to compete in the disciplines of dressage, show jumping and cross-country. The dressage test demonstrates that the horse is supple, obedient and calm; the show jumping proves his agility and carefulness over fences; the cross-country proves his boldness, speed and stamina. The sport is split into one-day, two-day and three-day events. At a one-day event the order of the phases is usually dressage, show jumping and cross-country. At a three-day event the cross-country, combined with some additional tests of the horse's speed and endurance, is held the day after the dressage. The show jumping is held on the final day, testing whether the horse still has the necessary energy, agility, obedience and desire to clear the show jumps following the tough test of his stamina the day before on the speed and endurance phase.

■ HOW THE SPORT DEVELOPED

Eventing was started in Europe by cavalrymen, when they were not away fighting wars. The sport was originally named "The Military." It evolved as a way of testing the skills a cavalry horse would need—the dressage represented his suitability for parade duties, the cross-country reflected the need to cross any terrain to seek out, confront or escape the enemy, and the show jumping showed that after the rigors of battle the horse was still fit, willing and obedient, ready to march on to the next challenge.

The first Olympic three-day event was held in 1912. Then and for some years afterward the sport remained the domain of the military. It spread from country to country through international military

A THREE-DAY EVENT

Day one	Dressage
Day two	Speed and endurance:
	Phase A roads and tracks
	Phase B steeplechase
	Phase C roads and tracks
	Phase D cross country
Day three	Show jumping

The sport of eventing involves three very different disciplines, all of which must be completed successfully in order to win. The dressage test comes first. While this is simpler than a pure dressage test, it must be remembered that it is being ridden on a horse who has been prepared physically and mentally for the cross-country phase. He knows what is coming next, so it is harder for him to settle for the discipline of dressage.

competitions and, as events became more numerous, the interest of civilian riders was aroused. Now eventing is a popular sport in any number of countries around the world.

■ ONE-DAY AND THREE-DAY EVENTS

At a one-day event you have to complete a dressage test, a course of show jumps and a cross-country course, all on the same day. The penalties incurred in each competition, or phase, are added together, and the winner is the rider incurring the lowest number of penalties. One-day events are an end in themselves for many riders, but their true purpose is to prepare horse and rider for the more demanding two- and three-day events.

A three-day event can actually last for four or five days, depending on the number of entrants. All the horses are stabled together at or near the event for its duration. Before the competition begins there is a veterinary inspection, where any signs of lameness, injury or illness will result in elimination before you have started. The next one or two days are taken up with everybody completing their dressage tests.

The second part of the competition—the speed and endurance section—starts on the following day. Phase A, roads and tracks, involves completing a set route within a set time. This is usually achieved comfortably at trot, although a very short-striding horse may have to canter some of the way in order to avoid time penalties. This takes you to the start of the steeple-chase, which is Phase B. All on your own you have to gallop around a course of steeplechase fences, again within a set time. The finish of the steeplechase takes you on to Phase C, another set of roads and tracks, which is meant to serve as a recovery period after the steeplechase. A steady trot has to be maintained for much of the way if you are to finish inside the time. You then find yourself in the ten-minute box which is a roped-off area near the start of the cross-country course. Here the horse is allowed to rest for ten minutes. He is usually washed off, has his tack readjusted and checked for security and comfort, and is then walked quietly around so that he does not stiffen up before the cross-country, which is Phase D. In the ten-minute box, vets check the horses over and eliminate any who are already overly tired or are stressed.

After the ten-minute rest you set off on the cross-country course, which is judged in the same way as at a one-day event. There are penalties for any refusals, falls or runouts, and also for exceeding the set time. The following day there is another veterinary inspection where any horse who appears to have suffered from his exertions of the day before is withdrawn or eliminated from the competition.

This is followed by the final phase, the show jumping. This is usually run in reverse order of merit, so that the overnight leader jumps last. Any penalties incurred for refusals, knock-downs or exceeding the time are added to the dressage and to the speed and endurance penalties to give a final score. The winners of three-day events do indeed prove themselves and their horses to be successful, all-around competitors.

■ LEVELS OF COMPETITION

Eventing is governed by the FEI and there are various levels of affiliated competition. There are also Pony Club, Riding Club and unaffiliated competitions, although these rarely offer classes at higher than

LEFT
The cross-country phase is the most important, and should be the most influential, of the three phases. For most event riders it is the favorite phase.

BELOW LEFT AND RIGHT
At a three-day event, the competitors have to tackle two roads and tracks phases, as well as a steeplechase course, before they even set out on the cross-country course. There is a ten-minute rest period between the end of the second roads and tracks and the start of the cross-country test.

affiliated intermediate level. Affiliated one-day events are graded into different levels along such lines as novice (or below, such as preliminary or pre-novice), intermediate and advanced. These classifications or grades refer to the ability of the horse, not the rider, so in the same novice class you may find a sixteen-year-old riding in his or her first event competing against the reigning Olympic champion. For many this is all part of the charm and attraction of the sport. It is far

more of an achievement to perform well against such experienced riders, even if you don't win, than it is to take first prize in a class where you knew your rivals weren't up to much anyway.

Affiliated three-day events are classified as one star (novice), two star (about intermediate level), three star (intermediate to advanced level) and four star (advanced and championship level).

In between the one-day events and the three-day events are the occasional two-day

events. These are usually offered at the preliminary and intermediate levels. They provide a great introduction to three-day eventing for the less experienced rider or horse. You perform your dressage and show jumping on day one, and on day two you complete a shortened speed and endurance phase. This still consists of roads and tracks, steeplechase, roads and tracks, ten-minute halt and the cross-country course, but the speeds and distances are less than for a three-day event.

Every horse has to qualify to take part in a three-day event. For each grade there are a set number of one-, two- or less rigorous three-day events that horse and rider must have completed to a set standard. You usually need to have gone clear on the cross-country, or at least have

incurred only a limited number of penalties. This adds another dimension to the sport, as it allows you to compete with your horse's long-term future in mind. You may well go to a one-day event and leave without a prize, but if you were able to finish the cross-country you will have achieved a qualification toward your target of the three-day event.

■ SKILLS REQUIRED

Bearing in mind what is required for dressage, show jumping and hunter trials will give you some idea of the myriad skills the successful event horse and rider need. But before you are turned off just think of it in terms of good basic training that equals good all-around performance. If you have put some effort into schooling

■ LEFT
During the ten-minute rest the horse is cooled down as much as possible by washing him off. His tack is checked and readjusted if necessary.

your horse well on the flat, and have carried through the same principles of rhythm, balance and responsiveness into your jump training, you are well on the way to producing a capable and successful event horse. Jump training, whether over show jumps or cross-country fences, requires the same technique and skills. The only difference is the speed at which you ride cross-country, and the fact that the natural terrain you have to cross makes it harder to maintain your rhythm and balance than when you are jumping in an arena. An additional factor is the

EQUIPMENT NEEDED

It is possible to compete in events with a minimal amount of tack and equipment but, because of the three disciplines involved, there is a greater chance that you will need to invest in various odds and ends. Many horses are better ridden in different tack for each phase—a horse may perform happily in a snaffle for his dressage test but may need a double bridle or a gag for the cross-country. Some horses need different tack for the show jumping as well. You should use a breastplate or girth and a safety girth with your saddle for the cross-country phase. You may also want to use different types of boots or bandages for the show-jumping and cross-country phases—show-jumping boots do not offer enough protection for cross country. If you can afford it, a dressage saddle for the dressage phase will help your seat and position enormously; some riders even opt for different show-jumping and cross-country saddles although this is a little excessive. In fact, it is now possible to buy saddles with interchangeable knee rolls that allow the same saddle to be converted from a dressage model to a jumping model.

You will need jodhpurs, breeches and boots, plus a show jacket and a certified safety helmet. You must also wear a body protector on the cross-country phase. At advanced levels you are expected to perform your dressage test in a top hat and tailcoat—these are expensive when new, but can often be bought secondhand.

■ ABOVE
You have to keep track of how much time you can allow yourself on the roads and tracks phases, the steeplechase and the cross-country course. Exceeding the optimum time incurs time faults. Most riders record all their times on a card that they carry on their arm, along with a stopwatch.

■ LEFT
At advanced one-day events and at three-day events the horses have to carry a minimum weight of 165 lb (75 kg). This includes the rider's clothing and the horse's saddle. If you weigh in under that, you will have to carry lead weights in a weightcloth under the saddle.

■ RIGHT
This horse is about to unseat his rider, having made a very big but steep jump into the water at Badminton. Under the circumstances, the rider has done well to keep her weight back and at the same time has slipped the reins to give the horse every chance of coping with the situation.

variety of fences you will meet on a cross-country course. Once your horse is familiar with show jumps he is unlikely to be fazed by anything he meets in the arena, unless you approach it badly. But the awkward obstacles that can be built into the natural terrain on a cross-country course are numerous, and each time the horse competes he may well be faced with something he has never encountered before. Cross-country training should concentrate on building up confidence and trust, and making the right decision about the approach you should take.

Water is one hazard that seems to cause more trouble than most. In the horse's early training it is important that he is never frightened in water. This means carefully choosing any water hazard you ask him to enter. Don't ask him to splash through a river unless you know it has a safe, secure bottom. If he willingly enters water for you, and then finds himself floundering in deep mud he is going to be frightened and he is not going to trust you next time you face him with water. So do not abuse his trust and willingness. Similarly do not allow the overbold or exuberant horse to frighten himself—

make him approach water quietly and calmly so that he puts in a sensible jump which allows him to land in a balanced and controlled manner. If your horse is introduced to water like this, and if you take care always to be in a good position to support and balance him as he lands in water, he should never have reason to refuse to tackle a water complex.

Fitness is another necessity for both horse and rider. As long as they are regularly hacked out and given some schooling and jump training, most horses and ponies will be fit enough to complete a novice one-day event. Once

you want to do more than this, special attention has to be paid to the horse's fitness and training routine. This requires knowledge and experience of how to achieve fitness without subjecting the horse's vulnerable joints and limbs to unnecessary wear and tear. You will also need to be fit, as a tired rider is of little help to a tired horse.

The event rider perhaps needs more determination and persistence than other equestrian competitors, simply because it is a lot harder to get three things to go well all on the same day than it is to get one discipline right.

■ LEFT
Commonly known as "hailing a cab," this rider has thrown her arm behind her in a tactic that many riders find helps them to keep their weight back behind the horse when jumping down into water.

Race Riding

Race riding, either on the flat or over fences, offers the best opportunity to experience the full power and speed that a horse can produce. The racing industry revolves around the thoroughbred horse and, to a lesser degree, the Arab horse. Point-to-pointing, the occasional unofficial horse or pony race and the growth in Arab racing all give the amateur rider the chance to experience the thrill of race riding, and the chance to race for the fun of it. Professional jockeys are either retained or employed on a freelance basis by race-horse trainers. They often work for a big training yard in order to supplement their income, exercising and schooling the race horses, as well as racing them competitively if they are offered the ride.

■ POINT-TO-POINTING

This is an amateur sport that tends to thrive wherever hunting thrives. A horse who is to go point-to-pointing has to qualify by going out hunting for a set number of days. The amateur status of the sport, and the fact that a great many who take part own just one horse that they hunt and race, all adds to its fun and social atmosphere. It is popular with spectators, even in winter when they usually end up standing around in the wet and cold, eating the traditional tailgate

picnic. There are yards where the owner makes a living out of training and racing either his own or other people's point-to-pointers, and this makes some of the races very competitive.

In most point-to-points the horses jump standard brush fences which may occasionally have a ditch in front, but some courses include banks and water as well. This reflects the sport's origins, when riders simply raced each other from one point, usually a church steeple, to another point somewhere in the distance. The standard of riding varies considerably; anyone who has seen the differing standards on the hunting field will know what to expect in a point-to-point race. It

is for this reason that in point-to-pointing there are more falls than in professional steeplechasing or hurdling. The point-to-point course is usually an oval-shaped track marked out over an area of grassland. The fences are well spaced out around the course and, because they make use of natural terrain, some courses are much flatter than others. Competitors quickly discover which tracks suit their particular horse best.

■ ARAB RACING

This is a well-organized sport that involves flat races between Arab horses. The racing is fast and competitive, but the sport is still small enough to allow you to train and

EQUIPMENT NEEDED

To ride in any of these races you will need to wear a safety helmet, lightweight breeches and boots, and a shirt reflecting your racing colors. In a point-to-point you are allowed to wear hunting attire. A body protector is compulsory for some types of racing, and advisable for all types. Goggles are a handy accessory, as a faceful of mud halfway around the course does little for your ability to steer your horse home. A weightcloth will also be needed. A horse can be raced in his ordinary saddle but most jockeys opt for a lightweight racing saddle.

■ BELOW
Despite its amateur status—which means the greatest reward is the fun to be had rather than the prize money to be won—the risks of point-to-pointing are probably greater than in either professional racing over jumps or flat racing. Falls are frequent.

compete your own horse with success. Races vary in length, which means horses tend to specialize in either the short, faster races, or the longer, slightly slower ones.

■ PONY AND HORSE RACING

There are a few pony and horse races held in most countries that give ordinary riding horses and their jockeys a chance to demonstrate their speed—or lack of it! Most of these are unofficial, although a few countries do have a national body that registers competitors and organizes races for them.

■ PROFESSIONAL FLAT AND JUMP RACING

The international racing scene is divided into flat races, hurdle races, steeplechase races and timber or cross-country races. Flat racing is mainly to test pure speed—many of the races are short sprints where

speed rather than stamina count most. Jump racing requires stamina, jumping ability and speed.

■ SKILLS REQUIRED

To race ride you need to be fit, have good balance and a feel for jumping at speed. These can all be practiced at home if you intend to race just for fun. But if you want it to be more than that, the best place to learn is in a racing stable, even if you only help out there at weekends. The more thoroughbred race horses you are able to ride, even if only on exercise, the better your fitness, position and balance will become.

Flat-race jockeys are generally quite short and also have to be lightweight. Jump jockeys, who ride with their stirrups a little longer, can be taller but need to keep their weight down so that they do not force the horse to carry more weight than he has been allocated.

■ ABOVE
If you want a career with horses, a job at a reputable race track can offer great variety, good experience and good friends.

■ BELOW LEFT
Dirt-track racing is common in America.

SUCCESS IS UP TO YOU

Competing with your horse can and should be an enjoyable experience for both of you. But if you take a look around you will see that this is not always the case—unhappy horses and riders abound at all kinds of events. Some horses are always going to be more talented than others; some will be more co-operative than others. But there will also be those who, either through lack of schooling or understanding, or simply through bad riding, do not fulfill their potential. Not everyone can afford the horse or pony of their dreams. Some think that this is exactly what they have found, only to be disappointed when things don't go as planned. A few horses, no matter how well ridden, simply lack the necessary ability or character to succeed at certain sports.

When things aren't going as well as you would like, remember too that very few talented riders are born—they have to be made. Riding has to be worked at; it doesn't just happen. You cannot be blamed for lacking a particular skill or aptitude for a specific sport—we are all made differently—but you can be blamed if you don't bother to work at your basic riding skills. So if you are going to ride, strive to ride well. GOOD LUCK!

Index

Page numbers in italics refer
to illustrations.

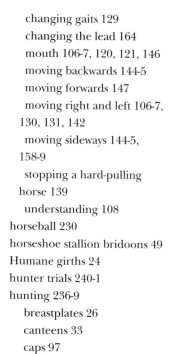

ACKNOWLEDGEMENTS

The author and photographer
would like to thank the
following:

Riders: Amanda Colbourne,
Thomas Cooper, Janine
Cornish, Charles Daniel,
Kate Eckley, Janice Peglar,
Sarah Rees-Elford, and
Jeremy Russell.
Facilities and equipment: Philip
Wellon for the use of land at
Vine Farm; Aubiose UK Ltd
for the outdoor arena; HAC
TAC Ltd for supplying close-
contact breeches; and
Keenthorne Saddlery, Bridg-
water, for clothing and tack.